Vladimir Antonov,

Ph.D. (in biology)

Ecopsychology:

HARMONY OF COMMUNICATION WITH NATURE
PSYCHIC SELF-REGULATION
SPIRITUAL HEART
SPIRITUAL DEVELOPMENT
MAN AND GOD. DESTINY
MEANING OF LIFE
UPBRINGING OF CHILDREN
ART. CHAKRAS. KUNDALINI
ECOPSYCHOLOGISTS COGNIZE AND STUDY GOD

Translated from Russian
by Anton Teplyy

Correctors of an English translation:
Keenan Murphy and Hiero Nani

2014

ISBN 978-1438257235

This book is written in a simple and easy-to-understand language by scientist-biologist Dr. Vladimir Antonov. It covers the essential issues: what is God, the place of human being in the Evolution of the Universal Consciousness, principles of forming and correction of destiny, ways of attaining health and happiness, most effective methods of psychic self-regulation, about spiritual development and cognition of God.

The book includes also texts of several lectures by Dr. Antonov. These lectures may repeat the main ideas of the book — in other words. It will help the readers to comprehend the material more fully.

The book is intended for all kinds of readers.

www.swami-center.org
www.new-ecopsychology.org

Contents

Ecology of Human Being in Multidimensional Space

Ecology and Ecopsychology

Ecology is a science that studies relationships between living organisms and the environment they live in.

Its branches focus on studying specific kinds of these organisms and are called respectively. For example: ecology of European beaver or ecology of sturgeon, etc. The object can be researched in terms of its habitat, places and conditions of reproduction, mating patterns and other kinds of interaction with representative of the same species, competitors and enemies (predators, parasites, etc.), or just neighbors.

Human being can also be an object of such research. It is being studied mostly in its working environment (sea, coal mines, space flight, etc.)

A separate branch of ecology of human being is protection of the environment. In many countries there are special ecological services as well as voluntary environmentalist organizations like Green Peace. Environmentalists struggle against pollution of water resources, air, and soil, as well as for preservation of natural forests and fauna. They protest against nuclear weapons testing, fight for banning of chemical, biological, and nuclear weapons and antipersonnel mines that cripple civilians and animals. They also call for banning of the usage of traps in fur trade, which cause incredible sufferings to animals...

The environmentalist movement deserves highest praise and every possible kind of support. The applied ecological studies of professional activities of man are also very important. But in this book we will try to show that this is not all that the ecology of human being can study.

Man is not only a body, but also, and primarily, a consciousness or soul. And man lives not only in close contact with air, water, soil, animals, plants, viruses, and bacteria... We also interact with non-embodied individual consciousnesses (spirits of people and animals) and — which is the most important of all — with God.

This is the subject of the science ecopsychology — as the most important branch of ecology.

In reality we live in a multidimensional environment. And the material world that we can perceive with our senses is just a small portion of it. Other layers (eons or lokas) of the multidimensional universe usually remain completely out of our perception, although they are filled with life that can see us and which influences us.

For the completeness of ecological perception, which allows us to live our lives on the Earth in the best way, we have to include in our worldview Him Who is the most important One in the universe — God.

For this purpose we need to have, first of all, the knowledge about God, about the Evolution of the Universal Consciousness, and about our role in this process.

And we have to realize that ETHICS is that field of philosophical knowledge which allows man to live in ECOLOGICAL HARMONY with God and with the entire environment.

What Is Man

In order to be really comprehensive the whole system of knowledge about human being should be based on the premise that man is not a body, but a consciousness, i.e. living energy, capable of self-awareness and possessing mind and memory. The body is merely a transient habitat for the consciousness. And throughout the personal evolution, every individual moves in and out of those habitats, dropping off old bodies and entering new ones.

Materialists and followers of primitive religious sects do not believe this. On the other hand, God has been telling us about this through Thoth-the-Atlantean (Hermes Trismegistus), Lao Tse, Krishna, Buddha, Jesus Christ, Babaji from Haidakhan, Sathya Sai Baba, and numerous other Divine Teachers and prophets [1-4,6-7,9-11,13-16,18-19,23,25-26,29,35-37,40-42, 45-56,58].

One may or may not believe in this. A small and weak consciousness, which associates itself with a contaminated and sick body, is generally unable to switch from blind faith (or lack of it) to knowledge. But one can experience this, if one starts to develop oneself as a consciousness. This process is also known as walking the spiritual Path.

It is this process of development of the consciousness, both qualitatively and quantitatively, that constitutes the meaning of man's life, as well as lives of all living beings.

But what is this all for, one may ask? The answer is — for the sake of merging with God, and thus enriching Him with oneself.

Everything material in the universe, including our planet and everything on it, exists only for that purpose: to ensure the possibility of development of individual consciousnesses on material mediums.

Evolution of any individual soul starts as follows. On the lattices of growing minerals the processes of formation and growth of the first rudiments of initially diffusive energy (called *protopurusha* in Sanskrit) begin. Subsequently the tiny amount of energy formed in this way gets embodied into bodies of plants, where it continues to grow, then it moves into animal bodies and finally into human ones. The soul grows from one incarnation to another.

One can observe some primitive emotional reactions and motor reflexes even in vegetable forms of life. Evolutionary advanced animals have a wide variety of emotions and feelings and, in some instances, even possess a well-developed intellect.

At the human stage of evolution, among other things, we have to get an understanding of the fundamental principles of consciousness' development and to take an active part in this process. Unfortunately, the majority of people do not do this, mainly due to philosophical and religious ignorance that currently prevails on our planet.

Multidimensionality of Space

In reality, the universal space is multidimensional. Just like sunlight and water co-exist within the same volume, sunlight moving freely through the water with little or no interaction with it, just like radio waves of different frequencies are present deep in the space in and out of our bodies — even so multiple worlds exist everywhere deep inside multidimensional space, in and out of all material objects, be they in solid, liquid or gaseous states. Those worlds are abodes of spirits and God.

The scale of multidimensionality is a special scale of energy states, which represent fundamentally different ranges. When studying this scale, the vector of one's attention should be directed not upward or downward, or in any conventional direction, but inward. Layers of the multidimensional space (eons in Greek or lokas in Sanskrit) are ranged by their *coarseness-subtlety*.

The plane of the subtlest energies is God in the aspect of the Creator. He is perceived as infinite and purest *Light*, which is similar to tender and warm sunlight at dawn-time. He is formless. All forms vanish on this plane.

His Name sounds differently in different languages: God-the-Father, Jehovah, Allah, Ishvara, Primordial Consciousness, Tao, etc. He is the God of Jewish prophets and of Jesus Christ, of Muhammad and of all the faithful ones of China, India and other places, where people have a correct concept of Him.

Only those deluded by ignorance or intellectually primitive people can think that different names mean existence of different Gods...

That first primordial plane, called the Abode of the Creator, is where the "construction project" of creating every new islet in the multidimensional Creation is realized from. Protomatter (protoprakriti, bhutakasha in Sanskrit) is used as "construction material" for creating solid matter.

This layer — if one enters it with the consciousness — is perceived from inside as infinite universal space filled with *Tenderness* and *Peace*, though lacking intensive radiance. It could be compared to a warm and tender starlit southern night.

An extremely important thing to know is that the Creator and the eons of akasha are somewhat on the other side of a "mirror" in relation to the Creation — in the "trans-mirror" realm, so to say. This universal "mirror" is somewhat like a regular mirror — it has its dark and light sides.

... When on a planet there appear conditions suitable for organic life to exist, small lumps of protopurusha start to incarnate into material carriers. This constitutes the beginning of concurrent evolution of organic bodies and souls that get embodied into them. The evolution of organic bodies has been thoroughly studied by biologists — the only "missing link" here that one needs to realize is the guidance of God over the whole process.

Our task as human beings here on the Earth consists in, having grown as souls, as consciousnesses, going all the way from the Creation back to the Creator, refining ourselves as consciousnesses — in order to merge into Him, to enrich Him.

This is what the intention of God was, when He created our planet. And this is the purpose of our lives.

It is important for us to realize that we are not capable of existing on our own. Therefore, we have neither right nor grounds to feel egocentric and to consider ourselves to be more important than other living beings. Since the only being whose existence does not need to be supported is the Creator. And He launched all of His Creation not for our sake but for the sake of His Evolution.

This sheds light on what determines our destinies: if we move in the right direction, then everything goes fine in our daily lives, if not — He brings our attention to this by means of our pain and of what we call "tough luck".

... In the course of an enormous period of time (in Earth's measures), billions of human bodies and even a greater number of souls of different ages and levels of development emerged on our planet. Those of them who attain perfection merge with the Creator and do not get embodied anymore (sometimes they do — but only as Avatars). The rest of the souls have to return to embodied states again and again — until the time period allocated for existence of this particular "islet" of matter is elapsed. When this happens, all matter along with souls that have not attained perfection get disintegrated down to the akasha state to serve as the construction material for creating new worlds of matter and various forms of life in them.

On the opposite from God end of the *coarseness-subtlety* scale there is a diabolic eon — a world of coarse black-colored energies, which induces eerie emotional states and is perceived as something "sticky", like petroleum. How souls get to this plane will be discussed later.

There is also the abode of the virtuous — paradise.

After the death of the body, the soul ends up in the eon it deserved while living in the embodied state. But we have to reach for the highest and the subtlest eons.

For us, raised in an atheistic environment and surrounded by religious ignorance, it may be hard, though absolutely necessary, to comprehend that God-the-Father does not live only up in the sky, on a high mountain, on another planet and so on. He is everywhere in the universe: in the *depth* beneath our bodies, beneath the entire material world, the entire Creation.

And the "stairway" to God does not invite upward, but *depthward*. The levels of refinement of the consciousness are its footsteps. And this stairway begins... in our spiritual hearts.

... Everything said above is the result of a thorough research and personal experience of the author of this book and is neither a compilation of other texts nor a reproduction of somebody else's words. And everyone has to make efforts and walk this Path to the end. But it is important to know that in order to advance one should go up one step at a time, from one "footstep" to another, without jumping over "flights of stairs".

... The Abode of the Creator exists *everywhere, beneath* every material molecule. Jesus said that the distance to it is "thinner than a sheet of the finest paper" [25].

God-the-Father is not in the physical sky; He is everywhere inside and around our bodies, underlying every bit of them. His Abode is extremely close to us! But one cannot get into it just like that!

In order to enter it, one has to receive a blessing from Him. But only those who have properly developed themselves in Love, Wisdom, and Power can receive this blessing.

* * *

The Path to the Abode of the Creator is the Path of gradual refinement of oneself as a consciousness. As the first step it is necessary, as Apostle Paul put it, "to avert from what is evil and cling to what is good" [6,7,11], which implies leaving companies of drunkards, cruel and rude people, learning to see the beauty of living nature and of the true art, making companions on the spiritual Path one's friends.

First steps in realizing the potential of the spiritual heart become the next stage of acquiring steadfastness in living in subtle states. Then one can proceed with cleansing the chakras and major meridians of the body, including chitrini (Brahmanadi). Successful completion of this process will allow one to find oneself right in the eon of the Holy Spirit upon exiting from the body through chitrini. And the *Pranava* meditation will enable one to merge with the Holy Spirit for the first time... In this manner, gradually moving deeper and deeper inside the multidimensional universe, stopping for a while to rest and to settle in the newly discovered states, we can reach the Abode of the Creator, which with time becomes our Home.

The described above is the true Way towards attaining God, as opposed to what sometimes is mistaken for it, i.e. crusades against "infidels" or declaring anathema on some particular otherwise-minded persons or sects, or even on whole nations! Those are ways to the development of devilish qualities, the way to hell.

God

So, we have discussed where one should seek God: not somewhere up in the sky but in the *depth* of the multidimensional universe. And one has to begin searching for Him not far in the cosmos but in one's own chest — in one's own spiritual heart, which begins its growth in the anahata chakra, which is called also the middle dantian.

We have also agreed that the word *God* (with capital G) in the first place must be interpreted as Primordial Consciousness that dwells in the deepest and subtlest primary plane of the multidimensional universe. This Primordial Consciousness is One for the whole universe and therefore for all living beings, including people who live on our planet. And the fact that the word *God* sounds differently in different languages does not mean that there are many Gods or that various nations that inhabit the Earth have their own God. The words *Sun* and *Earth*, too, sound quite differently — when spoken by people of different nationalities in their native languages, but it does not mean that people of each country have their own sun or that each nation lives on its own planet.

But we have not discussed yet all the aspects of the definition of the word *God*. One may ask: "What is the meaning of the thesis that God is *Everything*, which was proposed by Vedanta?" Or other questions may arise, like "What is Christian Trinity?", "What is Brahman?", "Are there planetary Gods-Demiurges?", "How should I understand the assertion that Jesus, Babaji, Sathya Sai Baba — each of Them — is also God?", "How can I reconcile the Vedantic thesis that Brahman is Absolutely

Everything with Krishna's assertion that there is a yet higher level of the Divine Consciousness — Ishvara or God-the-Father?"... Let us make it perfectly clear.

First of all, we should not regard various pagan deities since they have nothing to do with the ideology of a serious seeker of God. Those deities are what people were fantasizing about before they received the knowledge about One Universal God. There was plenty of those pseudo-religious fairy tales in ancient Greece, Rome, India, Arabian countries, and Russia. Let us leave those characters to folklorists' studies and continue with a serious scientific approach based on experimental study of Truth and information provided directly by God.

So, what is the Absolute? This word means *absolutely Everything that exists in the universe*. And what does exist in the multidimensional universe? First of all — it is the Creator Himself. Material constituent of the Creation and consciousnesses of all levels, other than that of the Creator, are just a small Part of the Absolute. Furthermore, the Creator pervades the whole Creation with Himself. The Creation, consisting of various manifestations in various eons, is like a multidimensional layered pie, in which the primary layer dominates the rest. At the same time this "pie" is *One Whole*.

There exists only All, One Whole Multidimensional All — this is not only one of the most important themes for meditation, but also an undoubted truth that reflects the Absolute.

But we, people, are we integral parts of the Absolute?

The answer is yes and no.

On one hand, we are like blood-cells in the multidimensional Body of the Absolute: we are negligibly small compared to It, incapable of separate existence and dependent on It in everything, although having a certain freedom of movement within Its Body.

But on the other hand, from the standpoint of these "cells" as opposed to the Body of the Absolute as Macro-Organism we, as souls, are undoubtedly separate from Him. Moreover, we possess a significant amount of free will, which the Creator granted to us.

The point is that we, having come into existence as separate souls have to return to the state of non-separateness, or non-duality, with God in His "basic" eon.

The thesis that we are originally identical to the Creator and even that we do not have any free will at all, proposed by some, can serve only as a theme for meditation, though quite an effective one, that calls upon us to merge with Him.

In reality, the free will is the mechanism of natural "sorting" of people by the ethical criterion: do we observe the rules of life suggested by God, do we aspire to merge with Him in Love? How our destinies form depends on decisions we make in this respect.

The level of our philosophic and religious knowledge and the intensity of our efforts on transforming ourselves in accordance with the Will of God determine our moving from one eon to another, in particular. As it should be clear from everything said above, it depends not on our actions, but on our prevailing emotional status: whether we accustomed ourselves to living in coarse or subtle emotional states.

If we have accustomed ourselves to living in the "heavy" and coarse states of malice and hatred, we are going to share the diabolic abode with those who feel the same way.

But if we have lived in the subtle and tender states of love, we naturally get into the harmony and purity of paradise.

If we have lived a dull life without falling into particularly coarse emotional states but without pronounced subtlety of the consciousness, after the death of the body we find ourselves in the "gray" eons of the Creation.

But it is not even paradise that should be our goal; it should be the Abode of God-the-Father. He tells us about that all the time [6,11].

In order to settle in it, one must possess not only subtlety of the consciousness but also Wisdom. One can gain it through increasing the level of one's erudition, intellectual work, active service to other people with good deeds and persistent aspiration for cognition of God.

... The Holy Spirit is an aggregate of Divine Individualities coming out of the Abode of the Creator. The cosmic function of the Holy Spirit is to supervise the evolution of all souls of lower levels of development. It is the Holy Spirit Who organizes and supervises our destinies. He does it Himself, directly or by calling to assistance numerous spirits that possess various qualities, either "paradisiacal" or "diabolic".

When we perceive the waves of bliss coming from somewhere in response to our righteous thoughts or actions — this is the Holy Spirit manifesting Himself. In such instances people say that He is granting us His Blessing. Special meditative techniques allow one to get into frequent blissful contacts with the Holy Spirit quite easily.

... In order to clarify the meaning of the word *Brahman* we need to say a few words about the ancient Indian philosophical system of knowledge called Vedanta. This is important for us since Sathya Sai Baba, the Avatar of modern age, addressing Hindus, educated within the Vedanta tradition, often uses the terminology of this particular philosophic school.

The Vedanta philosophy originated in India even before Krishna and was based on the pagan teachings of the four Vedas. At that time Indian people did not know about the existence of Ishvara — God-the-Father (i.e. the Creator Who dwells in His Abode). This was the reason why Brahman was considered by the Vedanta philosophy as the Supreme Godhead and even as the Absolute.

It was Krishna Who told people of India about God-the-Father. Later God declared the same Truth through Jesus Christ and Muhammad to the people of Israel and of all modern Christian and Islamic worlds. But people of both India and the Christian world failed to preserve this knowledge about God-the-Father, which exceeded their ability to comprehend. They almost completely forgot about His existence, having switched their attention to ancient fairy-tale characters (in India) or to some imaginary deified characters in mass Christian sects (for more details see [9]).

... There is the last question out of those listed in the beginning of this chapter that we have not answered yet, namely: what is the *Trinity*?

There exists God-the-Father — the Supreme Primordial Consciousness — Who dwells in the subtlest eon of the multidimensional universe, on the other side of the *Mirror* relatively to the multidimensional aggregate of the Creation. He is the Highest Goal for all people.

His primary Manifestation, His Representative, an active Manager and Supervisor of all life on any populated planet is the Holy Spirit.

Sometimes God-the-Father manifests Himself by incarnating in a human body. Those embodied Parts are people who attained the Creator in the past. In different languages They are called Messiahs, Avatars, Christs, etc.

In other words, the Trinity is the Creator, the Holy Spirit, and a Christ; in Bhagavad Gita's terms, it is Ishvara, Brahman, and an Avatar.

But, as Jesus Himself explains [25], the term *Son* is not at all felicitous in this context, since everyone should learn to see God as their Father-Mother and themselves as His son or His daughter.

God — and Us

God is not at all an invisible flying person, as some primitive religious sects depict Him. God is a Universal Ocean of Consciousness. What size is He? Can we imagine the distance of one *light year*? This is an astronomical space measure equal to the distance that light covers in one year in Earth's time measures. Astronomers discovered cosmic objects located at a distance of billions of light years. But God is still larger, for the universe is infinite. He is INFINITELY LARGE!

However large we consider our planet to be, when we walk, tired, across its surface or fly around it, the Earth is negligibly small compared to the Greatness of the Ocean of the Creator's Consciousness.

The Earth is just one of the countless islets of matter created by Him within the Ocean. Here on the Earth, as on many other planets in the universe, the conditions, favorable for life and evolution of organic bodies, developed. It is in the bodies of plants, animals, and humans that the Evolution of the Universal Consciousness takes place. Every one of us, people, is a lump of energy of consciousness, which has gone through the stages of its evolution that took place in the bodies of plants and animals and at the present human stage has to make vigorous efforts on self-development.

We have to try hard to become worthy and capable of "plunging" into the Abode of the Creator and merging with Him. Then we will attain the ultimate Peace in the Supreme Bliss of Eternal Oneness with Him, the Bliss of being Him.

He has been reminding us about this goal over and over again by incarnating Parts of Himself into human bodies. But the majority of people have always been unable to comprehend this Truth and to keep it in memory. They always tend to forget about, distort, and pervert the Teachings of God that He grants to us. This is how various religious sects emerge [9].

... The lifetime of each planet — of that "islet" of matter in the infinite Ocean of God — is limited to a certain period of time. When this period ends, the "islet" comes to its *end of the world*. Those consciousnesses (souls) that failed to reach Mergence with God get destroyed, disintegrated. But those who have attained the state of Mergence enrich Him with themselves; thus they completely realize the meaning of their lives and their love for God in Mergence with Him.

The Meaning of Human Life

The question of the meaning of life gets inevitably raised before any person who matures in his or her development, moving up from the instinctive-reflexive stage to the really human one, at which the intellect begins to dominate in choosing one's way of living and conduct.

Many philosophers racked their brains over this question. But the majority of them were not able to comprehend the true God's philosophy, while perverted conceptions created by numerous sects could not satisfy them. As a result the question about the meaning of human life was "declared" by many philosophers to be a "pseudo-question", i.e. the one that cannot be answered by its own nature. This atheistic concept assumed, in fact, that man is not dramatically different from animals and the objective meaning of man's existence on the Earth is just... reproduction, ensuring the survival of the human race and creation of material values for the descendants. Therefore no spiritual efforts are necessary, and ethics in relationships with other living beings can be neglected...

"What's our life? — A game... Good, evil — only dreams... Work, honesty — just tales for the females..."[1] And suicide "when the time comes" is the only right move for those worthy of respect...

But the truth is that there *is* a meaning of human life.

It consists in development of the consciousness: both qualitative and quantitative.

Qualitative development consists in intellectual and ethical self-perfecting, as well as in refining of the consciousness. The quantitative aspect implies a direct increase of the amount of the refined energy of the consciousness.

The latter reflects, among other things, the level of so-called *personal power* — the psychoenergetic might of an individual consciousness that depends on the quantity of its energy, or in other words on the size of the soul.

According to this quantitative criterion, God classifies souls into "small" and "large" ones [7]. But regardless of this classification, each of them can possess both positive and negative properties. God calls "small" souls that have developed negative properties demoniac ones; if in addition to this they have accumulated a significant amount of *personal power* they are considered diabolic, or devils. They can be encountered either in embodied or non-embodied form. Their abode is hell while they are in the non-embodied state. When they get embodied, this takes place in "hellish" conditions, where they will be experiencing the results of their bad karma (the fate they created for themselves). In this way God suggests

---

[1] Quote from P.Chaikovsky's opera based on A.Pushkin's *Queen of Spades*.

that they experience what the pain, which they were causing to other living beings, is like. He does this in order to help them to become better, to urge them to think about their ways, about the meaning of human life, about God and the Path to Him...

But those developing in the right direction rush into the embrace of their beloved Creator; their lives become filled more and more with Divine happiness and exultation of Divine Love.

So, what does God want us to become, specifically?

Destiny and It Correction

Living in our physical bodies we ordinarily think that we can be "alone", that we can have secrets which "nobody is ever going to know". But in reality this is our naive illusion. It is because with our physical eyes we can see only the bodies of other incarnate people, from whom we can really conceal or hide something.

In reality we are literally naked before the eyes of God and numerous spirits. They not only watch our activities, hear us speaking, perceive our emotions, but also know all of our thoughts.

There is no way for us to stay absolutely invisible to all. When we are having sex in any variation — we are being watched, too. In the desert, in the woods or on a tiny island in the ocean, day and night — we can be seen by God and by many non-embodied beings. Even if we lock ourselves sitting in a bathroom, we are still visible to them — from all around and even from within. Neither clothes, nor any other kind of covering can be an obstacle that could prevent them from seeing us.

In light of the above said, the following meditative theme could be very effectively used: "I am on the Palm of God". If we see ourselves as being always before His

Eyes, it will make it easier for us to cleanse ourselves of impurities, to get rid of all that is unnecessary.

… But they (God and spirits), while being invisible to us, can influence us in various ways.

In particular, they can easily affect our emotions, especially if we do not have sufficient control over our the emotional sphere.

For instance we can be easily directed into falling in love, or, in the same manner, in growing suddenly bored with someone.

Or walking down the street we may suddenly "feel like" stopping, turning right or left, or increasing our pace… and there we encounter…

Or a thought may "occur" to us. And we readily take this thought for our own.

Or by stimulating our brain they can make us lose balance, slip, fall down or hurt ourselves. Or miss when shooting.

And if criminals attack me and injures me in some way — it is not only because they are fierce and malicious hell-bound primitives, but also because God has led them to me in this situation.

It should be noted here that the more intellectually primitive people are, the easier it is to manipulate them: they do not have steadfast ethical principles of their own, thus they show no resistance to manipulation.

Animals can be manipulated even more easily. So, if a dog bites someone — it was not just the dog's intention.

God and spirits can control people and animals. But they can exert influence over inanimate objects as well. A bullet can be deflected from its trajectory if needed, and a bomb, a shell, or a grenade can be prevented from going off, a fire can be made to go out. And vice versa — fire, water, or anything else can appear out of the blue in an unexpected place and at an unexpected time.

The evidence of that are various poltergeist phenomena as well as the miracles that Messiahs perform not only around the places where Their bodies are but also at any distance. At present this is demonstrated by Sathya Sai Baba [6,11,36-37, 45-54] and David Copperfield [7].

Upon realization that God is present everywhere and that He is omnipotent, we need to learn to see that no external powers can do any harm to us, unless it complies with God's will. (All spirits are also supervised by Him). And if something unpleasant does happen to us, we should search in ourselves for the cause of it — our deeds and mistakes: either recent or those of remote past.

... We have previously mentioned that God created His entire Creation not at all for the sake of us, humans, but for Himself! We, humans, are not at all capable of existing independently. And we are not objectively separated from God. On the contrary — we are in Him, and our separateness is nothing but a silly illusion, which is the cause of all our adversities and misfortunes.

We are totally dependent on Him. He shepherds us as His flock, sending us to the "pastures" of the Earth to develop and to mature. Here, in close interaction with our peers and objects of the material world, we acquire and strengthen our personal qualities, whether good or bad.

We need to learn to see, to hear and to obey our Pastor, as well as to love Him. Some people take delight in learning this, while others keep trying to hide from Him, pretending that it is not He Who exists, but they do — being strong and all-around nice.

The humble, kind, loving, and intelligent — them He nurtures with care, draws near, and lets in Himself fast.

The rest have to keep coming back by accepting births in new bodies. In between incarnations they live among similar souls for a long time — in the states of the consciousness they accustomed themselves to while living on the Earth.

God never stops caring about us — up to the very *end of the world* — constantly reminding us about Himself through His Messiahs and prophets, as well as through holy scriptures. He also shows us what it is like — to be malicious, lying, mean, covetous of somebody else's property — by subjecting us to attacks of criminals or fierce animals... By this He wants to explain to us what pain, fear, being robbed are like... — to teach us to never do these things to others.

People call it the *law of karma* — the law of cause and effect in formation of our destinies. He will continue to "strike" us until we rid ourselves of our vices, until we become what He wants us to be: gentle, caring, altruistic, absolutely honest, free from self-importance and arrogance, not capable of being angry, of using violence (we may use it only in cases when we are protecting good people from somebody else's cruel violence).

He is Love. In order to merge into Him or even to approach Him, we have to become Love as well.

But what is love? So few people understand what this word means!

Love is primarily emotional states. What is the principal and the most precious thing about these states — is subtle tenderness accompanied by inner PEACE. Also — caring attention, benevolence, esteem, respect, gratitude, and so on.

Emotions are not the same as thoughts, mimics, behavioral reactions or electrical processes in the brain. Emotions are not at all generated by the brain, as materialistic physiologists hold. They are generated in the chest, in the neck, or in the belly. They are generated in special emotiogenic structures — chakras and meridians.

Variations of love, listed above, are generated by the anahata chakra, located in the chest. In fact, they are known only to people whose anahatas are developed and function properly. For the rest of people — tenderness, benevolence, etc. are just words devoid of any emotional content. And if we live without ever experiencing cordial love — that means that we live "far off" from God and have little chance of spiritual success, of cognizing God and His Love or even of getting to paradise as yet.

LOVE and PEACE are two states, living in which we have a chance of rapid spiritual advancement, of getting closer to God.

Various kinds of anger (hatred, fury, irritation, condemnation, jealousy, discontent, etc.) and fear — those are the states that conduct us in the opposite direction from God — to hell.

These two pairs of emotional states are opposite and mutually exclusive.

Learning to feel anger and fear is simple. Almost everyone can feel them. But do we really want to go there? How can we confront the evil that is drawing us to hell? By hating those who "staged all this"? This would be the simplest — and the most foolish — decision! It is this decision that will ensure for us not only bad karma for the current and future incarnations, but also abiding in hell in between them.

The conditions, each of us lives in, are the karmic consequences of our past lives, which were devoid of spiritual aspiration. Do we want our future to be even worse?

Only LOVE and PEACE — if we feel them regardless of circumstances — can lead us to a favorable fate, to paradise, and to God.

But how can we learn to always feel LOVE and PEACE?

The first way that God has been suggesting from all times is harmonious sexual love — love that is free of passion, lust (selfish desire) and jealousy, love based on mutual respect, on giving the whole of oneself to the partner, acting for the sake of overall harmony and not only for the sake of one's own good.

The second method is the bringing up children — in the atmosphere of harmony and happiness.

The third is harmonious contacts with nature.

The fourth is spiritual art. In particular, the art that in the first place contributes to development of LOVE and PEACE in us.

The fifth is visiting spiritual meetings, churches and temples, where harmonious collective meditations, which make for development of Love, are practiced.

In addition to this there are special esoteric methods of self-perfection, where the development of the spiritual heart — the main organ of emotional love — must be of paramount importance. The next stages include methods of refinement of the consciousness, of cognizing first the Holy Spirit and then God-the-Father.

Over the course of our personal evolution we, as souls or consciousness, have developed some individual qualities, called also *character (or personality) traits*. These traits can be both good and vicious.

Among our vices can be tendencies to be aggressive, angry, violent, sarcastic, arrogant, greedy, selfish, boring, untruthful, rude, tactless, etc. There may be in a person such small, but unpleasant for other people vicious traits, as biting the nails, trembling the knees while sitting at a table, sniffing, using obscene language or talking too much or too loudly.

The absence of some positive traits can also be considered a vice, for example, the absence of inner peace, absence of the ability to love sincerely and tenderly, lack of fidelity and reliability in relationships with other people, lack of faith in the existence of God, absence of aspiration for spiritual Perfection and of sincere willingness to help other people in everything good.

How can we fight our vices? Recommendations differ depending on the situation. Sometimes the mere realization of the viciousness of some of our actions is enough to break this particular behavioral pattern. For example, the author of this book quitted smoking, drinking alcohol, and eating bodies of killed animals as soon as he realized that God and the meaning of life do exist, that eating animal corpses is not a necessity for us but only a means of satisfying our cruel whim of gluttony.

In other words, there are vices of ignorance — and they disappear easily in the light of knowledge.

But there are vicious traits like a habit of lying; or being constantly irritated, angry, or bored; as well as arrogance, greediness, selfishness, cowardice, etc. that cannot be eliminated quickly. It takes certain intellectual efforts to overcome them — efforts on understanding their vicious nature, on developing new correct patterns of thinking, emotional reacting, and conduct. Reading serious religious books, some psychoenergetic methods like tuning up the system of the chakras and serious penitential efforts could be of great help here.

Now let us discuss the nature of repentance: what its meaning and mechanism are.

Degenerated religions, too, may have the practice of repentance, but it lost its effectiveness there. The reason is that those religions lost the understanding of the true relationships between man and God. They picture God as some kind of terrifying judge who — for some reason — examines people for sins, of which they have not repented yet, and then sends them on this basis either to paradise or to hell, to abide there eternally. According to them, the saving "repentance" consists in duly informing the local "pastor" of the particular sect of the sins one has committed. Then the pastor would "remit the sins" and thus save one from hell. In other words, it is perfectly fine to sin, since everyone does. If one does not sin, they say — one may become proud of one's righteousness and this would be the most deadly sin. Therefore, one may sin as long as one keeps coming for a saving confession.

Intelligent people clearly see that this "method of repentance" is but a means of intimidating the congregation, a method of forcing people to visit churches and temples and to pay "voluntary contributions" to support the "pastors".

In the context of this book, it can be interesting for us to find out what allowed the establishing of this absurd scheme of repentance theoretically. The point is that the concepts of those "Christian" sects have lost the knowledge about God-the-Father, Who waits for us to merge back into Him — after we have become all that we can be: perfect, Godlike.

This implies that the meaning of repentance consist not in merely "reporting" our sins to someone and thus escaping hell, but in complete elimination of vices as qualities of the soul in order to become Pure Love like God, and upon gaining Wisdom and Power, to merge with Him forever, to become a Part of Him.

In other words we have to prepare ourselves as a worthy gift to God, as a gift of our love for Him, as a Holy Offering. And this Offering must be Divinely pure!

It must be perfectly clear for us now that regardless of how many times we have "reported" and "apologized" for our sins, this practice can neither save us from going to hell nor bring us any closer to paradise and to the Creator, as long as we keep on living in emotionally coarse states!

... The primary mechanism of repentance consists in feeling a deep remorse about the transgressions that we have committed. Any harm to any living being that we do either out of self-interest or negligence, or due to our bad temper — this is the main type of sins that we commit. We harm others not only by our evil deeds or words, but also by our negative emotions. Moreover, every time when we exit out of the state of love, we not only alienate ourselves from God but also contaminate the space of the Absolute with the energies of our bad emotional states. And God points out to us that these states are also sins and that they, too, result in the accumulation of bad karma.

Our sins can be pictured as beads stringed on the threads of our bad traits, or vices. In order to get rid of vices we need to recall all the situations where each of them was manifested, to try to feel all the pain that we caused to the other living being and, having repented that we did it, to mentally re-construct this situation in the correct way. It is by using this method that we can destroy our wrong behavioral and thinking stereotypes and prepare in advance the patterns of ethically correct decisions.

... Truth (i.e. the correct understanding of what God, man and Evolution are) — Simplicity — Love — Karma Yoga (serving God through serving other people in everything that is good) — Abandonment of the lower self for the sake of merging with the Higher Self of God — this is the scheme of spiritual work that was offered to people by Avatar Babaji. By transforming ourselves in the way preferable to God we change our lives in the future, filling them with more opportunities for spiritual growth and advancement, making them happier, getting closer to the Ultimate Goal of our personal evolution — the Bliss of Merging with God-the-Father.

Love, Wisdom, and Power

Once God explained to me that His main qualities are Love, Wisdom and Power. This is why those who aspire to merge with Him should develop themselves according to these three fundamental parameters [9]. Many years later the same words came to us from God through *The Book of Jesus* [25].

Mastering each of the mentioned qualities of God is possible both in the course of "ordinary" life, provided that it is inspired by the right aspiration, and by means of special psychoenergetic methods.

Jesus taught and is continuing to teach the same thing [6,11].

Our great Contemporary — Messiah Sathya Sai Baba — is giving detailed explanations of the same principles for the modern people [6,11,45-54 and others].

Invaluable advice on bringing oneself up to the highest ethical standards can also be found in lessons of other Teachers, Who attained God, such as Juan Matus, Rajneesh, and Others [6,11,16].

… So, we should start developing the ethical aspect with studying what God wants us to be in this respect, with tracing our vices and eliminating them, through repentance, in particular, and with cultivating positive qualities. And for those who advance boldly on this Path, who aspire to practical cognition of God and are full of sincere love for Him, the crucial stage of their ethical self-correction (in terms of controlling one's emotions) will be trainings on psychic self-regulation. These trainings begin with acquiring proficiency in shifting the concentration of the consciousness from one chakra to another. Since chakras are organs responsible for the generation of emotions and other psychic states.

For instance, the anahata chakra is the organ that generates emotion of heart love. Therefore, if we have purified and developed this energy structure by special exercises, the mere entering it with the concentration of the consciousness will be enough to get us out of states of fatigue, irritation and anxiety and into the light and pure states of love and tranquility.

Those who practice such methods notice that people's attitude towards them starts to change gradually. We begin to create favorable energy fields for those around us, which makes people feel better. They find communicating with us easier and more pleasant; so the change in the attitude follows.

If we need a burst of energy for some activity, then we will find the well functioning manipura chakra or even the whole set of the three lower chakras (the structure also known as *hara*) very helpful.

Mental activity cannot be effective if the chakras located in the head are impure and undeveloped...

The condition of the chakras directly impacts functioning of the organs located in the corresponding parts of the body. The mere cleansing of the corresponding chakras can easily cure many chronic diseases.

... Development of the Wisdom aspect includes two main stages.

The first one is accumulation of knowledge and development of the thinking abilities. Ability to discern false teachings and concepts from the true ones and creative abilities of the intellect (i.e. the ability to find fresh decisions, ingenuity in small as well as in big matters) indicate a high level of its development. Studying in various educational institutions, reading books, intellectual games, intellectual efforts in scientific, professional, and educational activities — all of this contribute to positive evolution of human souls.

Engaging in a serious religious practice without a developed intellect is extremely dangerous. In this case it is very easy to get under the influence of false and destructive concepts like those, for example, which assert that drinking one's own urine in great quantities makes for spiritual progress of a person or that *Liberation* can be achieved by casting off all ethical norms and through "spontaneity" of behavioral reactions... These people cannot distinguish between love — and lust, tenderness — and sugariness, subtlety — and coarseness, God — and devil. They take voices of demons and devils for God's voice and surrender to them in their actions, they take great delight in possessing and using what they call their *personal power*, while being attuned in fact to the diabolic coarseness.

Psychoenergetic work is not for the mentally weak! The task of such people for the time being is self-improvement through service, strengthening of their faith, accumulation of knowledge, and through ethical self-correction.

The second stage of development of the Wisdom aspect relates to real exploration of multidimensional space by the consciousness of the seeker and cognizing of the consciousness that dwells there, including the Consciousness of the Creator.

This process brings about a gradual displacement of original human egocentrism with God-centrism.

The most profound Wisdom can possibly be achieved by an incarnate man through the ability to see the phenomena of the material world with God's eyes, literally *from God*, instead of seeing them from the small self attached to the body, as it is the case with almost all people.

"Fix your mind on Me," — God teaches us in the Bhagavad Gita [11]. In other words, we have to try first to gain an understanding of what God is and what role we play in the Creation in light of the fact that He exists. If we succeed in this, then through special spiritual practices we can gain the ability to submerge ourselves as consciousnesses into Him, to get closer to the full and final Mergence with Him.

The ability to control the orientation of the mind and consciousness — as opposed to mere reflexive reacting to the stimuli coming from outside or inside the body —

too, cannot be gained without special psychoenergetic training. I am talking about working with indriyas.

Indriyas is a Sanskrit term. It denotes "tentacles" of the consciousness.

An ordinary person is not the master of the body that he or she lives in, but rather a slave of the body. He or she is attached to the body just like a driver hand-cuffed tightly to the steering wheel and chained to the seat of the car. The "cars" differ from one person to another — someone's is new and well functioning, whereas another one's may be decrepit and falling apart. Man, as a consciousness, is usually "stuck" in one particular chakra, which is often contaminated and not functioning properly, and moves to some other chakra (if at all) not voluntarily, but only when being forced to do it by the needs of the body: when it hurts somewhere or there is a sort of sinking or pleasant sensation somewhere else... Man looks out of this "vehicle" only through the senses: vision, hearing, smell, etc. When doing this, man as if stretches the "tentacles" of the consciousness through the sense organs.

We can watch ourselves, for example. Here I am, listening to the radio. My indriyas are stretching from my ears to the radio set. But suddenly the phone rings. I instantly shift my indriyas to it, having taken them off the radio set. Now they are on the phone and there is no radio to me anymore.

We also stretch our indriyas through the mind to objects or to people, when we think about them. Sensitive people can perceive or even see other people's indriyas directed at them or at someone else with clairvoyance. Depending on the emotional state of the sender, his or her indriyas may have a favorable, neutral, unpleasant, or even pathogenic impact on the object. The latter phenomenon is called the *evil eye*: if an unkind and at the same time psychoenergetically strong person touches someone with the indriyas, he or she infuses the energy of his or her bad emotions into that someone and that one starts to feel bad or may even get sick as a consequence.

Let us make the following conclusion out of this: our emotional state, especially if we already possess some amount of *personal power* — is not only our personal business anymore. We need to remember that we can do considerable harm to others with our bad emotions, even involuntarily. On the other hand, we can help others, heal them, in particular, if we send our love to them.

... As we develop ourselves as consciousnesses in the right direction, we gradually free ourselves from the fetters that chain us to the body. First, we become capable of moving freely with the concentration of the consciousness within the body from one chakra or major meridian to another and acquire the ability to rid the body of various impurities. All this dramatically improves our health. After that, it becomes feasible to us to move outside the body, to grow in size as consciousnesses, to develop *personal power*, which allows us to move from one eon to another, thus exploring the multidimensional nature of the universe.

A developed consciousness, which has moved out of the body, can be compared to an amoeba, which stretches its indriyas freely without the aid of the sense organs of the body to objects and draws itself to them. As we progress in refining the consciousness, we become able to enter into more subtle eons in this manner — up to the Abode of the Primordial Consciousness, the Consciousness of God-the-Father.

... Man's *personal power* is not the power of the body but that of the consciousness. It may become either diabolic or Divine — depending on which direction we follow in our personal development. And this in turn is determined by what emotional states we are accustomed to.

Correct development of the *personal power* cannot be achieved unless we keep the body healthy and active. Therefore, physical work, athletic workouts, physical conditioning, and proper nutrition are very important, especially if they are cultivated from the childhood. The body has to become strong and healthy in order to make one really capable of high spiritual achievements.

The energy structure necessary for intensive growth of the individual consciousness is a set of the three lower chakras — this is called *hara* (or lower dantian). But it would be a gross mistake if one starts spiritual work with development of this structure, since gaining *personal power* before having the developed function of love and without being profoundly adequate from the ethical standpoint can tempt one into cultivating ethical vices. In this case, psychoenergetic training, instead of bringing one a great benefit, will be tremendously harmful.

This is why development of the spiritual heart must be given priority in psychoenergetic work, especially in the beginning of the Path. The ability to look at the world from anahata and to preserve this state even in extreme situations should be used as the criteria for judging whether a disciple can be taught the methods of increasing the power of the consciousness.

What Is Love

Love has multiple aspects. It manifests itself as care, tenderness, devotion, self-sacrifice, active service to God, which is realized through service to other people called Karma Yoga (work not for reward, but in order to please God), and in many other ways.

The "foundation" of living in the state of love is constant staying with the consciousness in anahata, transforming oneself (as consciousness) — through this —

into constant emotion of love which is being radiated to all people, all living beings.

One of the principal manifestations of love is tenderness, including the sexual aspect of it. It should be noted here, that the ethically correct sexual life directly contributes to developing the ability to love.

God is Love. If we want to Merge with Him, we have to transform ourselves into Love as well — into consciousness, constantly living in the state of Godlike Love. This is when we become these disciples of God whom He grants all other aspects of wisdom and then accepts us in Himself. This is the principal pre-condition for the ability to walk the Straight Path to Him.

But those who oppose love — oppose God.

Upon developing the spiritual heart, a follower of the Straight Path learns how to expand it beyond the bounds of the body — first, for several meters, then filling the entire Earth with it and then — even wider. This is the optimal way of breaking the identification with the body, the correct way of developing the consciousness, and of gaining experience of being and acting without the body while it is still alive.

Those who have developed themselves to such a level, shed all attachment to the body and do not fear death anymore: they find out that now it does not matter to them whether they possess a body or not and that the death of the body will be liberation from unnecessary Earth's troubles.

For such spiritual warriors, the moment comes when the Creator will reveal Himself to them and let them come in His Abode.

Love for People

Love can and should be expressed in both emotions and actions.

We talked about emotional love already and will continue to talk about it below. Here we will just reiterate, making a special emphasis, that developing love in oneself is a major method of spiritual self-perfection. This is the method by which we transform ourselves (as consciousnesses) into Godlike Love first and then into Divine Love, uniting and merging with God.

This love must not be confused with lust — selfish sexual passion.

True love is not the same as sugariness — a travesty of love, something, which takes place when one is attempting to demonstrate love when the spiritual heart is void of this emotion.

A feature of true love is a lack of elements of violence and compulsion in it. Otherwise it is not love anymore, but constraint, rape.

Love is subtle, tender, and free from egotism and egocentrism. It rests on caring about the other, not oneself.

Maturing of love must be based on the true knowledge of God and knowledge of the meaning of human life.

As this love accumulates knowledge and experience, it becomes wise.

As it develops in helping others, including fighting for their welfare, and by means of practicing special meditative techniques — it becomes strong.

Love, Wisdom, and Power — these are qualities of God. Those who have mastered them up to the Divine level infuse themselves easily into the Primordial Consciousness, thus completing their evolution in the human form. After that they continue to exist in the capacity of an active Part of God-the-Father.

But one cannot walk this Path to Divinity to the end just by thinking about It. This is a long and difficult work of transforming oneself. This work can be compared to the work of an athlete who spends many years in persistent and exhausting trainings in order to bring the body to perfection. But working with the consciousness is much more difficult. In this work, just like in athletics, the person, as a rule, cannot achieve serious results without the help of an instructor. On the spiritual Path this can be either an embodied Guru — a person who has already walked the entire Path (or the most part of It) and knows personally the Goal of the Path. Or God Himself may become one's Guru, like it was the case in my life [7].

Karma Yoga is a universal method of self-development on the Path to Perfection, which God constantly suggests to us. This is a way of perfecting oneself trough service to God, which is carried out by helping people in their evolution. This can be sharing spiritual knowledge with them, teaching them reading and writing, working in scientific, pedagogic, or medicine fields, practicing art, building homes, manufacturing clothing, producing food, protecting people from various criminal scum — the dregs of the Evolution. What is important about this is that every kind of activity has to be performed not for a reward, nor selfishly — but for the sake of helping people to advance to Perfection, including supporting their existence on the Earth, in this School of God.

This principle of Karma Yoga does not necessarily imply that work should be unpaid — this would be absurdity. But those who received help as a gift must think about giving something back. People who do not respond to gifts with gifts are considered by God as thieves (see Bhagavad Gita in [11]).

It should be noted here that activities that cause harm to people are not Karma Yoga and cannot be considered righteous. These are, for example, production and distribution of alcoholic drinks, tobacco products and other psychedelic substances, taking part in aggressive wars, preaching any type of hatred and aggressiveness, promoting fear, killing animals for using their bodies for food or for utilizing the skin torn of their bodies, unnecessary destruction of plants, etc. In other words, Karma Yoga implies helping people only in what is good.

Love for Nature

Contacts with living nature are essential for spiritual growth. Retreats to the forest or to other natural landscapes are one of the important ways of "exposing" oneself to God so that He can teach us more effectively. "In forests seek My instructions!" [40: *Leaves of the Morya's Garden. Call*]. This is where one can expand oneself as a consciousness over the harmony of the environment — in contrast to "sitting" in the head chakras while living in the city, "feeding" oneself with information about people's earthly desires and getting polluted by energies of their negative emotions.

Although cities, being big cultural centers, are also necessary: there are libraries, as well as other excellent opportunities for intellectual development. It is also easier to find like-minded people and partners on the spiritual Path there.

It is also beneficial to expose the body to sunlight, especially in the morning when the sunlight is particularly tender. This light exists not only on the material plane, but also penetrates other — the subtlest — dimensions inside our multidimensional organisms, reviving them, filling them with its pure power.

It is good for people who live at high latitudes to have an "artificial sun" — a quartz lamp — and to have sun-baths at home. This is also a wonderful remedy for various diseases. For example, exposure to ultra-violet radiation can easily cure catarrhal infections if performed right after appearing of their first symptoms. Light burns on the chest and the back made with a quartz lamp —

where mustard plasters are usually applied — make a cough go away quickly.

Summer and autumn is the time for collecting and storing mushrooms and wild berries, which are very important components of pure nutrition.

Any time of the year meditations can be performed at special *places of power* — zones that have a significant energy impact on human beings. They are very different and can be used depending on this for healing oneself, for talking to God, for refining the consciousness, for increasing personal psychoenergetic power or for dissolving oneself in God and Merging with Him.

... Early spring morning is the time when nature confers on us the greatest harmony and bliss — when birds start singing even before dawn and the entire space around us gets saturated with the energy of their love. Attuning to their state allows us to get closer to God and constitutes attainment of a certain level of refinement of the consciousness.

Those who like to sleep until late have much fewer opportunities for spiritual advancement.

... Sunset time in spring also provides a wide variety of the subtlest impressions. During this time the singing of birds gets superimposed against the background of sublime SILENCE, HARMONY. The energy of the consciousness "spills" out from the body by itself and expands over the forest saturated with bliss, filling it and merging with it. In this way the consciousness becomes more mobile, more fluid and established in harmony and inner purity.

... But at any other time of the year a morning or an evening spent in the forest or by the water reminds us of the spring dawn or dusk times. They are very important for those who have learned to deeply feel the beauty of spring!

... Nature also consists of a multitude of living beings: animals, plants, which, as a rule, are more refined as a consciousness and enjoy incomparably greater inner peace than most people. An average modern person has to come a long way in order to attain their level of LOVE and PEACE and has a right to say that he or she started to develop spiritually.

Moreover, only in open natural landscapes — in contrast to "boxes" of city apartments and "corridors" of streets — is it possible to expand, to open wide the refined consciousness in order to literally grow its size.

... Let me repeat that emotions are states of the consciousness. And the consciousness is what we are. Depending on what states of the consciousness we experience — we can be closer or farther from the Creator.

God in the aspect of the Creator is the highest degree of refinement of the energy of the consciousness. Is it clear to us now, which direction we should move regarding development of our emotional sphere?

... Very few people have witnessed what is going on at a display ground of black-grouses in spring, when pre-dawn mist gets filled with loud ecstatic singing of these big, beautiful, and passionate birds. But the majority of those who have been there, were cutting short those beautiful songs of love with gunshots, pain, blood, and death... And enjoyed themselves with voluptuousness of sadist-murderers.

Raised in the tradition of having a "right" to kill animals, not having absolute inner taboo against inflicting any suffering on other living beings, atheists, as well as members of mass sects in our country, easily switch to mass killings of people...

... In spring evenings, after the sunset, when twilight is enveloping the forest, male woodcocks fly smoothly over glades, forest openings and lakeshores overgrown with shrubs. Their song, consisting of beautiful, soul-touching tender "grunting", sends to us waves of love emotions of these lovely birds. In the shrubs, over which the males fly, sit female woodcocks — choosing the one who sings the best... Here — this one! She flashes to show herself to him... He rushes after her, seized by passion of bird's love... And then they spend the night together. In the morning they fly apart, having become tired of each other... — to look for new adventures and new friends at the next sunset...

The mysterious beauty of big curlew's song, wafting to our ears from the nearest swamp, "celestial bleat" of a snipe performing courtship ritual high in the sky with vibrating tail feathers, songs of robins and thrushes, all-night rumbling of frogs in puddles, flashing of spawning fish in the reeds, smell of a fire, swimming in a forest lake with the first rays of the sun and then — puffs of steam coming from wet and blissful naked bodies, exultation of souls, "exploding" from overflowing with joy of love for God and for every living creature — this is the emotional base that God wants us to have so that we could develop faster and more effectively in His direction!

* * *

... Plants are living beings, too. Souls live in their bodies, like we do in ours. Usually — these are the souls of *vegetative*, i.e. "rudimentary", stage of development. Although I know several humans-trees, which are quite developed, large, and strong human souls. But those people did not attain the required degree of Peace during their past incarnations — and God, in order to help them become better, embodied them into trees: so that they could calm down, become quiet after several hundred years of living as a plant.

It is easy to communicate with such people-trees on the emotional and even on the mental level. They get strongly "attached" to people who are capable of understanding them; they feel sad if no one visits them for a long time. When someone comes to see them — these plants meet them with joy, which is mixed with pain sometimes...

... What is peace then? Doing nothing? Living a lazy life? A sleepy inertia? No! Peace is the absence of emotional agitation and restless thoughts. It is possible to perform physical, mental or meditative work fast and for a long time while experiencing inner peace. It goes hand in hand with an energetic way of living. Maintaining inner peace allows one not to waste the energy in vain. Every kind of activity performed with inner peace as a background is done more efficiently. But what is most important is that it allows one to maintain contact with God, to be guided by Him and thus to avoid making many mistakes. In other words, it is conducive for positive evolution of man. But restlessness results in increase of one's isolation from God and in growth of the lower self. This is a drag on progress.

... All ordinary plants are capable of perceiving human emotions. This was proven by many scientists of various countries, which discovered changes of electric parameters of plants in response to emotions of people (see [7] for more information).

Once, long after I switched to the cruelty-free diet, I was working in a forestry on sanitary thinning-out of woods. In the beginning of my work, I thought about it as of something useful in general, and even enjoyed cutting "superfluous" trees — so that the rest of them had more space for living. But at some point, when I attained greater sensitivity, feeling the pain of those creatures, being cut down by my axe, became unbearable to me, and I quitted this job promptly.

Sure, we cannot live without eating plants. We inevitably use their bodies in construction and as firewood. And it does not make sense to wait until a tree grows old, falls down, and starts to decay; this is why it is "mature" trees that are cut down.

But one must not kill plants unnecessarily, or thrust a knife or an axe into a tree just for fun, or cut green branches without absolute necessity, or "mechanically" pluck and throw down leaves from trees, grass blades, or flowers. Disrespectful attitude towards food is equally inadmissible: since food was made of bodies of living beings that died for our sake. Throwing out food — even when one eats only plants — is also a sin, it is a sin of unnecessary killing.

And absolutely absurd from an ethical standpoint are those "ritual" killings of millions of fir-trees and pine-trees before Christmas and New Year, as well as picking flowers in order to put them in a vase and then admire their dying...

It is important that the reader does not start trying to remember now: this is allowed and that is — not... What is important is not "to learn by heart" certain "rules" but to realize and accept the ethical principles of compassion for the others' pain and respect for others' lives.

And those who do not understand or accept this — should not resent their own pain: through our pain God teaches us to understand the essence of the pain phenomenon: how unpleasant this sensation really is. In this way He teaches us to spare others and not to hurt them unnecessarily.

And even to a greater extent than to plants this principle of compassion must be applied to animals, since they can feel pain incomparably more acutely than plants.

The necessity of total adherence to the principle of compassion, in application to nutrition in particular, has been taught by God [6,11,13]. God is Love. If we want to get closer to God — we have to totally accept the principle of LOVE. But what is LOVE without COMPASSION? Only a parody of it?

Let us realize that however persistently "pastors" of various sects teach us the opposite we will not be able to make any progress in our spiritual development without total acceptance of the COMPASSION principle and resolved switching to *killing-free* diet (i.e. the one that excludes bodies of animals: mammals, birds, fish and so on) — on ethical rather than egotistic (for the sake of improving the personal health, for instance) motives!

... One can learn ethical lessons regarding plants not only in the field of nutrition. Tent pegs can be made not only out of green plants but also out of dry sticks that are still strong. And a fire can be made on the place of an old fire or on a trail, etc. — and not right on green plants.

Another thing — a fire must not be made on dry peat: huge areas of forest can get burned out, thousands of plants and many animals will die in the fire. Also, during dry periods a fire should not be made under tall spruces: thick perennial layer of fallen needles will smolder — the roots of the tree and surrounding plants will get burned as a result. One must be extremely careful during spring, when last-year's grass catches fire very easily. When it happens, a lot of green plants, insects, birds' nests with eggs or fledglings, as well as seeds get burned and die. And a great mass of the old grass that could serve as a natural fertilizer and enrich the soil is also wasted in the fire.

Also, it looks like a wildly immoral act when someone intentionally, for fun, sets this old grass on fire, which very often becomes the cause of destruction of haystacks, houses, and other constructions...

In some temples people sing, trying to convince God that He is "forbearing and merciful"... But would it not be better if they gave up this useless occupation and started living in accordance with God's Principle of Love themselves? But this is impossible without Compassion for all people and every living creature, including ants, worms, plants, and many others...

God Is Love

Jesus Christ gave us this highest formula, the key to cognition of God.

But why are there so few people who, considering themselves Christians, make use of this Truth for their spiritual advancement? Why didn't this formula inspire masses of materialists to accept faith?

One of the reasons for this is that the distortion of the Teachings of Jesus Christ began as early as when the New Testament was compiled, which took place just several centuries after Jesus' Incarnation on the Earth ended [9].

His Teachings were deprived of the part where Jesus talked of man as of an evolving consciousness, whose goal of development is attaining a Godlike state and then Merging with God-the-Father. The description of God-the-Father was also taken out of His sermons. But they included irritated demands of Paul regarding what one should and should not wear, as well as which hairstyle is appropriate. Also the Apocalypse, devoid of love and common sense, overflowing with threats of seas of blood and bowls of pus. (This is not only an opinion of the author of this book; the attitude of Jesus is the same [25]).

The result of this distortion of the Teachings of Jesus Christ was that the mass movement called "Christianity" almost from its very beginning ceased to be a religion of love — the love that God sent Jesus Christ to establish. We can recall the Inquisition, wars between the Orthodox and Catholics and *crusades*. In Russia we saw mass persecution of *Old Believers*, pogroms of Jews...

Outstanding Russian people — Alexander Pushkin, Leo Tolstoy, Fyodor Dostoevsky, Vladimir Vysotsky, and many others — although they acknowledged the existence of God, did not accept Christianity in this form.

Questions got raised also by "simple" people to which the Church could not give clear and perspicuous answers: how can one assert that God is Love if He promised these things in the Apocalypse, if what we see around us are wars, violence, cruelty, diseases, and suffering? No, if He is omnipotent and these things happen, if everything that surrounds us is evil, if I do not see any love anywhere, however I ask Him for it — then there is something wrong about this kind of faith, and I do not need a God like this!

It is important for us to realize that the fathomless abyss that appeared between the masses of "Christians" and God and that isolated people from Him and that opposed God to them, making them beg various mercies from Him — instead of inspiring them to change themselves in accordance with His Will and merge with Him in Love — this abyss has not been created by Him but by people who warped His Teachings.

In reality God is not somewhere far and high in the sky but, as Jesus said, the distance between the Abode of the Creator and every one of us is not greater than the thickness of finest paper [25]…

But in order to travel such a small distance to His Embrace of Love we have to become pure Love — like Him, rather than anger, fear, or selfish desire…

Emotions are states of the consciousness. This is a fundamentally important thing to realize.

We are consciousnesses, the energy of consciousnesses, not bodies and not minds.

God is also a Consciousness, although infinitely greater than ours.

And in order to fulfill what He wants from us, we just need to learn to live always in the state of subtle and pure love and to never exit from it.

God is Love. He has compassion for us. He is willing to help us, guiding us all the time on the Path to Him, to His Abode, to our ultimate happiness...

But we do not go to Him! Instead we squabble for the material welfare of this world, exhaust ourselves by hating others because they get dressed, have haircuts, etc. in a different way, or because they perform prayer bodily movements "different" from ours, or because their skin is of a different color or their nationality differs from ours...

... But God wants us to establish ourselves in the emotional state of love. And then — we can get in!

"Every Instance of Leaving the State of Love..."

"Every instance of leaving the state of love results in accumulation of bad karma..." God told me this once many years ago. This statement can be put as a second point right after *God is Love.*

What is meant here? Is this just another threat? Will He punish me? Will He send a dangerous illness on me? Or will He cause me to suffer during my next incarnation?

No, this way of thinking is incorrect.

God never punishes anyone. He teaches us. We build our destinies ourselves. For example, we ourselves postpone the happiness of meeting Him. And we will continue suffering from our separateness from Him as long as we do not have love within ourselves. Various misfortunes are what we attract to us ourselves; this is not God punishing us.

I will give a couple of striking examples from my own life.

Once I saw an illegal publication of my book about David Copperfield, which was made not only without my consent and financial calculations, but this time its content was distorted — it contained some preposterous scheme inserted in the middle on my behalf...[2]

This exhausted my patience: I exited the state of love and disposed myself to a hard conversation with the delinquent publisher...

And in the evening of the same day I got inflammation of the gullet — esophagus: spasms were so bad, that I could hardly swallow...

In the morning I could see a big black spirit, which grasped my throat, stuck to it and would not let go, trying to strangle. I rush into the Abode of the Creator, returning to the state of love — instantly recalling: "Every instance of leaving the state of love..." And the spirit disappeared — the inflammatory process was gone almost immediately.

The mechanism here is the following. When we are in subtle states of the consciousness — we are out of reach of evil spirits: they are not capable of entering subtle eons. If we coarsen emotionally — then we immediately get closer to their state and become easy targets for their aggressive attacks.

About thirty years ago I had a much more dramatic experience. I discovered that my colleagues in Moscow in their activity suddenly started to twist into different direction behind my back [7]. I regarded this as a betrayal of God's work by them. God Himself then ordered to immediately close the spiritual center that had been created in Moscow.

And that was actually all that I had to do in this situation. But I fell into a lingering state of anger towards them.

---

[2] I knew several such publications: among them there was one with a distorted portrait of David on the cover, in another one several important chapters about David were missed (only introduction and foreword remained, and it looked as if I promoted myself with the use of His name...).

And I immediately attracted devilish powers: without any obvious occasion I was attacked by a gang. After that I was on the verge of death of my body for a long time, suffering from severe pain. I experienced clinical death twice and ended up physically disabled for several years.

Only a "burning-through" of the destructed spine bones with the Kundalini energy, which I learned later, ensured an almost complete healing…

… In the same way, we attract either happiness or suffering for ourselves: if we enter the state of Divine Love — we get closer to God, if we take on coarse states — then devils and demons "stick" onto our bodies and we become sick and suffer.

This is how we punish ourselves for not complying with God's Will.

Jesus Christ expressed this Will very clearly: love God and love each other — regardless of anything! [6,11]

The opinion that God allegedly has to provide us with material welfare of various kinds is absolutely erroneous. He never promised to do this for everybody… He is not a slave to us at all! He is — the Lord, the Master!

He loves us and tries to help us. But to help not in procuring earthly comfort, not in satisfying our selfish desires.

His Love is manifested in His guiding us to our ultimate happiness in Unity with Him.

He is the Master, the Absolute Lord. We need to learn, accept, and realize His Will and His Law. In this case we will live in harmony with Him. This Law is: the Way to Mergence with God is steadfast Love, and whoever abandons it loses the protection of God and falls a prey to hell-beings.

Let us obey His Will: this is in our interests — to go to God, having accepted His Law!

He created the entire Creation and every one of us — not for our sake. This constitutes His Evolution and

His Life. And He is going to implement His Will firmly: if we want to go to Him — we have to live with love and to be happy, if not — we are going to suffer in our separateness from Him!

Self-Centeredness versus God-Centeredness

It is clear that the God-centered worldview cannot become the ideology of every one of us right away, for example just as a result of reading this book. What will be necessary is not just to think this concept over, but also to really feel God. Only then will we be able to learn to look at Earth's situations with His Eyes, from His standpoint. But what we can do right now is to set attainment of God-centeredness as our goal. And we need to prepare ourselves to this by fighting against our egocentrism.

Voluntary renunciation of personal pleasures for the good of other people along with the elimination of arrogance — this is the beginning of the struggle against egocentrism.

An alternative to egocentrism is true CARING — that which is sensible and free from violence and rudeness.

With that, the interests of others must be given higher priority over the personal interests.

Taking responsibility for the well being of other people — in the family or in any other group — is an opportunity for developing needed qualities. The leader's feeling of "I" must disappear and give place to the feeling of "we", where there is no personal interest left whatsoever.

Sexual relations are the sphere where egocentrism as well as the absence of it can manifest themselves in a very pronounced way.

"Do I act in my sexual relations out of my personal interests or out of those of my partner?" — this is the fundamental question that everyone should ask themselves as a part of self-analysis and self-control.

Any type of violence and constraint in sexual relations is a manifestation of one's disgusting qualities. A similar situation is when a man does not take care of prevention of unwanted pregnancy of his female partner.

Another example is when after a defloration, the man proceeds with the sexual intercourse for the sake of his personal satisfaction, ignoring the pain that his "beloved" is experiencing.

Many more examples can be given here.

The behavior of many women is no less disgusting than that of many men.

Now let us look at the nutritional habits. The overwhelming majority of people eat things made of corpses of animals without even bothering to think that they experienced pain and suffered, dying just for the sake of satisfaction of our cruel gustatory habits, for our pleasure!

People do not necessarily have to eat *"killed"* food (one that is made from meat or fish): we can get all essential nutritional elements out of plants, milk products, and eggs. Eating *"killed"* food just leads to contamination of our organisms with salts of uric acid (which causes various kinds of gout) and with coarse energies that remain in the animal corpses as a result of fear and pain that the animals experienced when dying.

Eating corpses of animals is incompatible with any spiritual progress — for the ethical reasons, first of all. God has been telling people about this constantly [6,11,14]. But now we are seeing that eating dead bodies of animals is what multiple religious pseudo-pastors demand from their followers — otherwise, they say, you can grow proud!

They should stop and realize that by doing this they act against God and against the Evolution, that they cripple the souls of people who trust them!

For what God wants us to possess is Love.

* * *

The use of special meditative techniques can be of paramount importance in one's attempts to free oneself from the egocentric lower self. This concerns the step-by-step mastering of the *total reciprocity* meditation. Its essence consists in actively shifting the consciousness into the state of *non-I*, distributing it beyond the body, outside of it, with the vectors of attention directed towards the body.

This is how just another break of egocentrism takes place and a fundamental step is taken towards Mergence with God and towards the ability to see the Earth's situations from His standpoint — with His eyes, as it were.

This is the meditative technique that allows one to attain complete Mergence with Him in His Abode.

Love for God

For those who move boldly and in the right direction, the spiritual Path is the Path of increasing bliss, joy, and happiness!

But why do so few people walk this Path? And why are such a great number of people quite content with performing pseudo-religious acts like coloring Easter eggs, drinking heavily on holidays and ritual killing of animals and plants?

Is it only a lack of intelligence that makes them do these substitutive actions, which are often nothing but crime in the face of God? Or maybe the reason is that they lack love for God?

Love for God does not imply performing rites "just in case": what if He really exists and will punish us! Love for God implies being lovingly attracted to Him: to cognizing Him and Merging with Him! It is like a sexual passion: those who are in love with Him miss Him and get saturated with bliss at times of rendezvous: successfully performed meditations.

In order to love God like this one has to know already what it is like to fall in love. For those who cannot love, God is unreachable. Jesus told about this: learn to love one another first — then you will be able to direct your already developed love towards God-the-Father.

But one does not have to spend the entire incarnation learning hard and long the art of earthly love. One may speed up studying significantly by using special methods of developing the organ of love — the spiritual heart. It is also important to understand who God really is: fairy-tale characters that "pastors" of various degenerated religious schools propose to worship cannot inspire serious people for love, can they?!

… God-the-Father can be cognized only if one lives a monastic life. But monasticism means not just wearing special clothes of certain color — black, white or orange… As well as not proudly assuming a new name — most often foreign. All of this is just childish games of grown-up people playing "religion".

True monasticism does not necessarily call for living in a monastery, as well as for giving up caring about the family or social service, or for a strict celibate or "mortification of the flesh" by rejecting elementary hygienic routines with wearing chains and enduring diseases.

True monasticism is a state of being connected with the indriyas to God rather than to objects of the material plane. This is a result of soul's being in love with God, which has been developed through meditative trainings.

A monk — in the true meaning of this word, which God assigns to it — is a person who lives in a permanent alertness, in the state of "total war" with his or her vices and shortcomings. This spiritual warrior also fights for the well being of his or her partners on the spiritual Path.

An important attribute of a spiritual warrior is a cell: a room or a house where one can sleep and spend most of the time alone with God, also the possibility to seclude close to nature for meditative work.

It is also very important to have the possibility to wash the body with soap every day. Maintaining an external cleanliness of the body promotes good health, freshness of feelings, and subtlety of emotions.

It is also good to have a quartz lamp, especially if one lives in the northern latitudes — so that one can sunbathe all year round. Sunrays — not only "living", but also artificial — confer good health on us; they are very favorable for the well-being of our bodies and souls.

In addition to this in the life of a monk there should be spiritual books, friends-companions on the spiritual Path, and — what is the most important — God as the constantly present Teacher and Advisor, tender and caring, but inexorable to our deviations from the Path to Him, Universal Father and Mother.

Criterion of the spiritual warrior's success is the disappearance of egocentrism (which is manifested in susceptibility to the offence an in the desire to obtain something "for oneself") and gradual increase of God-centeredness.

The latter does not imply mere intellectual acknowledgement that there is God but a real feeling that He is everywhere, in everything, that He is *Everything*. Feeling of "I" disappears: one's lower self — due to "concretion" with God with the indriyas — gradually dissolves in Him. This changes the ecological status of a person fundamentally, does it not?

The Creator allows spiritual warriors, who are ardently in love with Him and who do not see the meaning of their lives other than Merging with Him in Love and helping others with it, to enter into His Abode, into Himself. Having placed ourselves there as the spiritual heart, we can for the first time really embrace with the arms of the consciousness our main Beloved.

The subsequent consolidation of the Mergence with Him allows one to start acting from His Abode, perceiving oneself as a part of Him.

This is the complete spiritual self-realization, the ultimate Liberation, the highest Nirvana, the completion of the personal evolution as a human being, the total cognition of God and of oneself and Mergence with Him into *One*.

Sexual Aspect of Love

Every one of us, as well as actually all embodied people, appeared in the material world owing to sex. Is it not absurd to deny sex then?

Yet sex is not only a means of reproduction, but also a way of developing the emotional sphere in the right direction, a method of attaining subtlety of the consciousness, tenderness, and caring attention — which are the most important qualities on the Path to the Creator.[3]

Various taboos against sex and its defilement in some religious sects are indications of perversity of those sects and their being engrossed in the tamas guna[4].

On the other hand, God does not approve of being obsessed with sex, when finding new sexual adventure becomes the main purpose of one's life. God points those

---

[3] Since sex is not only a means of reproduction, a problem of contraception arises (prevention of unwanted pregnancies). It is both partners who should take care of this.

One of the convenient contraception methods is interruption of coitus immediately before ejaculation; in this case ejaculation takes place outside of the woman's genitals.

[4] Gunas are qualities of souls. They are subdivided into three groups: sattva (purity, harmony), tamas (coarseness, ignorance, filth of the soul), and rajas (intermediate stage characterized by passionateness, vigor).

people at their being deluded by, for example, sending them various diseases.

Sex plays a socializing role in any healthy person's ontogenesis (development in the current incarnation) starting from pubescence (this has been demonstrated also in experiments on animals; see [7]). Sex hormones generated in the body make people attracted to each other, start studying features of other people and ways of communicating with them.

Sexual relations highlight sometimes completely opposite personal qualities of people. Some people GIVE themselves and their love to their partners; they care for them. People of the opposite end DEMAND pleasures for themselves, express selfishness accompanied by violence, contempt, and even hatred for their sexual partners.

This is how people express and develop qualities of one of the gunas and proceed either in the direction to God or to hell.

God controls all of us to a significant extent. Among other things He does — He throws us together with our sexual partners. He does it in order to provide people with learning situations, in which they would have to make their own decisions — right or wrong. In this way, in particular, people improve or worsen their destinies.

And if someone is having problems in their sexual life — they need to look for their mistakes here taking into account that in all situations God guides them. They need to find these mistakes and draw conclusions for the future.

Sometimes we find ourselves in a tight corner because of the mistakes we made in our past incarnations. This means that sometime in the past I did to somebody what I have to experience now. It is the *law of karma* manifesting itself — God showing me what victims of my past transgressions felt. Let us draw the right conclusions!

How should we behave in our sexual relations in order to advance to God through them, instead of moving in the opposite direction?

The main rule here is that no constraint should be used — large or small, not even in one's thoughts. Everyone should be absolutely free in giving their love, willing to fill and to saturate their partner with it.

One cannot ignore psychological differences between people of the opposite sex. And those differences are significant. For example, a man feels like having a sexual contact with a particular woman as a result of a predominantly visual perception, whereas for a woman it is her tactile sensing, responding to tender touching and fondling that plays a primary role here.

We all should try to be always tender and caring with each other! Tender words, a sincere smile of love, a touch with a hand or with the lips — these are the ways we can express our caress. (The lips must be relaxed and not wet when kissing somebody. One should also keep them closed. "Slobbery" kisses arouse only dislike for the one who gives them).

During a sexual intercourse an intensive energy exchange between the partners takes place. Especially powerful energy emission occurs during the orgasm; the feeling of bliss that accompanies such an emission is what orgasm actually is.

These kinds of energy are very important for the proper functioning of the human organism, as well as for spiritual work. This is why everyone should try to give their energy to their partner; this is a very valuable gift, of course provided that the energy is pure and subtle.

... The problem of saving energy for meditative work does exist. We certainly should try to get rid of everything that is unnecessary, of everything that interferes with our spiritual growth (acts of service according to Karma Yoga principles are necessary). Sex with inadequate partners is a typical example of energy squandering. One is really wasting energy when having sex in such a way.

Who are inadequate partners? And who are the adequate ones? The adequate partners are people whose level of energetic purity is similar to each other and who are at about the same level of spiritual advancement, including the level of subtlety of the consciousness. If one of the partners is at a fundamentally lower stage of personal evolution for the time being, is energetically coarser, and keeps a non-spiritual way of life, possessing gross ethical vices — than such partners are inadequate.

Sexual relations of adequate partners do not cause the waste of energy but the exchange of energetic purity and activation of both partners' psychic energy, as well as its growth. They also create a greater energetic stability of both spouses.

Sex has been granted to us, people, not only so that we could use it for reproduction. Sex is supposed also to contribute to the spiritual progress of those who are capable of such progress. Through sex we learn to love another person emotionally, develop structures of our emotional sphere, learn to care for the other, and get to know the states of peace and bliss. We also develop these states in ourselves, thus preparing ourselves to Great Peace and Supreme Bliss in the Abode of the Creator.

Spouses can use sex as a meditative training. For example: both partners may look at each other from their anahatas, merge by spiritual hearts with each other into one — and with God.

I want to mention that in low-grade literature on "spiritual sex" one can find recommendations to avoid one's own orgasms. This, they say, allows one to accumulate energy in the body and tremendously contributes to spiritual growth... But in reality any attempts to improve one's well being at the expense and to the detriment of others have nothing in common with spirituality. This is propaganda of a variation of energy vampirism. This is a disgusting manifestation of egotism. God can in no way call this love, and this has nothing to do with the Path to God.

And one last thing: who can become the spouse of a spiritual warrior? What is marriage for this kind of people? And what is adultery and fornication for them?

General rules here are the following:

Marriage is a stable union of two people, who walk the spiritual Path together, sexual relations being one of the components of their communication.

And on the contrary, "any (sexual) connection of dissimilar people is adultery," [6,11] — this is what Jesus Christ taught to His closest disciples and this is what Philip the Apostle wrote in His Gospel.

Dissimilar are people who significantly differ from each other in the level of their spiritual advancement. Among the dissimilarities are their psychoenergetic characteristics: the purer and subtler one's energy is — the closer this person is to the Goal, to the Creator.

During a sexual intercourse an intensive exchange of energies between the partners takes place. Therefore, marriage with spiritually inadequate partner hinders the progress of the more advanced one and such a marriage is not pleasing to God.

God also considers it as fornication if someone is too obsessed with sex, which is manifested in searching for new sexual contacts. Tendencies like this distract one's attention from God and lead one away from the Path.

We see that both adultery and fornication may take place only when speaking of religious people. These terms may not apply to earthly people who live just by satisfying their bodily needs, thus the rules for them are different.

God throws people together in marital relationships Himself. He did not delegate this function to any earthly "pastors". State registration of marriage makes sense only in regard to solving any proprietary issues and children-related problems.

It is also necessary to mention that demands of various religious sects (and sometimes those of mundane morality) that people get married "blindly", without getting to know each other from the sexual standpoint, are invalid.

When it comes to sexual disorders or failure of sexual function — men's problems usually come to mind: impotence, fast ejaculation, etc. Sexual failure of women is not that clear and is not that widely discussed. Women also less often ask for this kind of medical help.

But some women cannot reach orgasm under any circumstances, and because of this they suffer after each sexual contact from sacrum pain, headaches and feeling overall exhausted. Sex becomes a nightmare to them. The genitals of some women instead of being erogenous — only possess an increased sensitivity to pain, even in the absence of inflammatory processes. Sexual contacts cause unbearable tickling sensation in some women. There are also women whose sexual energy (udana) is so coarse that no partner can make a sexual contact with them last longer than a few seconds. The erogenous part of the genitals of some women is not the clitoris, not the entrance of the vagina or its front side, but only the deepest part of the vagina, which not every man is able to reach.

In all such cases spouses cannot enjoy deep harmony in their relationships, and these marriages will not be stable, whatever splendid rites were used to "sanctify" them.

Only those marriages which are based on spiritual as well as on sexual harmony can be harmonious and favorable in spiritual respect.

So, marital relationships are important lessons in the School of God. Let us be sensitive to His Will and comply with it!

* * *

Let me draw your attention to the fact that Krishna not only had wives and children, but also talked about relationships of Ishvara (God-the-Father) and Brahman in sexual terms, as well as emphasized the Divine nature of *sexual power* in all beings [6,11].

Sathya Sai Baba also blesses marital relationships.

Babaji taught and teaches now the same.

David Copperfield demonstrates the Divine beauty of tenderness in eroticism of His "magic" dance.

Jesus, when He last time lived on the Earth, exemplified for His disciples the important role of sexually colored tenderness in the correct development of the consciousness [6,11]. At present He suggests that people view the exchange of sexual energies between spiritual aspirants as a truly sacred communion [25].

But I want to emphasize especially that these words in no circumstances should be interpreted as recommendations of casual sexual relations or "total sexualization". The conclusion that sex by itself can ensure one's spiritual growth will also be incorrect. No. Only ethically impeccable sexual relations between spiritual aspirants will render them invaluable help.

Only those sexual interactions that are performed with emotional subtlety, that are filled with tenderness and gratitude to the partner — can lead us to God. They represent an antipode to egotistic satisfaction of lust, which God disapproves of.

I would like to point out one more characteristic of spiritual sexual relations: each partner acts in the interests of the other, attunes to him or to her, feels the partner, trying to make his or her pleasure more intense.

This is what ensures the attainment of full harmony. Each partner learns how to penetrate (as a consciousness) into the body of the beloved one; as a result of this their bodies get purified and healed and the consciousnesses merge into one.

In this way we can practice merging of consciousnesses in the embrace of subtlest love. And this in turn prepares us to future Mergence with the Main Beloved — with God.

In conclusion I will cite the Gospel of Philip: "Get to know pure marriage — for it possesses a tremendous power!" [6,11].

Upbringing Children

God embodies us on the Earth so that we could learn Divinity here — in this School called *Earth*, where God is the Teacher. This study is threefold: we study Love, Wisdom, and Power. We study here under His guidance — invisible in the beginning, which later becomes evident.

There are theoretical and practical lessons in this School. The theoretical ones consist in studying the Will of God through reading books and by other means. Upbringing of children is one of the practical subjects.

In the beginning, children need to be taught elementary things: speaking, walking, rejoicing, etc. But as children grow up — parents should try to teach them many skills and make them as broad-minded as possible. They should teach them how to ride a bicycle, how to run, how to swim, how to pitch a tent, how to make a fire, how to sing, how to draw, how to play various games, and so on. Let them watch TV so that they can get to know people in different parts of the planet and the diversity of their religious quests... All this will prove useful to them in the future and will allow them to solve problems of the adult life.

One can work for the Evolution of the Universal Consciousness by upbringing not only children from one's flesh and blood, but also many other children. We all are children of One God! We all are one family. One has to learn to treat other people's children as one's own!

By living this way we will learn to expand our love and to treat people the way God does, we will learn Divine Love.

Nutrition Recommendations

God once gave people principles of nutrition through a prophet: "… See, I have given you every plant yielding seed that is upon the face of all the earth, and every tree with seed in its fruit; you shall have them for food!…". This commandment was written in the Jewish Bible (Genesis 1:29). After some time He added through another prophet: you may eat everything, "… only, you shall not eat flesh with its life, that is, its blood" (Genesis 9:1-4). What did He mean in this phrase? He was talking about the *killing-free* diet: you may eat any edible plants, use milk, eggs but do not kill for food those creatures in whose bodies you see blood.

But what did sly and gluttonous Jews, who received this commandment, contrive? They started to let the blood of animals that they were killing flow out into the ground and to eat their meat after that… — yes, without blood. They pretended to have understood that the animal's soul is its blood… Later gluttonous "Christians" began using the same way of fooling God. And… they simply did not include the protests of Jesus Christ against this in the New Testament [6,11]…

But true Christianity is Teachings of Love. Is it possible to call these people Christians who are capable of causing other creatures to suffer just for satisfying their own gustatory cravings?

True Christians are not those who have been formally baptized but do not follow the Teachings of Jesus Christ. And especially not those who were baptized at a very young age. Or those who wear crucifixes around their necks. It was crusaders who wore crucifixes, was it not?

True Christians are people who follow the Teachings of God that He has been giving to us through Jesus Christ and other Messiahs. The essence of these Teachings can be expressed in short in three phrases:

1. God is Love.

2. We have to infuse into Him for the sake of enriching Him with ourselves.

3. In order to do this we need to become Love, like Him.

Those who do not follow these Teachings do not have a right to call themselves Christians. They are simply perverts: "Christians" in quotation marks.

… In this incarnation I was born and grew up in a family of communists and atheists. Nobody thought about sin and compassion there, as almost in every "soviet" family. And I, too, ate meat and fish since my childhood: this was widely accepted. I even became a hunter and a fisherman — and I tortured and killed animals without even thinking that somebody other than myself could feel pain.

Only when I became a senior research assistant, I started to question my right to kill animals. But I immediately came up with a justification for myself: we cannot live without eating meat and fish, therefore I have an objective right to procure this kind of "food" for myself without any assistance from anyone else — since I can and know how to do it.

But then there was this incident. Once I came up to a lakeside and flushed a duck family: a mother-duck and about ten ducklings, which could not fly yet. They swam away from the shore heading towards an island fifty meters away — they swam in a tight group close to one another. But an unknown hunter was hiding on that island. And when the duck family swam up to the island he shot them all down with two gunshots...

This was the first time when I took the death of the victims of this cruel entertainment — hunting — as a drama. My confusion was aggravated by the fact that I became the cause of their death. And right after this I saw a contradiction: I would not get upset if I were the hunter who killed them! On the contrary — I would rejoice at such luck of getting a great hunting trophy!...

Later I happened to ride on a bus in Karelia with workers of a forestry. They drank vodka after work and were going night fishing — to spear fish with a fish-fork in a beam of light. But one of them got "deeply moved" and started to think aloud: "How is it possible: to spear live fish with a fork?! It is live, don't you see! With a fork!..." He repeated these phrases many times in a heartfelt way, addressing these questions both to himself and to his friends. It was obvious that he was on the verge of illumination, of awakening...

But his friends just smiled at him slightly without saying anything: this happens if one has drunk a bit too much...

Then, seeing no support from his friends he suddenly felt ashamed of his "weakness" and exclaimed: "Yes! We are going to spear live fish with a fork!"

And the issue was removed from the agenda...

Once I was hunting ducks. I wounded one. I was shooting again and again trying to kill her off, but the duck saw me firing and managed to plunge every time before the shot reached her. Then I resorted to cunning and, steering my boat, drove the duck to a shallow place, where she could not plunge. And she realized it — and gave up. I was shooting at her again and again and every time her little body got pierced with the leaden hail. Severely wounded, with her wings broken, she cried from terror and pain, unable to escape. Her screams, as perhaps, the screams of all those innocent creatures, which get cruelly killed, sounded like this: "What for?! I did not do anything bad to you or to anybody else! Have mercy! Why are you causing me such terrible pain?!" But I rowed up closer and closer and kept aiming and shooting..., but she just would not die. And only after I got next to her I shot her head off.

We ate her body, riddled with shots, afterwards, but somehow I could not enjoy it then...

My last hunt was an elk one. The beaters drove an elk-cow to the shooters' line. The hunters started shooting and wounded her. She dashed back to the beaters' line, but they opened fire, too. Two of my bullets broke her spine. Other hunters kept shooting. I recall that the chasseur got into ecstasy over the sound of many shots and was screaming rapturously: "Here's what I call music!!!" She fell down, eventually.

By the time I came up to her she already had stop breathing. But the hunters told me that after she had fallen, she crawled about fifty meters, leaving a wide bloody trail behind her. They laughed and felt happy when they were telling this. There was no compassion in a single soul...

I was shooting as well, thinking about meat and not about the pain, which this beautiful animal was experiencing...

Since that incident I quitted hunting and even sold my gun.

... When I later met a person, whom I respected and who for the first time seriously told me about the existence of God and that He did not want us to eat bodies of animals, — by that time I was quite ready to completely give up this terrible vice...

Later, I studied scientific literature on physiology of nutrition and learned that in the bodies of animals there are no nutritional components essential for the human organism, which can not be found also in vegetable products, milk or milk products, and eggs. Moreover, milk and eggs contain all the indispensable amino acids — the most important protein components. I came to the conclusion that eating meat and fish is not at all a necessity, but a striking manifestation of the human vice of gluttony, of the desire to satisfy one's gustatory whims regardless of the fact that others have to suffer pain and to die for that!

And let no one seek an excuse like this: "I do not kill anyone — 'they' do, I just eat the meat." No, we are those for whom "they" kill. We participate in this killing of innocent creatures, which have been embodied not for us to kill them at all, but in order to undergo the next stages of their evolution in the bodies that were granted to them by God. The souls that live in those bodies are just like us, only younger — they are like children...

... I killed lots of animals.

From my childhood I was taught to bait live worms onto a fish-hook. It never occurred to me then what it is like what each of those worms feels... And later fish suffered on those hooks.

Fish do not "fall asleep", as many cruel parents comfort their children who show compassion for dying fish. Each fish experiences terror, pain from wounds, and sufferings of asphyxia...

Then I began shooting at living targets: birds and animals.

Later, I became an ecologist-zoologist — and thousands of animals died from my hands. This time I did not kill them for food but for purposes of "scientific research"...

Later, working in the medicine field, I used to cut and kill rats and rabbits — these gentle, lovely animals...

When awakening finally came to me, I suddenly realized all their pain... I repented and asked them for forgiveness... But apparently I did not suffer all their pain through in my repentance...

And when many years later a two-meters-tall primitive attacked me from an ambush — without any external cause and when I could not resist him, and fatally injured my body — then, dying in severe pain, I could also be puzzled: "What for? — I did not do anything bad to anyone, didn't I?..."

And some day, perhaps, in their future incarnations, he and all the members of that gang will be dying in pain, groaning: "What for?!..."

Often people, who never cared before what it was they were eating, upon hearing a sermon about compassion and having agreed with it suddenly get perplexed: what is there to eat if not meat and fish?! So, here we will talk very briefly about general principles of nutrition.

First, as a rule, it is advisable for our diet to include all five groups of nutritional components: proteins, fats, carbohydrates, vitamins, and microelements. Deliberately scanted diets including mono-diets (those, which imply only one product — for example, only rice, wheat sprouts, oats or apples, etc.) can be very successfully used for therapeutic purposes, but they should not be adhered to for an excessively long time. So, after consulting with a specialist one may get on a diet like this for 1, 3, 7, 30 or 45 days — depending on how serious the disease and on the tactics of the treatment.

Complete fasting (with obligatory drinking of water!) that does not exceed three days is also helpful for therapeutic purposes and is an effective means of purification of the body. If one is willing to fast for a longer period of time, one should do this only under the supervision of a specialist in therapeutic fasting. Break of the fast must be gradual. Best things to eat first, when you break a complete fast, are juices and fruits. No salt is allowed for the entire recovery period, which may last for several days — otherwise there is a high risk of edema of the body tissues.

Almost every natural type of food: milk, grains, vegetables, etc. — contains proteins, fats, and carbohydrates, though in different proportions. Depending on these proportions, they are usually classified into *proteins*, *carbohydrates*, and *fats*.

Milk and lactate products, curds, cheese, eggs, nuts, mushrooms, soybeans, peas and beans belong to the *protein* group. Proteins can be different, depending on the type of the amino acids that they are composed of. The amino acids in their turn can be divided into two groups: the dispensable (i.e. necessary, but which can be generated within the human body) and the indispensable (which are also necessary, but usually are not generated by the body, therefore their external supply with food is vital for the human organism).

So, the most valuable from the standpoint of supplying the organism with proteins are those foodstuffs that contain a complete set of indispensable amino acids. These are milk and eggs. Milk and eggs, if included in one's diet, make it protein-balanced. If there are neither milk products nor eggs available — one should compensate for this by diversifying other components of one's diet, especially those of the *protein* group.

But it would make sense to take into account that beans, when consumed in big quantities, result in generation of gases in the intestines. This also can be caused by barley and rye, and in case of adults — by milk (but not curds and cheese). In such cases, it is better to drink milk in the evening in small quantities and without combining it with anything else. By the way, in cases like that substituting milk with clabber would be even better.

Gases form also as a result of combining large quantities of protein or fat food with sweets.

One should not eat eggs and fat food before going to bed at night: these products remain in the stomach for a long time, but during a night sleep the digestion process in the stomach slows down (in contrast to that in the intestines). Food can stay undigested in the stomach for the whole night, which causes the multiplication of microbes in it and inflammation of the stomach walls first and then of the walls of the intestines.

Let us discuss also two issues in regard to eating eggs.

First, there is a postulate that we should not eat eggs for ethical reasons, since chickens could hatch out of them. But chickens can in no way be hatched from the eggs, which were laid by battery farm hens. The point is that domestic hen is a unique biological species (bred through a selection process), which lays eggs without being impregnated by a cock. Chicken cannot hatch out of these eggs. (At battery farms, cocks and hens are brought together only for making those eggs that would go to incubators for subsequent hatching of chicken).

But it would not make sense not to eat even impregnated eggs: since there is no embryo in a non-incubated egg, therefore it has no embodied soul; such eggs can feel neither fear nor pain when fried or boiled.

Eggs that we eat are merely ovules. But if we are to spare all ovules — how much more we should grieve over dying human ones! Since every menstruation is a sign of the lost opportunity of a human being to be born! Does not it follow from this line of reasoning that all women should be constantly pregnant in order to save all ovules from dying unnecessarily? (Joking!).

The second objection against eating eggs comes from the physiologists: eating eggs, they say, inevitably causes atherosclerosis, since eggs contain great amounts of cholesterol.

Once I participated as a laboratory assistant in the experiments on rats conducted under the supervision of academician N.N.Anichkov — the experiments that subsequently allowed him to "pronounce an anathema" against eggs. I myself then, with my own hands, was making atherosclerosis in those rats. However, they were fed not with eggs but with pure cholesterol powder mixed with oil. And the doses of that chemically pure cholesterol were quite impressive compared to the weight of the rat's body: they measured grams per one intake, several times a day. And this is for a small rat! Of course, the rats developed atherosclerosis. But the doses of cholesterol were exceeded by millions of times — as compared to those contained in several eggs a day for a human being!

In reality cholesterol is quite an important substance for the human organism, since it serves as a material from which all sex hormones — both male and female — are formed.

Cholesterol gets generated within human bodies as well. And its high concentrations can be found not only in eggs but also in the bodies of animals, especially in the liver, brain, and fat tissues.

But in order to identify the cause of atherosclerosis one should start with finding out first whether those people, who adhere to the *killing-free* diet, suffer from it.

... Fats can be of vegetable and of animal origin. The latter include both butter and fats obtained from corpses of killed animals.

Scientists say that consumption of fats significantly increases risk of cancer, but we need to know that for butter this is not true.

Both vegetable oils and butter are good for people. The former contains vitamin E among other things and can dissolve cholesterol deposits, if any. Butter is rich in vitamins A and D.

It is better to use butter for frying and heating of food, since all oils get oxidized when heated in presence of oxygen, forming harmful substances. The more liquid the oil is the quicker it gets oxidized.

There are also margarines, which represent mixes of various oils. If someone wants to use them, it would be better to read the list of ingredients on the package first.

All vegetables, fruits, berries, cereals, greens, jam, honey belong to the group of *carbohydrates*... All bodies of plants and grains are rich in fiber, which is important for proper functioning of the intestines, and in vitamins, especially of the C and B groups. Sugars among other things provide the body with energy that is easily assimilable.

It is currently widely known that bread is a source of the necessary vitamins of the B group. But it is important to know that bread made of high-grade flour contains almost no vitamins of this group, as well as almost no proteins. Bread made of coarse grinded grains or with bran added is a much healthier food.

The same can be said about rice. Unpolished rice is rich of the vitamins of the B group and in protein.

As for vitamins, we have discussed them enough already. I will just add that if we drink milk and eat eggs, vegetable oil, butter, carrots, greens, fresh fruit and berries, — then we provide our bodies with all necessary vitamins. In case one doubts it or if there are special medical indications — one can buy poly-vitamins or specific combinations of them in a drug store according to a physician's recommendations.

Vitamin C is worth special attention. It is important for the resistance power of the organism; in particular, it helps in curing catarrhal diseases. But it is not heat-resistant. This is why herb, fir needle, or hip brews should be made without bringing the water to a boil. Garlic and nettle contain great amounts of vitamin C.

We provide necessary microelements to our bodies when our menu is diversified to include milk, mushrooms, and many other kinds of foodstuff. But the best source of microelements, which contains a full set of them, is sea kale (laminaria). It is sold in many grocery stores either canned or dried (the latter is also sold in drug stores). One can simply add sea water or sea salt to food.

... Lives of those, who love and know nature, not only are full of beauty, healthier and more efficient in terms of spiritual growth but also require less money. A true nature-lover will always store up jam and self-made flower honey and dry up delicious herbs for using in place of tea for the winter. But the most useful thing to store is, of course, mushrooms.

Fried or boiled mushrooms are very delicious, but they are hard to digest, since the membranes of their cells are not easy to destroy for our peptic enzymes. Drying mushrooms up also does not improve this situation. But prolonged exposure to acetic or lactic acid — when mushrooms are marinated or made sour (salted) — destroys the membranes and makes mushrooms easy to assimilate.

One can store salted mushrooms in one's own house; the only thing that needs to be done regularly is taking off the mould from the surface over the brine (approximately once a week). But do not try to pickle honey fungus (armillaria) only with salt separately: the process of its fermentation goes without producing lactic acid — thus the result will not be good. One may either add this kind of mushrooms to the vessel with other salted mushrooms or pickle it using vinegar and salt.

The most important thing about correct nutrition is adherence to the fundamental ethical principle of *not harming*. Only those who have developed compassion for the pain of other living beings can make progress on the spiritual Path, for God will let get close to His Abode only those, who become embodiments of the principle of LOVE.

The Divine Teacher Huang Di taught this way of life in ancient China. Pythagoras, Gautama Buddha and then Jesus Christ taught the same [6-7,11]. (Jesus made several exceptions only when He talked to fishermen and to crowds of common people, when He was feeding them with bodies of fish). Nowadays God is teaching the same through Babaji and Sathya Sai Baba [6,11,19,45-55].

This opinion of God seemingly contradicts to His words in the Quran. But we should keep in mind that during the first years of the establishment of Islam, which were marked with the continuous state of war, the situation was not appropriate for introducing new nutrition habits among cattle-breeders and desert inhabitants. God, Who guided prophet Muhammad at that time, had another purpose — to establish a monotheistic faith in that region of the Earth. And only after Islam had been established and accepted by people, Muslims were presented with an opportunity to think about the ethical aspect of their nutrition.

If one ignores the ethical aspect of nutrition, then one becomes subject to special mechanisms, created by God, that make for the development of diseases.

Deposits of salts of uric acid, of which meat and fish dishes are the major sources, start to form gradually in the blood vessels, in the skin and in the cartilaginous tissues. This disease is called gout. Among its symptoms there are memory failure, headaches, disturbed sleep, sexual malfunction, and muscle and joint pain. And an urgent need to eliminate the states of discomfort of the brain provokes smoking and alcoholism.

Energy aspect of such nutrition should be considered as well: the chakras and meridians get contaminated with the energies of dead bodies, and this causes disorders of bioenergetic supply of multiple organs and contributes to the development of cancer. The same energies adversely affect the organs of digestion, thus acute and chronic inflammations and ulcers develop. This also provokes the development of aggressiveness in people. Their energy of the consciousness coarsens, and they become incapable of attaining subtle states.

The well-known postulate that meat and fish are the only sources of necessary proteins, as we have discussed above, is absolutely invalid, and those who defend it only demonstrate their ignorance in medical issues. The complete set of amino acids (the elements of proteins) necessary for the human organism is found in milk and eggs.

The best testimony to the correctness and adequacy of the *killing-free* nutrition is the dramatic improvement of health and disappearance of diseases in those who switched to this type of diet. In addition to this, their ability to perform various kinds of activities increases.

I want to note also that people, who eat bodies of killed animals to satisfy their gluttonous habits, should be aware that the time may come for them to experience their own pain. This is the way God teaches us Love. This is the *law of karma* in action: those who disregard the pain of others have to learn compassion through their own pain, experiencing it themselves.

The ethically correct behavior in regard to the "pure" foodstuff — plants, milk and milk products, and eggs — is to use them sparingly and with respect. They should not die in vain.

One should avoid using too much salt as well as drinking alcohol, which by no means contributes to attaining Perfection, also to restrain from excessive consumption of caffeine-containing drinks (coffee, cacao, tea, etc.) and from frying food using vegetable oils. And of course, under no circumstances one should drink urine, which has become quite popular "foodstuff" in Russia recently. Regular drinking of urine intoxicates the brain and causes mental disorders.

What should we eat then? What is the best diet for one and for one's whole family? Of course, everyone has their own tastes and nutritional habits. The set of the four basic products: rice, mushrooms, eggs and tomatoes (fresh or as various sauces, ketchups, or pulp) — became the basis of my nutrition. In addition to these, I use mayonnaise, greens, potatoes, carrots, wheat bread, jam, berries, butter, vegetable oil, cheese, and other. This type of diet is satiating and provides a sufficient amount of energy for any kind of work, including meditation. Only at the last stages of my spiritual ascent I had to give up eggs: the energy derived from them was not favorable for settling down in the Abode of the Creator.

And the last piece of advice: we should not think about food too much! Upon eliminating vicious nutrition habits, you should establish a new thinking "algorithm" — and think about God and your Path to Him, including your service to Him. Beware of repeating the mistake, which so many people have made by focusing all their attention only on "nutritional rules" and forgetting about more important things.

Clothing

One should walk a lot, communicating with God in the surroundings of living nature. So, let me say a few words about clothing. The first important rule for those walking the spiritual Path is to try not to wear clothing made of synthetic fabric, especially that having an immediate contact with the skin. Synthetic fabric accumulates static electricity, which has an adverse impact on the energy systems of human organism, and prevents proper energy exchange between the organism and its environment.

Synthetic clothing is particularly inappropriate for psychoenergetic work — both indoors and outdoors.

This is not to say that one should not wear polyethylene raincoats when it is raining or rubber boots during a wet weather.

In cold winter, the rubber boots should be 2-3 size points larger than one's regular size, so that one could put 2 insoles inside it and put on 2 or 3 woolen socks and regular socks over them so that the former do not get worn out too quickly.

It is better to put woolen socks on bare feet, since wet wool does not make the body cold.

It is the same with outerwear: if you happen to get drenched just wring your clothing and put a woolen sweater on first and all other things over it.

Another thing that we need to make sure is that the upper surface of the sole of our footwear is smooth. If there are any prominences under the heel, then long walks will cause heel bones periostitis.

Or, in some kinds of footwear the sole gets warped in the toe area: this happens because the card layer that was inserted in the sole gets pursed. As a result, toe joints may not function properly, which sometimes causes severe inflammation accompanied by edema of the entire foot. In order to bring that footwear back to the appropriate condition, one needs to detach the sole, tear the card layer out and then glue the sole back on.

Night Sleep

One should not work during the night. The best time to go to bed is 10 o'clock in the evening, and the best time to wake up is from 4 to 6 o'clock in the morning. This regime provides the best night rest to the body and ensures vivacity and agility of the consciousness. It is best to start every day with doing spiritual exercises.

Getting a good night sleep is important: its primary purpose is to ensure the bio-chemical cleansing of the brain. If one does not sleep enough, the brain gets inflamed. This can be seen with clairvoyance as a darkening of the brain.

In this connection I want to mention that sleeping with another person in one bed which is not too wide is a mistake: body movements of one of the partners disturb the sleep process of the other. As a result both do not get a good night's sleep, and their activity the next day is carried out with an inferior energetic level.

One should sleep in a bioenergetically favorable place. Favorable and unfavorable places for sleeping can be located within an apartment or even within a room. The origin of unfavorable places is primarily people's coarse or sick states that got imprinted bioenergetically in material objects. It is possible to correct such defects by influencing those places meditatively.

If one ignores this factor when choosing a place to sleep and makes a bed anywhere, one can easily catch the unfavorable energy states, traces of which were left by someone who was there before. In this way one may end up getting insomnia or nightmares, the previously refined consciousness may coarsen or one may even develop the symptoms of the disease of which the previous inhabitant of this place suffered.

If you need to examine your home for the presence of such places, do not look for "psychics" who use dowsing rods or other similar devices: none of them is able to interpret the indications obtained in such a way. Only those who succeeded in refining the consciousness can make a proper examination. And they will not be using any "tools": they perfectly feel everything with themselves — as pure consciousnesses. May all of you become like this too!

Regarding dreams: sometimes we have dreams, in which we sin. This is an indication that we have not completely eliminated our vices yet. In these cases, we need to work over our "weak points" using the mechanism of repentance.

Medicine, Health, and Destiny

Two diametrically opposite approaches in regard to medicine can be observed sometimes.

Some people rely completely on medicine. They "live on pills", call for a doctor and try to get on a sick leave every time they feel indisposition. They do not want to make any effort to keep a healthy life or to heal themselves. But most diseases are easily cured just by changing the nutritional habits, quitting smoking and drinking hard, and starting to regulate the emotional sphere.

Another extreme typical of neophytes is the attempts to renounce completely all medical services and rely on various "panaceas", like fasting, walking barefooted, or keeping to some type of a mono-diet. These "novations" are not bad for a start, although they are not sufficient for attaining spiritual results.

But some "neophyte" passions can turn out to have disastrous consequences. For example, drinking large amounts of urine causes intoxication of the brain, mental degradation, and various psychic disorders [7].

Having enema every day used to be quite popular some time ago. This disturbs the proper trophism of the organism: since the large intestine is the place where many vitamins and other useful elements of food get absorbed.

Declaring first salt, then sugar, bread or even oxygen "main enemies of man" relates to the same kind of mistakes...

... Diseases can be classified into three groups.

To the first group belong those which occur naturally due to the physical wearing out of the body (for example, teeth decay as one grows old) or as a result of the natural lack of experience when we are learning something new, or due to an overstrain, etc.

The diseases of the second group develop as a result of our indulging in various vicious habits, for example, an addiction to toxic substances (alcohol, tobacco, etc.), gluttonous habit of eating *"killed"* food or living in angry states: condemnation, irritation, and hatred — instead of states of love and peace.

The diseases of the third group are caused by ignorance in hygienic or religious issues. It may be, for example, a wrong direction of religious aspiration, when the attention of "believers" gets focused not on God but on demons, black magicians, and "vampires". By thinking about them people attract them and attune to them instead of attuning to God. And this provokes mass schizophrenia among the members of such sects.

God uses the diseases of the second and third groups to show us that we are wrong, to prompt us to seek correct decisions.

Forgetting about the inevitable death of the physical body may become one of our tragic mistakes. But death can come very soon, nobody knows for sure — when exactly. And it puts an end to all our dreams that sometime in the future, when we retire...

But after the death of the body, one will no longer be able to achieve any fundamental change of oneself and of one's status in multidimensional space. One will have to wait the next incarnation, which is going to happen in the conditions according to one's destiny. To people like this — who must make spiritual efforts but do not make them — God sends, for example, cancer, which makes the inevitability of death more apparent to them.

The material mechanisms of diseases vary. It may be genetic factors, fetus injuries, traumas, poisoning, eating *"killed"* food, unbalanced nutrition, impact of microbes, viruses or parasitic fungi, information overload, excessive tiredness, wrong life purposes, energy contamination of the chakras and meridians, as well as entering of spirits of different levels of development into one's body (spirits of either vicious people, animals, or even plants). All this causes a wide range of various diseases: mental, oncological, and so on, including common inflammations and "aches" of unknown origin.

All these diseases occur in our bodies and souls as a result of combination of two types of will: the person's own will and the Will of God. All of them are realization of our destinies.

The destiny of every one of us is composed of two interlacing destiny lines — the "inborn" and the one acquired in this life.

For example, if children are born with some kind of bodily defect or acquire it at a very young age — this is their "inborn" destiny, or complication of their life as a result of their making gross mistakes in the previous incarnation.

As children grow up, they acquire the ability to make ethically important decisions. As a result of these decisions, the destiny line in the current incarnation forms. It gradually starts to prevail and then even to dominate over the "inborn" one.

Thus, an unfavorable destiny can be completely changed if we develop ourselves in the right direction.

And vice versa, a good destiny can be degraded by our own ethical mistakes in the current incarnation.

Destiny is not some sort of a mechanical law defined by "stars" or "planets", as astrologers claim. Destiny is the direct guidance that we receive from God — the Supreme Consciousness, Who possesses Omnipresence, Omniscience, absolute Love, Wisdom, and Power. He leads every one of us to Himself, into Himself. If we move the right way — then He encourages us by giving us a feeling of bliss, but if we turn away from the Straight Path to Him — He points out to this by causing us some kind of pain. Everything is that simple.

And there is no point in complaining about "bad living conditions", because the Path to Him is not at all something like walking or riding public transportation. It consists in transforming oneself as a consciousness, as a soul. This implies the inner work on self-improvement.

God outlined the Path towards Him through the Avatar Babaji in the following formula: Truth — Simplicity — Love — Karma Yoga — Abandonment of the lower "I" (lower self) for the sake of merging with the Higher "I" (Higher Self). This is the entire Teachings of God, in short. All other knowledge and instructions are simply explanations of this formula.

One of the things God wants us to possess is Wisdom: without Wisdom, walking this Path is difficult. One of the lessons regarding health is getting to know the structure and functioning of one's own body and taking care of it. Upon learning this, we will be able to take care of other people and to enrich them with our experience.

... I heard an opinion that syphilis, for example, should be treated with a specific set of Hatha Yoga asanas or that prayer is the only medicine that should be used for the treatment of any disease, or even that no treatment at all is needed — that any disease will go away by itself, that one should just let the organism strengthen its resistance, while all medications can only do harm.

But syphilis does not go away as a result of doing asanas; it goes to the next stage of its development while the diseased person is performing asanas. And to no reasonable person will it occur to extract a splinter with a prayer: it should be taken out using the nails, a needle, or tweezers. Life in the body was granted to us not that we squander it in suffering from diseases, wasting energy and precious time for this. Life in the body is granted to us so that we actively develop the Divine qualities — Love, Wisdom, and Power.

My approach consists in curing any disease promptly without letting it develop and using all available means.

Even if I get a splinter in my finger, it will be appropriate to think about the causes: have I been doing the right thing or did I lose a state of love and peace? But it does not make any sense to think about it for too long with a splinter still in my finger. The splinter must be extracted promptly and iodine probably should be applied to the wounded area.

The same applies to flu, tonsillitis, and even the common cold. They can be indications of our mistakes, our loosing peace, for example, or our associating with wrong people. But after drawing the right conclusions from the analysis of the causes, it would be wise to start taking appropriate measures: applying anti-virus ointment or calendula tincture on the mucous membrane, having quartz lamp radiation session, drinking brews of hip, nettle or fir needles, etc. Cleansing of the corresponding chakras and meridians and the *cocoon* can also help.

The same algorithm should be followed in cases of more serious diseases that require intervention of medical specialists. Even in case of cancer, it does not make sense to decline a surgery if a physician suggests it. But finding out the karmic causes of cancer and the correction of one's mistakes must undoubtedly be the main direction of one's efforts.

By the way, contemporary Divine Messiah Sathya Sai Baba, Who possesses unlimited ability of working miracles and Who personally healed a great number of people — including those at a distance, using the most unbelievable means from materialists' standpoint — nevertheless takes care of building conventional hospitals, some of them are even on the territory of His ashram.

After all, both doctors and patients have to develop themselves, to perfect themselves on the Path to God — through interacting with one another. As for miraculous healing, we have to deserve it by our own efforts; otherwise, it will not do us any good.

… Every good householder should have — not only for the family members, but also for guests — a set of the most elementary medications: bondage, cotton wool, iodine, calendula, phthalazolum (Phthalylsulfathiazole), analgin (Metamizole sodium), oxoline ointment, menovasin, indovasin (Indometacin), sage, etc.

Some of it should be taken along when going outdoors for a hike, especially in a group.

For example, phthalazolum (Phthalylsulfathiazole) is good for intestinal inflammations, sage — for gastritis or esophagus. Menovasin can be used not only for rubbing in muscles but also (if diluted 1 to 50) as eye drops in case of conjunctivitis or as nose drops in case of a cold. If diluted 1 to 10 menovasin can be used for throat rinsing in case of sore throat. Applying indovasin (Indometacin) to and tight bondage of swollen feet joints will let one continue walking if the joints have been injured or rubbed sore. Propolis possesses remarkable healing properties.

Everyone will benefit from becoming a specialist in this "household" medicine: this not only will make one's life easier, but also will make one able to help others in trouble. These are also lessons of Wisdom.

... It has been confirmed by statistic research that eating *"killed"* food, as well as smoking and drinking alcohol, dramatically increases the risk of cancer. People who adhere to the *killing-free* diet do not have cancer.

Moreover, usually just giving up eating *"killed"* food is enough to achieve a dramatic improvement of the health: gastrointestinal diseases, high blood pressure, various types of gout and other kinds of health disorders disappear.

In Russia, until 1917 a successful experience of using the *killing-free* diet for treating various diseases and freeing people from addiction to tobacco and alcohol was accumulated. There was also an ethical movement in Russian society that advocated moral nutrition [5,21,24,30, 34,39,44,61]. One of the initiators of this movement was the Russian writer Leo N. Tolstoy, cursed by the Orthodox Church for "free-thinking".

* * *

People who started walking the true religious Path get healed of many diseases, even of cancer, in a very short time. Yes, over the years of teaching, I had dozens of people with cancer in my groups. Several of them had it in the inoperable stage and official medicine gave up on them having classified them as hopeless. All of them recovered after they accepted the correct spiritual orientation and started to make real efforts (each one — according to his or her own abilities) on self-development.

I need to mention that not any kind of religiosity is a salvation from diseases. This can be illustrated by the fact that the percentage of sick people among the members of modern mass sects is not lower than that among atheists.

Moreover, those sects, where mystical fear is cultivated instead of love, become hotbeds of mental disorders.

There are also sects in which people massively take psychedelics or alcohol, which are incompatible with the spiritual Path, let alone with health.

Another popular occupation of modern sectarians is drinking urine — in large amounts and for long periods of time — which results in the intoxication of the brain and… in further decline of intellectual faculties of those who practice this.

We need to realize fully that all our diseases are consequences of either our ethical mistakes or of our ignorance. Behind all our pain we need to try to see the guiding Hand of God, Who wants — by means of this pain — to point out something that we need to change in ourselves.

Diseases can result, for example, from smoking, alcoholism, or eating dead animals' bodies. But did not God warn us about this? And if the leaders of your sects bless such things — is it not the time to turn our back on them and seek guidance from God?

Some diseases are a result of human laziness: for example, when a person lies or sits most of the time. Some originate from ignoring the necessity to temper the body. Or some of them occur because we forget that every day brings us nearer to the death of the body and that we have to make spiritual efforts — in order to have time to advance as much as possible. Cancer is the example that we have already discussed above. One gets it as a reminder that death is inevitable. It is something that helps us feel that death is approaching, something that makes it more evident for us. And if a person gets this hint and wakes up, cancer goes away.

Some healers can develop diseases that they "take up" from their patients: if they try to heal the body of the patient instead of focusing on healing the soul first — by eliminating ethical causes that brought about the disease. All such causes can be classified into three groups:

a) lack of aspiration for God (or aspiration in a wrong direction); b) lack of love, and c) ignorance.

I will give only one of many examples of this kind. Once I was sitting in the kitchen with two ladies — a mother and her grown-up daughter — who invited me to their place. We were drinking tea. Next to us on a stove there was an animal's dead body boiling in a saucepan. They were telling me about their ailments for a long time... I asked them about love — love for animals, in particular. Both of them started to "coo" about how much they loved them... I lifted the saucepan lid and asked: "Do you love them — as a soup? Or roasted, too?..."

Chronic anger as the cause of a disease is especially terrible — including the emotion of condemnation, as well as dislike, hatred, or jealousy. All this not only pushes one into hell but also is very detrimental for one's health. Through these diseases God warns us so that we can come to our senses before it is too late. Various medications cannot save us from hell: God wants us to make ethical decisions and to perform real self-transformation!

By giving us some types of diseases God suggests that we start studying the basics of anatomy and physiology and learning to identify the causes of common ailments.

For example, a combination of large amounts of protein or fat food with sweets causes flatulence.

Another example: heating or frying food using liquid vegetable oils, as opposed to butter, is a harmful practice and may result in the liver disorder. This is because *unsaturated* fat acids, which make up liquid oils, get easily oxidized forming harmful substances, when heated in the presence of oxygen.

One should avoid wearing clothes made of synthetic fabric, which have a direct contact with the skin — even if they look good and "everybody wears them", because this upsets energy processes in the body tissues.

One should not only brush the teeth but also floss them in order to get rid of small bits of food that get stuck in between the teeth; either a dental floss or a thin metal plate can be used for that purpose. Also, it is beneficial to massage the gums, at least occasionally or systematically if needed, by pressing lightly all intervals between the roots of the teeth: from the jaw to the chewing part of the tooth. If food gets there during chewing — then periodontitis may develop, which we may not notice for a long time: until we feel pain or someone points out at an unpleasant odor from the mouth. But any nidus of infection in the body poisons the whole body through the blood stream. And gingivitis can become the cause of diseases in other parts of the body (for example, sinusitis, tonsillitis, conjunctivitis, etc.).

Let me stress out that caries and inflammations of the gums (periodontitis) quite often cause conjunctivitis. Conjunctivitis which is not caused by dust or sand contaminating the eye may be a sign that one needs to visit a dentist.

There are a great number of silly and harmful opinions in regard to health.

For example, if a "fever blister" swells up on the lip — people say that this is just a "cold" and there is "nothing to worry about". But in reality, this can be either a highly contagious herpes virus or sometimes a lesion of lips caused by trichomonad. In both cases one should not kiss anyone but should seek medical treatment.

Or when a woman feels pain in the ovary region, they say that she has been simply overexposed to cold and needs to warm this area. Then they recommend that she use a hot water bottle or get wrapped in a shawl. But this can be either harmless ovulatory pain due to a regular follicle rupture — in this case it is all right and no heat therapy is needed. Or this can be an inflammation, caused by microbes' activity — in this case it must be treated seriously with antibiotics (namely, modern cephalosporins).

Among causes of chronic adnexal inflammations there can also be bioenergetic lesions from sexual contacts with energetically coarse partners, as well as from wearing synthetic lingerie.

Hemorrhoids sometimes is attributed to a low-mobility lifestyle, whereas the cause of it is that small bits of feces, which stay in the rectum, rub the rectum walls; thus an inflammation of the mucous membrane results, which spreads to the vein walls. As a preventive measure, it is recommended to keep the lower section of the intestines absolutely clean and with first signs of inflammation apply a bactericidal ointment over it.

Some say that it is impossible to get pregnant at all days except the few in the middle of the ovulatory cycle. In reality, the probability of getting pregnant during the rest of the cycle does get reduced but not to zero.

Some people claim that male potency can be improved by drinking more coffee and eating more meat. In reality, both should be avoided in such cases. What can really help is the correction of the emotional state and cultivating deep inner peace. This comes as one advances along the spiritual Path.

Or there is a neophyte slogan: "I will not take any medications!" This is not wisdom but something contrary. We do not have time for illnesses! It also does not make sense to yield the body "at the mercy" of microbes, because the body suffers from this incomparably more than from the adequate usage of medications.

Once I was astonished by a statement of a woman, about 30 years old — she was a senior coach and a graduate of a University of Physical Culture — who said that the best means of contraception which "was always effective for her" is... to urinate after sexual intercourse...

She did not know the difference between her womb and urinary bladder!

I could not even object, just said nothing to her. How could one discuss this "difficult" matter with such a person...?!

Years later, when I told this story to a female physician, an acquaintance of mine, she did not laugh and was not surprised. "Many women in our country think that; I can hear this opinion quite often!" she said...

By the way, why did not this woman, who loved new sexual adventures, get pregnant? Most likely the reason was a chronic inflammatory of the uterine appendages affected with a venereal disease.

... God wants us to be wise. One of the ways to acquire wisdom is through accumulating knowledge about everything, including the anatomical structure of the human body, possible threats to it and ways to prevent them, as well as methods of treatment of diseases.

I recommend that everyone get a *Handbook of a Practical Physician* and read it through, at least once. This, of course, will not make one a specialist in medicine. This also is no substitute for getting qualified medical help. But after reading a book like this one will get an idea of the variety of possible diseases: from sexually transmitted ones and fungal skin infection — to mental disorders. It will also make it easier for one to avoid dangers to health.

For example, several times I had guests who had fungal infection of the feet — and they put on my slippers without ceremony and feeling conscience-smitten...

Or when some neophytes get venereal diseases they usually do not worry: only "those" — "non-spiritual" people — can have such diseases, they think, but not them. They think that it is "okay" and "will soon disappear"...

You may also accept this advice if you want: it is best to stay healthy, but if you do happen to get sick — it is better to start complex treatment using all available means: analysis of the cause, repentance, meditative and bioenergetic methods, non-specific means that increase the resistance of the organism (vitamins, hot baths, ultraviolet radiation by quartz lamp, *winter swimming*, etc.) plus specific medications and other therapeutic procedures recommended by a physician.

Incidentally, one of the methods of preventing many diseases and ensuring one feels well is to wash the body with soap every day. For successful spiritual work this is absolutely essential.

Let us remember: one can gain good health by advancing along the spiritual Path! And it is better to be healthy while walking this Path!

Work in the Material World

In regard to work, two principles are important for any person, even if he or she is not mature enough to be able to comprehend the highest religious truths. These are — honesty and striving to learn as much as possible. The second principle implies not only aspiration towards study but also quite frequent changing of the field of applying one's efforts and change of places of work. We come to every new place enriched by the experience we gained at all of our previous places of work. This significantly enriches our experience, develops us intellectually, and creates an objective prerequisite for respectful attitude from other people.

For religious people, the attitude towards their work implies a more serious approach. Namely, they should regard their social activity as their service to God.

This is called Karma Yoga. Karma Yoga is the path of self-development through helping God in His Evolution. This consists in various kinds of help to other people — help in what is really useful for them, including spiritual help.

We have to try to serve people with our highest abilities, as well as to aspire to master even higher skills for our service [6,11].

This attitude towards work implies that personal material gain moves far down on the list of our motives, because this kind of service is a way to express our love for God and for people. But is it right to sell love?

Krishna said about this: "Regard only the work and not the reward for it!... Miserable are those who act for the sake of getting reward for their activity!" [11] (Bhagavad Gita, 2:47, 49).

Karma Yoga does not imply working for free. But Karma Yogis eat "remains of their sacrificial offerings", as Krishna figuratively put it. [11] (Bhagavad Gita, 3:13).

Those who receive help must not forget that the one who helps them also has to pay for food, transport, accommodation, and so on. Let us recall the words of Jesus Christ that relate to this: "Laborers deserve their food" (Matthew, 10:10), "Laborer deserves to be paid" (Luke, 10:7), and important words from the Bhagavad Gita: "The one who receives gifts and gives no gifts in return is verily a thief" [11] (Bhagavad Gita, 3:12).

Man develops Love, Wisdom, and Power through constant spiritual quest, which has to be accompanied by service according to the Karma Yoga principles.

... We have talked much about Love; now let us talk about Wisdom. Without this quality one cannot achieve Perfection and merge with God.

Wisdom is the knowledge of the most essential things: what is God, what is man, what is the meaning of man's life, and what is the Evolution of the Universal Consciousness. It also implies being familiar with the diversity of human souls, as well as the ability to classify people according to their qualities, faculties, and psychogenetic age. Wisdom consists also in knowing the Straight Path to Perfection and the ways people may diverge from it. Also — knowing how one can help people in their evolution by determining what kind of spiritual help would be most appropriate for them.

One acquires Wisdom by performing theoretic research and by gaining practical experience. The former consists in studying the instructions that God has been giving to incarnate people, as well as in getting acquainted with the experience of people who sought for God, their errors and successes. One gains practical knowledge by studying oneself and God, as well as by engaging in spiritual service and creative spiritual work.

Spiritual Service

We cannot reach the end of the Path to God without helping other people spiritually. This is objectively necessary for the process of the Evolution, since this makes the number of people initiated into spiritual knowledge grow. This also contributes to our own development, providing us with lessons in psychology, in particular. After all, the process of spiritual development can be considered as a "course of learning to be God", and God is the perfect Psychologist, the perfect Soul-Knower.

On the spiritual Path, just like during a war, some of the human qualities get manifested in a dramatic way, such as stupidity of some "superiors", which turns out disastrous for many people, and the wise heroism of the others, which saves many lives.

In these battles, emotions of people get activated; human cowardice, which makes those of little faith insane, gets highlighted. Manifestations of both vicious and high soul qualities also become more intense.

Spiritual warriors temper themselves in rebutting attacks of envious persons and aggressive fools.

Betrayals of "best friends" teach them not to get attached to people.

The warriors develop themselves saving those who walk by their side the spiritual Path or those who follow them. In the battles before the face of God, the warriors cultivate Love, Wisdom, and Power and thus gradually attain Divinity.

What must be the initial spiritual help to other people? First, it must consist in explaining to them the correct concept of God and of the Path to Him; second — in teaching them the methods of regulating one's own emotions.

Those who deserve it, by intellectual and ethical criteria, may be taught the art of meditation.

But before aspirants begin serious meditative work, they have to purify the body of energetic impurities: it is impossible to enter subtle eons, where God abides, from a contaminated and therefore sick body.

This is why it is allowed to involve in esoteric practices only those aspirants who have renounced eating *"killed"* food, taking alcohol, tobacco and similar toxic substances, and have abandoned close relationships (including sexual) with energetically coarse people.

Aspirants have to set as their primary task the establishment in love and peace.

And those who deviate from this path or do not make progress — they should be debarred from further studies — for their own good. This is because the same psychic methods can bring those, who are focused on refining of oneself and growing as love, — to God, but others, who go in the opposite direction, — to hell, transforming them into devils.

I have witnessed the latter many times in various cities and countries, including those where they used the methods developed with my help. Some instructors, either for money or fame, or simply due to their culpable irresponsibility, started to teach psychoenergetic methods to everyone interested without a careful prior selection of candidates. This led to personal tragedies and in one case even to formation of a criminal gang [7].

Once I was careless enough to show wonderful *places of power* to many of those who subsequently proved undeserving. Now… I meet sometimes downright black magicians there, who leave traces of their energetic coarseness, defile the sacredness of those places…

But there is no place for violence on the spiritual Path. I do not have any right to demand that those perverts do not go there to grow devils out of themselves… God gave them free will, and they have a right to move in the direction of hell. Maybe after having lived in hell, they will want to escape from there. And then my books will probably help them…

One of the wise things to know is that no one can be "dragged" into the Abode of the Creator. He does not need this, let alone it is impossible: the spiritual Path is primarily qualitative self-transformation, as opposed to, say, climbing a mountain. And it is we ourselves who can and have to walk this Path; other people can only show us the way.

Everyone has to be absolutely free in building their own personal relationships with God. This is why there must be no "religious discipline" or strict subordination of people or spiritual groups. Everyone has to develop in total accordance with their own free will, given to them by God. Breaking this rule distorts the harmony of the Evolution and interferes with God in His leading us to Himself.

True and False Attachments

The philosophical term *attachment* denotes the state of being firmly and for a long time attached by the indriyas to some objects. These can be parents, children, spouses, objects of sexual attraction, money, luxury items, high social status, favorite work, friends, one's own body, gaming, various kinds of food, alcoholic beverages, tobacco or other toxins...

In other words, we can see that attachments can be apparently harmful, not apparently harmful, or even quite useful at certain stages of the person's development. It is the latter that at times "get us moving" in various situations, and "moving" with quite an emotional uplift. It is much worse to be inactive and live a lazy life.

Let us look at the following analogy: one can steer an automobile or a ship only provided that they are moving; but if they do not have their own motion — it is extremely hard or impossible to direct or turn them anywhere.

The same true is with everyone of us: if we live an active life, even though without correct understanding of its meaning and of our Supreme Goal, — then our moving allows God to create many learning situations for us. Only in this case can we develop and prepare ourselves for further spiritual ascents.

... In religious books one may sometimes encounter a character of a seemingly positive hero, who suddenly gives up taking care of his family and leaves to become a hermit in hope of spiritual achievements. It is presented as an exemplary "cutting of attachments".

But there is no truth in this. This way of "detaching" oneself is not only unjustified from the ethical standpoint but also does not make any sense. Attachments should be replaced, as opposed to being dropped through an "act of volition". We should try to fall in love with God. This is difficult to accomplish overnight. But we need to set this as our goal and ask God to help us. And then love for God will grow, as we study Him with an inquiring mind through reading books, engaging in spiritual conversations, and personally asking Him to show, to reveal Himself, to let us feel His Love in full, to instruct us through a Revelation... This is what correct initial distribution of our indriyas would be.

Later on, when we start to feel real reciprocity of our love, the relationships with God progress even faster, love gradually turns into passion, into a new attachment... And this new — true — attachment and passion gradually displace all the others.

... This is how I have lived my life. Raised in a atheistic environment, I heard for the first time about the reality of God's existence only at the age of 27. But at that time nobody could explain to me what hides behind this. The Orthodox Church provided first mystical experiences, but it failed to answer the question about what God really is: God-the-Father was lost there, although He was the central figure in the Teachings of Jesus Christ. Reading books allowed me to widen my spiritual horizon, but at that time there was no book in which everything would be presented in such a detailed and simple way as in the one you are reading now.

I have never had an incarnate Guru — a spiritual Teacher, who would know all the way to God. There was none of them around me at that time apparently. And this is good in a certain sense, since having an incarnate Guru, on the one hand, allows one to receive explanations and learn practical methods for working on self-development. But, on the other hand, relationships with Him creates attachment to His incarnate form, instead of Divine Consciousness; in this case the goal is not the Highest but an intermediate one, and not all disciples in this situation are capable of switching to the Highest Goal — the Consciousness of God-the-Father.

At that time God set before me, a scientist possessing significant research experience, the Highest Goal — Himself in all His Universal Totality.

And I fell in love with Him.

And then everything was quite simple: I started, as they say, to "push my way through". I started going to Him. Other people started following me — many of them were joining and leaving. But they could not keep up with my speed and with my intensity. Some stepped aside quietly, some protested and demanded a "special" kind of love for them, and hated me when they were not getting it. Some people betrayed me, doing mean things to me; others defamed me, sometimes in public. Some people robbed me. There were even those trying to kill my body.

But I went on without looking back, without falling in love with people, without getting involved in quarrels, or avenging myself for the mean and cruel murder, although I found out the names of my murderers. I did not allow myself to stop because of the "attachments" to my honor, reputation, or my body, in the end.

I have never had disciples to whom I would sell the highest knowledge. What I did have were friends, whom I loved very much. And I was giving to them my spiritual experience and myself. I lived for them and for God. I could not… sell my love for money! Their progress was my reward.

I loved them very much. But when they left — I was not "attached" to them and forgot about them right away.

I have never made — quite sincerely! — a slightest attempt to make any of those who left me, come back. On the contrary, I encouraged them to leave — so that not to overburden them with a load of knowledge unbearable to them.

Some were leaving, being unable to understand me anymore — God was bringing to me others, who were more prepared… I loved them even more, for they understood me better… But I still did not get "attached" to them: I was totally focused on my main love — the love for God!

And whatever amounts of mud envious people, betrayers, and slanderers were throwing at me — I came out victorious of all the arguments: God accepted me in Himself; I learned to merge with Him in the Embrace of Love. I have won! It was not someone else that I conquered. No! I conquered myself, without causing any suffering to anyone, having become another kind of person: the kind that God needed.

I have won, and now I am calling you to the same Victory!

And I am grateful to God and to all of those, who were going together with me, for my Victory, those who loved and hated me: through you God enriched me and directed my life. Peace to all of you!

Teachings of God versus Sectarianism

After creating our planet and populating it with us, people, God did not forget about us at all. On the contrary, we are His major concern; we are His children, whom He cannot wait to see in His Home. The whole Creation was created only for that purpose, so that after maturing here we could enter the Home of God.

God teaches us in two ways: He gives us direct instructions concerning the way we should live, and then He offers us a free will and teaches us how to fulfill these instructions in relationships with other living beings and with Him.

Presenting us with the free will in choosing our ways of living and in making decisions in particular situations is His wise intention, which allows Him to discern clearly those who sincerely move to Him — and those who move in the opposite direction.

We have a right to move in either direction as well as to stay where we are. Yes, He gave us this right and we are free to exercise it.

But when we are moving to Him, we really increase the amount of happiness and bliss in our lives.

Otherwise, we are inevitably going to attract diseases, misfortunes, and suffering.

We even have a right to experience a nightmare of being among our likes in the diabolic eon. But do we need this? Is it not better to become humble and obedient to His Will? He wants good for us and gives it to us — all we need to do is to take it!

But why is there so much suffering on the Earth then? Why don't people go to Him? Why are crimes, darkness of primitivism, and absurdity of ignorance typical of both "believers" and atheists?

Is it not because people, especially those endowed with power, due to their ignorance or out of self-interest have been concealing and distorting the plain truths about the Path to God and to happiness?

It is quite simple to secure power and money by declaring oneself, for instance, an intermediary between people and God. Someone puts on the "priest" clothes and declares solemnly: "Here, I am endowed with the power to ask God to grant you well-being and with the right to forgive your sins. Come to me, pay money, otherwise... — you will be burning in hell forever!..."

This is a typical sectarian version of a greedy lie.

This lie may be reinforced with the following scheme: "Our Church traces its history from Adam and Eve. All other Churches are its illegitimate offsprings. So, who does God love more — His legitimate child or illegitimate one?"

But in reality God loves all His children. So, can sincere believers be capable of making such an outrageous lie?

Several sects emerged recently that sell "rights to communicate with God" for enormous amounts of money: one needs to paint a certain symbol, they say (it is that symbol that they are selling), — then God will be responding to your requests and sending "Divine Energy" to you or through you... As if God is a sort of a slot machine operating on tokens!... But a lot of people believe this and similar kinds of lies. And they pay money for these kind of things!...

But however stupid this is, it is not as terrible as when "pastors", wrapped in magnificent clothes, on behalf of God send members of their organization to hate, extirpate, and kill those who interfere with their (the "pastors'") lying. As a result, coarse base passions flare up, the "righteous wrath" starts raging... — and the whole "congregation" ends up going to hell...

Anger and fear (especially the mystical fear — fear of devils, demons, sorcerers, and vampires — which is a necessary attribute of intimidation and enslaving of the "congregation" in the cruelest and most ignorant sects; and this is so typical of Russia today) — if people cultivate these emotions, they destine themselves for going to hell. Woe to them who do not understand this, who follow this path and especially to those who instigate others of doing it this way! You are enemies of God!

... But God is Love. And He accepts in Himself only those who have become like Him.

... God always teaches us through all Messiahs and true prophets only one thing, but using different words and stressing different aspects for different people. These Teachings of God is His Eternal Law (*Sanatana Dharma* in Sanskrit). It holds that we have to strive to cognize Him, to merge with Him in Love and serve Him, that we have to love people and help them, love all creatures, develop ourselves for the sake of ultimate spiritual self-realization.

What on earth prevents us from accepting this Law and from turning our back on all of those who distort this Will and Law of God?

Eternal Law — Sanatana Dharma

So, sects are those religious associations that deviated from the true Teachings of God.

But the Teachings of God were brought to us through sayings and writings of Thoth-the-Atlantean (He was Hermes Trismegistus in His next incarnation), Krishna, Lao Tse, Pythagoras, Jesus Christ, Muhammad, Babaji, Sathya Sai Baba and other Divine Messengers, prophets, great disciples of God, and spiritual heroes. (The essence of their preachings is summarized in our books [6,11]).

One can also find several valuable passages in the Old Testament.

But we can see that in the entire Bible, there is no description of God-the-Father — the main object of worship of all believers. How can one lovingly aspire to Him, about Whom... one does not know anything? Is not this the reason why He got almost forgotten in the mass Christian Churches?

The Bhagavad Gita provides a comprehensive description of Him and of the Path to Him. The only problem is that the Bhagavad Gita has been translated by people who did not quite understand it. Only those who put into practice the entire Teachings of Krishna could do a reliable translation.

Throughout the entire history of mankind God has been teaching people the same thing: how we have to develop ourselves, seeking Divine Perfection and aspiring to Mergence with Him. But people tend to forget the essence of the concrete Teachings given to them, distort something in them, sometimes to their exact antithesis, and start conflicting with those who perverted the Teachings in a different manner [9].

This is why God needs to incarnate Parts of Himself into human bodies again and again or to speak through new prophets — in an attempt to revive Sanatana Dharma. But people tend to consider His Envoys as enemies of their "true" faith, to taunt at Them and to kill Them.

Currently, the Avatar Sathya Sai Baba preaches these pure Teachings in this way (His Teachings are integrated in the books [6,11]).

The essence of Sathya Sai Baba's Teachings as well as of the Teachings of all other Divine Teachers can be summarized in short as follows.

The main goal of man is to merge — as a developed consciousness — with the Consciousness of God. In order to realize this, one has to study oneself and God as multidimensional phenomena, including cognition of the Abode of the Creator and settling there with the consciousness.

In order to accomplish this, one has to prepare oneself by spiritual practices — such as pranayamas, techniques of pratyahara, and meditative trainings.

But no training is of use if we lack steadfast faith and longing for the Creator, or do not have a developed ability to love. Love is a function of the spiritual heart, and one has to start developing it through interaction with people and other incarnate beings.

Basic principles here are compassion for every living being and serving every living being according to Karma Yoga postulates. Karma Yoga is a practical expression of one's love for God and for people; it is the best method of self-development. Faith without active service is dead.

One should also cultivate faith by remembering constantly about God. Religious conversations, various rituals, and public worships that involve praising God's name, etc. can help one in this.

All main principles of one's relationships with people and other creatures are summarized in the short precept of Vyasa: "Help ever (in everything that is good), hurt never!"

Sathya Sai Baba gives detailed explanation of this precept with reference to a great number of concrete Earth's situations.

He teaches that there are two major landmarks in every person's earthly life: God — as the Goal, and the death of the body — as a reminder of our limited opportunity to improve.

Let us remember this! Let us cast aside all the insignificant and unnecessary things and devote ourselves totally to the realization of the meaning of our lives!

This is the way to liberation from bonds of karma, from diseases, from the necessity to submerge into the world of sufferings again. This is the way to Merging forever with our most Beloved!

Comments on the Patanjali's Scheme

In ancient times, Indian rishi Patanjali highlighted the principal stages of the ascent to spiritual heights, to the Primordial Consciousness.

He distinguished eight major steps of this ascent: yama — niyama — asana — pranayama — pratyahara — dharana — dhyana — samadhi.

However, since the first two of the above-mentioned steps are very similar and are supposed to be practiced simultaneously, it makes sense to regard them as one and view this system as a seven-step "octave".

Let us look at these steps.

Yama and Niyama

These terms are translated as "effort and relaxation" or "exertion and rest". This stage consists in mastering fundamental ethical and psycho-hygienic rules of the spiritual seeker's life.

The first rule is called <u>ahimsa</u> — non-harming. It means trying not to injure, as far as possible, any living being in deeds, words, thoughts or emotions.

This also includes the principles of ethically correct nutrition that we have discussed above and, what is no less important, getting rid of coarse emotions, which are the result of ill thoughts and often provoke rude words and actions.

We can make ethical mistakes, including crimes, as a result of either our ignorance, lack of understanding of the universal order and of our place and role in it, or as a result of our indulging in the emotions of spite, condemnation, jealousy, resentment, anxiety, despair, fear, etc, which are manifestations of the "sticking out" lower "I" (lower self).

Destroying the lower "I" by merging it into the universal Higher "I" of the Creator is one of the important tasks on the spiritual Path. This kind of work begins with the inner fight against all vicious manifestations of the lower "I" — first of all, those existing in the field of emotional reactions.

Repentance is an important tool in accomplishing this task — sincere repentance for ethical mistakes that one has committed, accompanied by a mental analysis of the corresponding problematic situations and finding the best ways of resolving them.

Many people do not grasp the essence of the principle of non-condemnation. Condemnation is an emotion, a form of anger. Identification and discussion of one's mistakes, as well as an intellectual analysis of them are not condemnation at all. An analysis is necessary since it helps us not to repeat someone else's mistakes. But while performing this type of analysis, one should be free from any kind of the emotions of anger.

Emotions are states of the energy of the consciousness. They emanate beyond the body, thus creating energy environment for people and other beings around us. People living in coarse emotional states produce a destructive and pathogenic environment for those around them. Communicating with such people can cause severe energy lesions and diseases, especially in children.

But people who live in subtle states of love make everything around their bodies healthy, spiritualized, and elevated; they heal with their mere presence. And the stronger their love and more powerful the consciousness is — the larger space they spiritualize — up to the planetary scale.

A spiritual seeker can achieve full control over the emotional sphere only through working with the chakras and other energy structures and then through merging (as a consciousness) with the Divine Consciousness. But he or she should start making efforts right from the beginning of the Path.

The second rule of yama is sathya — truthfulness, purity, honesty.

However, there are cases when we cannot tell the truth, because this will harm someone. In such instances it is better to evade answering the question...

But if we lie, we become sinners before God and captives to our lies before people, since we will have to apprehend a disclosure and to live in anxiety, instead of the state of steadfast pure peace.

The third rule is asteya — non-covetousness, renunciation of the desire to possess something that belongs to someone else. We have to be totally concentrated on the cognition of God! Craving for material objects, especially those belonging to others, is an utter perversion of the true orientation of the consciousness, which at the same time results in harming other people.

The fourth rule is aparigraha — limiting possessions to necessary things. Unnecessary things only distract our attention from the essential: from aspiration for Mergence with the Creator.

Brahmacharya — the fifth rule — literally means "walking the path of Brahman (Holy Spirit)". This implies renunciation of earthly desires (except for attending to the basic needs of the body) and redirection of the attention towards God, searching for Him first with the mind and then — with the developed consciousness.

This rule implies sincere renunciation of seeking earthly fame and honors, of accumulating the things that are unnecessary on the spiritual Path, and renunciation of the embellishment of the body.

Some people interpret the Brahmacharya rule only as celibacy (sexual abstinence). But this is too narrow of an interpretation. Besides that, sexual continence is unnecessary provided that one regards sex as a spiritual act. On the contrary, celibacy can result in adenoma of prostate in men, in energetic "fading" of women, and in the consciousness growing "callous" — in both. It really does not contribute to one's progress on the spiritual Path. What is important is not abstaining from sex, but freeing oneself from being obsessed with it and from sexual contacts with inadequate partners.

The sixth rule is saucha — maintaining purity of the body. The main thing here is to wash the whole body with warm or hot water and with soap, daily if possible. This cleans the skin from deposits of perspiration salts, which upset the normal functioning of the whole organism. Let us recall what we feel after taking a good bath, especially if we have not washed the body for a long time! This is the state of comfort that we can and should create for ourselves every day by washing the body in the morning.

Saucha also implies brushing the teeth and so on.

There are also special therapeutic saucha techniques, such as abstersion of the nose and of the nasopharynx by drawing in salted water. There is no reason for using them regularly, but they can be effective for treating chronic rhinitis.

The seventh rule is <u>mitahara</u> — pure nutrition. This has already been discussed in detail above. Here let me mention only that it is best to take food in an emotionally favorable environment. In no circumstances should one eat on the background of conflict conversations or bitter arguments, as well as in presence of malicious or irritated people.

One may perform a meditation before taking a meal in order to harmonize the inner state.

For example, the Orthodox prayer-meditation *Heavenly Father* suits this purpose very well.

The eighth rule — <u>santosha</u> — consists in maintaining a positive emotional attitude always. If we feel the presence of the Lord and devote our lives to Him totally, if we do not act out of self-interest, if we know that He is constantly watching us, leading us, teaching us, that He creates difficulties for us so that we can learn and then helps us find solutions to the problems — why would we not live in joy?

"You do your work; I control the events," — this is what He taught the author of this book once [6].

The ninth rule is <u>svadhyana</u> — philosophical discussions, conversations, and readings that make for a thorough comprehension of the meaning of life and of the Path to Perfection.

"Fix your mind on Me…" — this is how Krishna defined the first steps that man has to take on the Path to God [6,11].

The tenth rule — <u>tapas</u> — implies any kinds of self-restraint and efforts for the sake of overcoming our vices. Among other things, tapas teaches us the spiritual discipline as well as to follow the principle "it must be done!" as opposed to "I do only what I want!".

The eleventh rule is <u>Ishvarapranidhana</u>. This implies feeling that everything existing is pervaded with the Consciousness of the Creator (Ishvara), feeling His constant presence inside and outside my body, bodies of other people and material objects, seeing Him as my Teacher and a Witness of everything that I do and that happens to me.

There are also four very important rules:

— <u>kshama</u> — tolerance to those who think differently;

— <u>daya</u> — mercy, kindness;

— <u>arjava</u> — simplicity, absence of arrogance;

— <u>hri</u> — lowliness of mind, also absence of: self-admiration, self-pride because of one's actual achievements, and conceit — self-praise on account of one's imaginary virtues.

Asana

In this context, the word *asana* means a posture, a steady position of the body. There are special methods of working with the body in order to prepare it for further stages of spiritual work. Systems of asanas and other exercises of this stage of work are collectively called *Hatha Yoga*. They also help one acquire the initial skills of concentration and provide the entry-level development of the energy structures of the organism.

One should start doing asanas only after studying and accepting the principles of the previous stage. Practicing Hatha Yoga without switching to the *killing-free diet* results in coarsening of one's energy and in accumulation of coarse power, and this, in turn, makes one go astray from the true Path.

The best time for doing asanas is early morning — approximately 4-5 a.m.

Each session must be followed by shavasana — a deep relaxation of the body and mind while lying on the back for about 20 minutes. If one does not do this, health disorders may occur, such as deterioration of the eyesight, anxiety, insomnia, etc.

Attempts to do anything with Kundalini as a part of Hatha Yoga training are strictly prohibited: this can result in severe health disorders — both physical and mental. Working with Kundalini is a task of the Buddhi Yoga stage. Raising Kundalini is allowed only after all the chakras and major meridians have been cleansed and developed thoroughly.

One also needs to understand that Hatha Yoga is just a preparatory stage for the actual Yoga Path. This is why dedicating one's life to it, counting on any substantial spiritual success — is not serious. Only working with the spiritual heart within raja and then Buddhi Yoga programs can ensure serious advancement.

Pranayama

Working with energies within the body and within the *cocoon* that surrounds the body is the task of Raja Yoga. One of the methods here is pranayama, which is translated as "work with energy".

Sometimes this term is incorrectly interpreted as "breathing exercises". This is an atheistic error. In reality it is the energy of the consciousness that gets moving during pranayamas, but one may perform this — for convenience — keeping time with the breath.

The part of the consciousness that is working during pranayamas has to transform itself into white flowing *light*. With this *light*, we wash all areas of bio-energetic contamination located within our bodies. It results in general improvement of the health and elimination of various diseases. Also the consciousness itself turns into a mobile and active power.

Pratyahara

The word *pratyahara* means "removing the indriyas from material objects". At the stage of pratyahara, aspirants learn to control the "tentacles" of the consciousness which are called *indriyas* in Sanskrit. This allows one to achieve the ability to see in subtle and the subtlest layers of multidimensional space, as well as to exit from the material body into them and settle in them, accustoming oneself to their subtlety, tenderness, and purity.

The concept of indriyas exists only in the Indian spiritual culture. Europeans with their simplified and degraded religious ideas usually are not capable of grasping this kind of knowledge. Even in translations from the Indian languages they substitute the word *indriyas* with the word *senses*; by doing this they completely reject the immense methodological significance of pratyahara concept and of the principles of work at this stage.

Europeans translate the term *pratyahara* as "control over the senses". But senses are not everything that is denoted by the term *indriyas*, since the indriyas include the mind as well. It is also essential that the image of "tentacles" evoked by the word *indriyas* provides profound understanding of the principles of functioning of the mind and consciousness, as well as of methods of controlling them.

Krishna presented fundamental knowledge about working with the indriyas in the Bhagavad Gita [6,11]. He was talking about the indriyas of vision, audition, smell, touch, proprioception, and about those of the mind. And indeed: one's concentration on an object through any organ of sense or with the mind is very similar to extending a tentacle to it from the body. When one switches the concentration to another object, one detaches and moves the indriyas to it.

In the same manner the mind creates its own indriyas, when one thinks about something or someone.

People with developed sensitivity can perceive other people's indriyas touching them. In some cases they can even see those indriyas and therefore can influence them.

Krishna said that one of the things man has to learn is the ability to draw all the indriyas from the material world inwards, just as a tortoise retracts its paws and head into its shell. Then one has to extend the indriyas into the Divine eons in order to embrace God with them, to draw oneself to Him, and to merge with Him.

Now Sathya Sai Baba — our contemporary Messiah — also teaches about control over the indriyas. Many of His books have been translated into Russian but in all of them the information about working with the indriyas was lost due to inadequate translation.

One cannot achieve control over the indriyas without mastering the ability to shift the concentration of the consciousness between the chakras and main meridians, i.e. the meridians that make up the *microcosmic orbit* and the middle meridian. We will dwell on this separately in one of the following chapters.

Dharana

Dharana means "maintaining a proper concentration". Proper concentration means keeping the indriyas on God. In other words, this is a real manifestation of our aspiration for God, for Mergence with Him.

But God in the aspect of the Creator or the Holy Spirit is inaccessible for direct perception at this stage of apprenticeship.

Our loving thirst for God can be partially quenched by working with an Image of a Divine Teacher, for example, Jesus Christ, Babaji, or Sathya Sai Baba — the One Whose form from His past Incarnation is familiar to us.

If we hold such an Image in anahata on the background of the emotion of the most intense love that we are capable of, we gradually enter the state when it is not I who look at the world from anahata but He. This denotes the Yidam (this is what this Image is called) becoming alive; we are partially merged with Him. After that we may live in Unity with Him in anahata; having moved the concentration of the consciousness to the chakras located in the head, we can address Him in anahata as an Advisor and a Teacher.

This is not an illusion but the real Divine Teacher entering into His Image created by us. He may also become an Instructor in our meditative trainings. He will lead His devoted and loving disciples through Himself — into the Abode of the Creator.

"If you can visualize the Image of the Teacher in your consciousness with the most complete clarity, you can transfer your consciousness into His, and thus act through His Power, as it were. But for this, you must visualize the Image of the Teacher with utmost precision, to the minutest detail, so that the Image does not flicker, suffer distortion or change Its outlines, as it frequently happens. But if following the exercise of concentration one succeeds in invoking the steady Image of the Teacher, through this one may gain the greatest benefit for oneself, for those around one, and for the work." [2].

"You may be asked how the entrance upon the path of Service is defined. Certainly, the first sign will be renunciation of the past and total aspiring towards the future. The second sign will be realization of the Teacher within the heart not because it is one's "duty", but because it is impossible otherwise. The third sign will be rejection of fear, for the one who is armed by the Lord is invulnerable. The fourth will be non-condemnation, because the one who strives into the future has no time to occupy oneself with the refuse of yesterday. The fifth will be the filling of the entire time with labor for the future. The sixth will be the joy of Service and completely offering oneself for the good of the world. The seventh will be spiritual aspiration for the far-off worlds as a pre-destined path. According to these signs you will discern warriors that are ready and manifested for Service. They will understand where to raise the sword for the Lord, and their words will be from the heart." [2]

If work with Yidam does not bring immediate results, one may benefit from practicing visualization. One may practice creating images that help develop the chakras or visualize blissful pictures of communion with living nature, etc. But only those images, which are filled with exultation of happiness, harmony, joy, subtlety, and bliss, will make for one's correct spiritual development. Corresponding types of paintings, musical compositions and art photography, etc. may also serve as an aid.

Dhyana

Dhyana is the stage of meditative trainings that conducts one to Samadhi.

Meditation is work of the consciousness aimed at consciousness development on the path to Perfection, to Mergence with the Creator. Meditation is practiced at three stages of the Patanjali's scheme.

At the dharana stage, students learn, among other things, to expand the consciousness in the subtlest and the most beautiful that exists in the world of matter. By means of such attunement they establish themselves in the sattva guna.

And through working with Yidam they can immediately come in contact with a Manifestation of the Divine Consciousness and experience Samadhi.

At the dhyana stage, students work on increasing the "mass" of the consciousness and obtaining power in subtlety.

At the next stage, the stage of Samadhi, their efforts are focused on interaction of the individual consciousness with the Consciousness of the Creator and on merging with Him in His Infinity.

At the dhyana stage, meditative work is especially effective if it is performed at special *places of power* — areas on the Earth's surface that have a special energy impact on human beings. Among the variety of them only those should be chosen that make for expanding of the consciousness in the subtlest eons. A correctly selected sequence of such places ensures that the most complex tasks of correct *crystallization* (i.e. quantitative growth) of the consciousness will be solved easily and with little effort.

For the same purpose, one can meditate during athletic exercises, as well as practice winter swimming and *meditative running*.

The structure of the human organism responsible for meditation is the lower *bubble of perception* (this term was introduced by Juan Matus; see [6] for details) the principal part of which is the anahata chakra supplied with energy by the lower dantian (a complex of the three lower chakras).

From the very beginning of meditative training until the ultimate victory of Merging with the Primordial Consciousness, one must always remember that man's main merit is measured by the level of the development of the spiritual heart. This is by what man can merge initially with God. This is why it is the spiritual heart that man should develop and keep pure in every possible way. Everything said above allows us to take it not as a nice figure of speech or a metaphor, but as a quite practical knowledge and instruction.

The steps of one's spiritual ascent that we are discussing now are meant for teaching one how to position the consciousness, first, in cleansed anahata, then to ensure the growth of anahata within the body and then beyond it — within the *cocoon*, then within the Earth and beyond the planet in the highest eons.

In this way we can grow as Love. God is Love; this is why one can merge with Him only after becoming Great Love, a Great Soul consisting of Love (Mahatma)!

And there are no other ways of developing Divinity, except for these fundamental steps that we are describing here.

Samadhi

This stage includes a range of the highest spiritual achievements — from the first Samadhis — up to Mergence with the Primordial Consciousness and with the Absolute.

The consciousness of the spiritual seeker prepared at the previous stage becomes capable of getting in contact with the Consciousness of God in the highest eons. These first contacts give one a vivid novelty of bliss, which is what the term *Samadhi* denotes [6,11].

In contrast to Samadhi, Nirvana is a stable *Mergence* with the Consciousness of God in which the feeling of the localized "I" disappears. The term *Nirvana* means "complete burning away", i.e. losing the individuality through Mergence with God in the aspects of the Holy Spirit or the Creator. And it really happens.

In the Bhagavad Gita, Krishna speaks about Samadhi and about two principal stages of Nirvana: Nirvana in Brahman (the Holy Spirit) and Nirvana in Ishvara (the Creator).

But in India, the term *Nirvana* became widely used by Buddhists at some point in time, and later on, this term along with Buddhism, was "forced out" from India by Hindus. Instead of using the term *Nirvana*, Hindu schools started to expand the meaning of the term *Samadhi* by adding to it various prefixes. Various schools used these composite words, and because of this the term *Samadhi* became "diffused" and lost its unambiguity. This is why it makes sense to get back to the accurate terminology that God introduced into spiritual culture through Krishna.

So, in order to get from Samadhi (Bliss of Contact) to Nirvana (Mergence) one has to have a large and strong consciousness, developed by preceding trainings. In addition to this, it has to be firmly established in Divine subtlety.

If these conditions are fulfilled, then all one needs to do is just to find an entrance into the required eon, to enter it, and to dissolve oneself in its Consciousness using the method of *total reciprocity*, which one has to master in advance.

This task requires not only meditative skills but ethical preparation as well: destroying the lower "I" in every possible way and replacing it with the collective *we* first, and then with the universal "I", i.e. with Paramatman.

This is the only way man can connect to the unlimited Divine Power.

"... We have an inexhaustible reservoir of psychic energy!" [2] (Hierarchy: 394), says God.

But "if one were to expound the conditions and the aims of Yoga, the number of applicants would not be great. Terrifying for them would be the renunciation of selfhood..." [2]

In connection to the above said, I want to cite the Carlos Castaneda's book *The Power of Silence*: "… War, for a (spiritual) warrior, is the total struggle against that individual "I" that has deprived man of power." (see [6]).

… One explores the highest eons of the Absolute one after another. Before starting exploring the next eon, one has to accumulate the power of the consciousness for a long time, sometimes for years, in order to be able to enter it and remain in it. The only exception is people who approached these stages in their previous incarnations and maintained the necessary amount of *personal power* and the level of the subtlety of the consciousness.

Chakras and Meridians

Chakras have a form of more or less regular spheres with the exception of the upper sahasrara chakra, which is flattened vertically and looks like a horizontally lying disk.

Chakras do not have, as some authors claim, an internal lotus-like structure; this is a fantasy. Although, an exercise involving creation of temporary images of flowers inside chakras and even feeling their delicate aroma in them is a very good exercise.

Chakras also do not have a specific color inherent to them and they are not supposed to have it. This is also nothing but a popular fantasy. And attempts of coloring the chakras in accordance with colors of the rainbow constitute a downright and serious self-injuring or injuring of the disciples, who followed such recommendations.

One has to strive to cleanse the chakras as much as possible of all impurities that are energetically coarser than a tender white color with a slight goldish-amber hue. This is the path to cognizing Atman and God. But deliberate fixation of other colors inside the chakras means tuning them to coarser modes of operation, which cripples students and prevents them from attaining Perfection.

It is beneficial to let morning sunlight or scents of flowers into the cleansed chakras.

We also may invite our favorite Divine Teacher into anahata, learn to look at everything with His eyes and ask Him for advice...

God once gave me a wonderful method of cleansing anahata and other chakras — an exercise with a tetrahedron. If this exercise is supplemented with influencing the chakras by particular sound vibrations specific for each chakra (mantras), then in a couple of months of training the chakras transform into structures shining with tenderness and purity.

Working with a tetrahedron and with yidam as well as developing other chakras — this is the level of seriousness of exercises which must not be open to everyone interested.

Under no circumstances those who did not switch totally and forever to the *killing-free* diet on ethical grounds or those who do not show progress in the refinement of the consciousness, should do this kind of exercises.

Otherwise, the very methods that can produce a refining and purifying effect on the organism, will fix and increase its energetic coarseness. This is the path in the opposite from God direction.

This kind of psychoenergetic work is also incompatible with taking alcohol — even in the form of kvass, kumiss or industrially manufactured kefir. The reason for this is that the fine structures of the organism, which are being built, get destroyed in this case that results in dangerous illnesses. People starting this kind of work have to give up alcohol forever.

These methods increase the practitioner's sensitivity to energetic influence from other people as well as to information that spirits of lower levels of development may impose. Therefore there is a danger that people who are not intellectually and ethically mature will not be able to react adequately to this kind of influence, especially in precarious situations, be they real or imaginary.

Because of this people less than 20 years old must not engage in this kind of work. Actually, only few adults may benefit from it.

Psychoenergetic trainings that result in one's reaching high levels of refinement of the consciousness and — as a consequence — to feeling of its "nakedness" under no circumstances must be conducted for the masses of people. Only the selected ones can be admitted to them. The rest of people have a possibility to grow intellectually and ethically in the conditions of exoteric work on self-improvement: by accumulating new knowledge, by serving other people, and by strengthening one's own faith.

* * *

There are seven chakras, in total. Sometimes another number is quoted, but this is a result of misunderstanding. For example, other energy centers or even structures artificially created inside or outside the body are referred to as chakras.

There are also erroneous opinions as to localization of the chakras. For instance, in a range of incompetent publications anahata is placed in the stomach area and manipura "slides down" to umbilical region.

In reality the chakras are located as follows:

Sahasrara — a chakra that has a form of a lying disk and is located under the parietal bones in the region of the forebrain hemispheres. Its diameter is about 12 centimeters; its height is about 4 centimeters.

Ajna — a large chakra located in the middle of the head, coincident with the central parts of the brain.

Vishuddha — a chakra located in the lower half of the neck and at the level of collarbones.

Anahata — a chakra located in the chest between the collarbones and solar plexus.

Manipura — a chakra of the upper half of the belly.

Svadhisthana — a chakra of the lower half of the belly.

Muladhara — a chakra located in the lower part of the pelvis between the coccyx and the pubis bone.

The level of development of individual chakras corresponds with one's psychological features. So, when the following chakras are developed:

sahasrara — there is the pronounced ability of thinking strategically, i.e. the ability to see the "big picture", to comprehend the whole situation "from above", which allows such people to be broad-thinking managers;

ajna — one possesses a "tactical thinking" ability, which allows dealing successfully with particular problems in science, business, family life, etc.;

vishuddha — there is the ability for esthetical perception; good painters, musicians, and other artists are people with well-developed vishuddhas;

anahata — one possesses the ability to love emotionally (to love not "from the mind", but "from the heart");

manipura — the ability to act energetically; but sometimes it is accompanied with a disposition towards dominance of irritation and other manifestations of anger;

svadhisthana — a well pronounced reproductive function;

muladhara — psychological stability in various situations.

* * *

The next stage of work after cleansing and development of the chakras (it will be discussed in the next chapters) consists in bringing the main meridians of the body to proper state. These are the meridians that make up the *microcosmic orbit*, as well as the *middle meridian*.

When one has cleansed the *microcosmic orbit*, the energy of the two lower chakras can be raised through the spinal canals, leaped over the head meridians to the front side of the body and brought down through the *front meridian*, which runs like a flat hose along the front side of the body.

This exercise of circulating energy around the *microcosmic orbit* produces a strong positive emotional effect; it also "burns" coarse energies of the organism in the *front meridian*, which makes for further improvement of health as well as for the cleansing and refinement of the organism.

The *middle meridian* is a wide canal (corresponding to the diameter of the chakras developed at the stage of raja yoga), which integrates the entire "column" of the chakras.

Its significance is immense since it allows one to combine all the chakras into one complex with a spacious corridor. Working with it also allows one to perform *crystallization* of the consciousness in the subtle eons, in which this meridian exists, up to the volume of the body.

Cleansing the *middle meridian* and its walls results in further health improvement.

And on the highest stages of psychoenergetic work, this structure is essential for working with Kundalini.

Work with the *middle meridian* can be performed with the help of a special mantra on special energetically significant areas on the Earth's surface (*places of power*) or with the help of participation of a competent instructor.

The next principal stage is moving the consciousness into the energy *cocoon* that surrounds the body and *crystallization* of the consciousness in its volume.

After that, one has to realize the segmentation of the *cocoon* into two *bubbles of perception*: the upper and the lower. The upper one includes the three upper chakras; the lower one — the four lower chakras.

With our upper *bubble of perception*, we perceive the world of material objects; with the lower one we perceive non-material worlds.

Meditative Trainings

Meditation is one of the main means of developing oneself as a consciousness, as well as the only possible way of cognizing God and merging with Him.

There are four principal kinds of meditative trainings: a) refinement of the consciousness; b) augmentation of it; c) transferring the concentration of the consciousness within one eon, as well as to other eons, d) mastering the methods of merging the consciousness with the Divine Consciousness.

Actually, the entire Path to Mergence with the Primordial Consciousness can be expressed as an astonishingly simple scheme:

— developing the spiritual heart inside the body;

— growing it gradually up to the size of our planet;

— exploring more and more subtle eons of the multidimensional universe;

— and merging oneself (as a spiritual heart) with the Creator in His Abode.

In this context, it is becoming clear for us what we should cultivate in ourselves and what we should cut off.

We have to grow ourselves as wise, strong, and refined Love.

We need to purify ourselves of everything that is not Love: all kinds of rudeness, anger, and egocentrism, including emotions of condemnation, jealousy, greed, envy, violence, egotistic sexual desire (lust), etc.

The next principal stage of development of the spiritual heart will be its expanding, "overflowing" in lucid calm of mornings on open natural landscapes (for example, seashores, prairies, fields, hilltops or mountain summits).

Such meditations of love can be practiced throughout the year, but they can be successful only during daytime. The best season for this kind of work is spring, when exultation of nature tunes us to the correct emotional state and gives us its power — power of the emotion of LOVE.

The next step for those who have successfully mastered the meditations discussed above is hard work on filling all subtlest eons of multidimensional space with oneself as a spiritual heart. The last eon one needs to fill up is the Abode of the Creator.

* * *

Sathya Sai Baba says [37]:

"The task of meditation work is to dispel the illusion that God and the essence of each man, as well as the essence of the whole material world, are different.

"The right meditation is merging of all thoughts and indriyas with God.

"Correct fruits of meditation are... when all actions come out of the Consciousness of God and not from the mind.

"Mergence with the Absolute means removal of the veil of ignorance, i.e. of the illusion of dual existence of the differentiated parts — as opposed to the One Absolute.

"Man can observe the Absolute, manifested in the divided, in the life of an Avatar."

I can assure you that all of this is real!

Places of Power

Significant acceleration of the meditative development of the consciousness can be achieved at special *places of power*.

This term was introduced by Mexican Indian Juan Matus (don Juan), whose experience was described by Carlos Castaneda (see more details in [6]). This term denotes special places whose energy characteristics substantially differ from the background level (for human beings).

Places of power can be classified into positive and negative ones, according to the effect they produce on people.

Negative *places of power* can induce anger, depression, terror, anxiety, sensation of strange discomfort or drunken "knock-out", etc. Staying at these places can cause diseases, coarsening of the consciousness, and even death, especially if one makes one's home at such a place.

I particularly remember one large place like this, located to the west of Magnitogorsk city, near the Ural mountain range. Once, I was driving across this place on a rather flat highway. Along both sides of it there were numerous tomb crosses — this is how they traditionally mark the places of automotive accidents with lethal outcomes in this area. My companions, who lived in Magnitogorsk, explained that this had always been a mystery for everyone why so many drivers and passengers died there, on a smooth section of the road, and not somewhere in the mountain area.

This place induced the state that occurs if one has drunk too much alcohol and smokes a cigarette in addition to this. Those who know how it feels can easily imagine what happens to a tired driver there, especially during the night snow or rainstorm.

There was also a village on that *place of power*; it looked gray and depressed, with no people or animals in sight. I detected the "epicenter" even before we approached it. It turned out to be right in the center of that village. When we drove closer to it, we saw several abandoned half-ruined houses: apparently, all the people died in them; nobody could live there...

Surely, I wanted to help all those poor fellows. But how could I say anything about that? Who would believe me?

Places of power are not necessarily that big. They can be as large as several kilometers, or just hundreds of meters or even one meter in diameter. Sometimes one can encounter an energy column one meter wide through all floors of a high-rise building.

Sometimes I managed to destroy small negative *places of power* in houses forever, sometimes not.

Locating *places of power* with the help of "tools" like dowsing rods or pendulums is not effective. One can determine all features of *places of power* — including their qualitative and quantitative characteristics — only by feeling them personally: with oneself as a consciousness. But one can learn this method only on the spiritual Path — through refinement of the consciousness and by acquiring fluidity in moving along the entire *scale of coarseness-subtlety*.

The above said also relates to positive *places of power*. And they can be so wonderful!

They can provide us with standards of subtlety or shape the consciousness in various ways, filling this shape with their energy.

They can heal various diseases by washing the bodies through with fountains of healing energy or just by infusing the excess of its healing power, adequate for a particular organ.

They also can get one into the *non-I* state — this state cannot be explained by words. It can only be experienced, but it is an essential experience, nonetheless...

They can help entering the highest eons, make for cognition of Atman or be favorite places of Divine Teachers for appointments with worthy disciples...

People can pass through these Holy Places without noticing them. But the ecologist of multidimensional space, who is a spiritual warrior and spiritual seeker, has to learn how to find and use them.

Babaji's Formula

We have already examined all stages of the spiritual Path in the terms of Patanjali's scheme. Now let us discuss the same problem using analysis of the formula of spiritual development suggested by the Avatar Babaji [6-7,11,16,19,55]. This formula sounds as follows:

Truth — Simplicity — Love — Karma Yoga (Service to humanity) — Abandonment of the lower "I" for the sake of merging with the Higher "I" of God.

* * *

The advent of Jesus Christ — a Messenger of God-the-Father — had been prophesied by numerous Jewish prophets. But when Jesus did come — only some of the Jews acknowledged Him as Christ; those were the people who became His first disciples and spreaders of the Teachings of God, which were new for that region of the Earth. But the official Synagogue never accepted Jesus as a Messenger of God-the-Father and... for almost two thousand years has been waiting for another Christ...

A similar phenomenon happened in the near past: all mass organizations calling themselves Christians did not recognize God Who appeared before people of the Earth in the human form!

Jesus Christ Himself prophesied: "When you see One Who was not born of a woman, fall on your faces and worship. That One is your Father" (Gospel of Thomas,

16; see [56]). In 1970 Avatar Babaji came to the Earth exactly in this way — but "Christians" did not recognize Him.

(Now another Avatar — Sathya Sai Baba — works on the Earth, preaching the same Eternal Universal Teachings of God-the-Father — and again the hierarchs of all mass Christian confessions refuse to recognize Him!).

God became a competitor to many religious organizations: for He can "entice away" their "flock" to Himself. Who would then support all those for whom Churches are a source of income? This is why some "parsons" intimidates the congregation: "everything that comes from the East — is of Satan!", or "if you do not stick to us, you will surely go to hell!"...

But Jesus Christ was embodied in the Middle East — in Judaea. Krishna, Babaji and Sathya Sai Baba — all of Them are from the East. So, is God — "from the East"?

* * *

Babaji is One of the Representatives of God-the-Father, a Part of Him. He periodically embodies on the Earth as an Avatar in order to help people. One of His incarnations took place at the end of the 19th century; it was described by Yogananda [63]. The next one was from 1970 to 1984 — again in Northern India, where He appeared before people by materializing a body of a young man for Himself, in which He lived for 14 years.

Now Babaji, together with Jesus Christ, Sathya Sai Baba, Krishna, and other Divine Teachers, Who are Manifestations of God-the-Father, keeps on helping worthy disciples of God — but this time from the non-embodied state.

From His last incarnation on the Earth Babaji left people a concise and brilliant version of the Teachings of God, the "core" of which is the mentioned above short and exhaustive list of what we, people, have to accomplish.

The main thing for us now is to try to understand correctly what these words mean and then to fulfill all this.

Truth

This part of *Babaji's formula* implies understanding what God and the Evolution of the Universal Consciousness are, what our place in it is, and what exactly we have to do. Today almost everyone lacks this understanding.

In India at present, the favorite "folk's god" is fictious Ganesha: a man with an elephant's head, who was allegedly born in Heavens of copulation of other "gods".

In "Christian" world people sincerely believe that their God is Jesus Christ and that Muslims have another God — false, of course, — Allah, although Allah is simply a translation of the term *God-the-Father* into Arabic language. And it is love for Him and aspiration for Him that Jesus Christ preached.

At present most "Christians" have lost both God-the-Father, Who was preached by Jesus, and LOVE, which is essential for attaining the Creator...

This is why any intelligent person has to learn to see the difference between true *Christianity* as the *Teachings of Jesus Christ* — and those interpretations of them that exist under the same name. And among the latter, one may single out various degrees of distortion up to its absolute perversion, to its antithesis.

What have to do those who consider themselves Christians? They have to study the Teachings of Jesus Christ and follow them!

To make realization of this task easier, the Teachings have to be systematized on the considered subjects [6,11] and there must be a methodology of their realization.[5]

---

[5] This is the purpose of this book and of other books and films created by our scientific-spiritual School.

* * *

Some readers may think: the author is criticizing everybody — maybe he wants to present himself as a "Savior"?

No, I want to present as a Savior not me but God! I need neither fame nor popularity: I chose a modest and quiet monastic life for myself. I want to help people. And I serve God.

... Yes, God does not lead infidels to Himself by the Straight Path. These are the words from the Quran.

And the Straight Path to Him is the Path of Love: love for people, for all living beings, for the Creation and the Creator. This is the Path to Him as the correctly understood Goal. This is the Path of purging oneself as a soul of everything that is not Divine: including coarseness, violence and all kinds of egocentrism — and of replacing self-centeredness with God-centeredness. And all of this is real!

If you could embrace non-incarnate Jesus Christ Who appears in a human-like form and feel His Divine love, Subtlety, and Tenderness — combined with unlimited Power resulting from Unity with the Universal Consciousness of the highest eon, and Divine Wisdom — then you would realize right away what God appreciates in people and what He wants us to be like.

But in order for us to be honored with such an Embrace, we have to get closer to Him — not physically but by the characteristics of the soul.

* * *

One of the ways to answer the question "What is the Truth?" is:

"There is Evolution going on within the Body of the Absolute.

133

"Our Goal is the Creator. Our task is to transform ourselves from a part of the Absolute into a part of the Creator, to enrich Him with ourselves.

"In order to fulfill this task we have to become Love — strong, wise, and refined to the level of the Primordial Consciousness."

Simplicity

Simplicity means sensible naturalness of the way of life and behavior, as well as modesty and lack of arrogance and self-importance. Simplicity is a pre-requisite of Love. It is also an indispensable tool of spiritual warriors, which God wants us to be.

The best way to develop simplicity is to keep close to nature and to learn how to attune to its harmony. Here, in the solitude of forests, fields and lakes, without make-up on the face, earrings, fancy synthetic clothes or even with no clothes at all — we can love the beauty of the Creation and the Creator, accepting help from God in the optimal way, expanding with the consciousness in the beauty of the Creation and in the Holy Spirit.

Simplicity is also beautiful in expressing our love for other people: in a smile, friendliness, tenderness and openness with friends.

But it is important to know the limits. For instance, walking naked among those who do not understand you and propagating your understanding of "simplicity" in this way — this is tactlessness; this cannot be called a harmonious and spiritual action.

The same principle can be applied to sexual relations: the "simplicity" that results in sexually transmitted diseases and unwanted pregnancies, as well as that, which is connected with violence and selfishness — is not what God wants from us.

"Spontaneity" in expressing and realizing all of the whims, needs and desires, which is encouraged in some modern pseudo-spiritual sects and other organizations, also does not have anything to do with the true Simplicity.

Only the Simplicity of intelligent people who belong to the *sattva guna* and of those who have reached even higher spiritual heights is the true Simplicity.

People of the *tamas guna* understand simplicity as either sugariness or violence, rudeness, scuffle, and lying drunk in the mud.

The true Simplicity is one of the elements of the "training for God". It is not for those who are far from Him.

Love

Love is the main quality of God. In order to merge with Him (or even to escape hell, to begin with) we have to learn to feel emotions of love and to perform deeds of love, to eliminate all the opposite states and actions, whatever circumstances we may live in.

Love is the main thing that God wants from us. And we do not have any other possibility to cognize Him and to merge with Him, unless we transform ourselves into Love.

Love is a special emotional state; in other words — this is a state of the energy of the consciousness. And the consciousness (soul) is what every one of us is in reality.

Every time we leave the state of love, we alienate ourselves from God. "Every instance of leaving the state of love results in accumulation of bad karma" — this is what God told me once [7].

People blame their misfortunes and diseases on anyone but themselves. Although it is always they who are to blame.

It is of paramount importance for us to understand that the stable and confident state of love can be achieved only through practicing special psychic self-regulation techniques, which must include working with the chakras, primarily with the anahata chakra. (We will describe these methods in the following chapters of this book).

In the ancient Christianity a special method of "opening" the spiritual heart was developed, which got named *Jesus Prayer*. Adepts had to repeat constantly a special prayerful appeal to Jesus, and after years of practice some of them succeeded in making the prayer "break through" into their spiritual hearts — and this made them realize what love really is. When this happens, the whole life of such a person changes dramatically [59].

… Once God, seeing my sincere aspiration for Him and my strong desire to help people, helped me create a tremendously efficient system of methods of "opening" and development of the spiritual heart. Some of these methods were described in several books of mine and were widely taught in Russia and some other countries some time ago.

However, I need to mention that out of thousands of students, only a few were able to attain the actual and quite complete cognition of God-the-Father. What was the reason for the "dropping out" of the rest? It was their inability to thoroughly comprehend the points of the *Babaji's formula*.

The overwhelming majority of the students were lacking that intensive aspiration for cognition of God, which could allow them to switch their attention to Him from the objects of the material world. Others gave in to threats of sectarians.

The psychic techniques per se cannot make a person attain God; they can only play the role of wonderful and necessary aids. But the main prerequisite of success is the ability of the spiritual seeker to comprehend with the developed intellect the entirety of the Truth and to build a steadfast loving aspiration for the main Goal, in other words — to fall in love with the Creator.

The true spiritual Path necessarily implies the complex development of a person, which must include intellectual, ethic, and psycho-energetic components.

Also, a person cannot successfully cultivate real love only by performing exercises with the anahata chakra during meditation classes. Development of love must fill one's whole life and pervade all of his or her activities.

It must be manifested:

— in staying constantly with the concentration of the consciousness in the anahata chakra,

— in sincere respectful and tactful attitude towards everyone, whether one knows them or not,

— in the ability to forgive and forget insults quickly, without taking revenge,

— in behavior that excludes any possibility to offend or aggrieve someone wrongly.

Love has to include a sacrificial component of willingness to help others even if it goes to one's own detriment. Interests of those who deserve this help has to be given a higher priority than one's own.

Love must be directed not only towards God and people, but also towards animals and plants; nobody may think that their love is developed if they are still able to kill or maim plants unnecessarily, if they allow themselves to eat bodies of animals for the sake of satisfying their gluttony.

Love has to be irreproachable in relationships with children. This implies being incapable of getting irritated. Although, being demanding in teaching children discipline and honesty should not be excluded — in the interests of the children, in the first place!

Everyone should analyze the characteristics of their love in the sexual sphere, since this is where human vices usually are manifested very vividly.

Any kinds of violence or constraint in sex — even in the verbal form or in thought — are examples of a behavior opposite to love.

Carelessness of a man as to the prevention of unwanted pregnancy is another example of the same type of behavior.

Passiveness of a woman during a sexual intercourse when she is not aiming to give her love to her male partner, but only selfishly expects satisfaction for herself, being able to resent him for doing something "wrong" — is a phenomenon of the same nature. (Since all people differ by the features of their sexuality, and the new partner never knows in advance how to satisfy you better!).

True sexuality is the art of giving yourself and your love to the partner through sexual relations. And only a combination of sincere and giving love on the side of both partners can make such relations harmonious.

I am sure that many women would benefit from reading the wonderful book of Barbara Keesling [38], which promotes the practice for women of giving their sexual love as a gift. Although I would not recommend doing everything that is written there. For example, practicing oral sex regularly increases the risk of transmitting infections dramatically. Also, sexual relations with so many partners are absolutely incompatible with a serious spiritual Path: during a sexual intercourse an intensive energy exchange takes place between partners, which results in taking on possible energetic coarseness, impurities and diseases of the partner.

... Everyone builds their destiny themselves, using the freedom of will granted to us by God. Someone develops in sacrificial love by helping others. Someone cultivates capricious egotism, hatred, coarseness, cruelty. The former forbear and forgive, do not become immersed in hostility and thus preserve themselves in love and aspiration for the Creator — and attain Him. The latter become "refuse of the Evolution". The former can be truly called Christians. And the latter, though wearing crosses and visiting churches, — how should one call them?

Our sexuality was conceived by God not only as a means of reproduction but also as a method of spiritual development. It facilitates the cultivation of such aspects of love as tenderness, care, self-giving, merging of two consciousnesses into one, which prepares one to the Mergence with the Consciousness of the Supreme Beloved — the Creator. Sexual love can directly contribute to the development of the spiritual heart, which we have already discussed. It also teaches us Peace (if everything goes well), which is an indispensable component of Perfection, one of the qualities of God, which we need to master.

But all this relates only to the sattvic, pure sexuality of people who make real progress on the spiritual Path. In this case it does accelerate their advancement significantly.

But sexuality of coarse and egotistic people who do not possess developed spiritual hearts can be disgusting and bring them to hell.

The spreading of a perverted "Christianity" that has lost love became a damnation for the spiritual evolution of many people of the Earth. Among other things, it pronounced anathema against sexual love and declared renunciation of it a "Christian feat". It profaned all conceptions by calling them "defiled" as opposed to the "immaculate" (i.e. without a man) conception of the mother of Jesus Christ that allegedly took place. The human body itself, especially the female body, was declared shameful. In the past, "decent" people felt shy to say even the word *legs*. The words that related to the sexual theme were declared "indecent" and transformed into cursing — a means of defiling other people. In this way the obscene language was created — the language of the tamas guna.

And how could a pure attitude to sexuality form in people who regard it as an odious "vice", who hate sexuality in themselves and especially in others? But without this pure attitude towards sexuality one can hardly succeed in refinement of the consciousness, development of love, and getting close to God.

People started to fear what in reality could help them to become better!

Many men came to hate women exactly for what women could help them with. Since women are, in general, significantly more refined than men, if for no other reason than their hormonal status. And by this characteristic they are closer to God.

Jesus Christ taught the same [56] in addressing men:

"Respect her, uphold her. In acting thus you will win her love and will find favor in the sight of God…

"In the same way, love your wives and respect them…

"Be lenient towards a woman. Her love ennobles man, softens his hardened heart, tames the brute in him, and makes of him a lamb.

"The wife and the mother are the inappreciable treasures given unto you by God. They are the fairest ornaments of existence….

"Therefore I say unto you, after God your best thoughts should belong to the women and the wives, woman being for you the temple wherein you will obtain the most easily perfect happiness. Imbue yourselves in this temple with moral strength. Here you will forget your sorrows and your failures, and you will recover the lost energy necessary to enable you to help your neighbor.

"Do not expose her to humiliation. In acting thus you would humiliate yourselves and lose the sentiment of love, without which nothing exists here below.

"Protect your wife, in order that she may protect you and all your family. All that you do for your wife, your mother, for a widow or another woman in distress, you will have done unto your God." (Life of Saint Issa, 12:13-21)

But "Christianity" (and not only "Christianity")... declared woman... "the source of sin" and prescribed to cover her body in any possible way. In Russia for many centuries women had to wear special long dresses when bathing and even to sleep in clothes: "What if you die in your sleep — you will appear before the Lord naked! What a shame it will be!".

Another example of a similar kind of abomination is declaring some children "illegitimate" and holding up to shame the motherhood of these women to whom God entrusted the upbringing of these children!

... We need to understand that it is people of the tamas guna who are immersed in vice and who do not see anything except it, while possessing aggressiveness, seize the "reins of government" in the originally holy religious movements and gradually turn them around to the opposite direction, warping the doctrine of God to its exact antithesis.

In the sexual aspect of life they — while themselves belonging to hell, obsessed with passion for violence, defilement, and satisfaction of their egotistic lust — are unable to imagine that for other people, sattvic ones, sexuality does not mean lust, but a way of sharing their love, giving it to other people as a gift and that this may be their way of serving God!

* * *

But getting obsessed with sex is also not good. The term *fornication* is valid not only for people but also for

God. It denotes both too many sexual contacts and sex with inadequate partners (those who are not at the same level of the spiritual advancement). Sexually transmitted diseases are the mechanism that God uses for slowing down the tendencies for sexual amusements in people.

The truth here is that we have to try to direct all our attention towards searching for God, without distracting ourselves excessively for anything else. (And sex is just one of such distractions).

... So, in sex, like in everything else, everyone has to find the golden mean between two extremes...

* * *

Refinement of the consciousness and true sattva, as a necessary stage of cognition of the Holy Spirit and God-the-Father, are impossible to achieve without accepting and understanding concepts of BEAUTY.

"Beauty: Cosmos establishes Evolution on this formula" — this is what God taught us through Helena Roerich [26,40].

Spiritual beauty exists at two levels of the scale of gunas: rajas and sattva.

Rajas is, in particular, boldness, self-discipline, and beauty of exploit. It is manifested in a spiritual warrior with unbending will.

Rajas can be found in the states of nature; it also can be expressed in dancing, music and fine art. Examples of the latter are paintings of Nicholas Roerich.

Sattva — spiritual purity and beauty, refined and saturated with tender love — is the last step on the stairway leading to cognition of the Holy Spirit.

In nature we can observe sattvic states in the purity of sunlight at dawn, in singing of spring birds, in charming silence of a tranquil evening, etc.

Among the most vivid examples of highly sattvic music are some compositions of Ananda Shankar.

Sattvic beauty of harmonious human body is also spiritual and can attune the one who observes it to tenderness, tranquility, and peace, which so many of us are lacking.

* * *

And another comment on the subject of love.

One day I was traveling by train, perfecting lowliness of mind when studying the situation: among my fellow travelers were a mother and a son. She had a huge body and was very rude. Her son — a military cadet — was about fifteen years old. All the way she constantly shouted. About what? It… was just her regular manner of talking to her son, shouting everything that was coming to her mind: all her thoughts. For example: "Darling! I am going to go to the toilet and throw out the apple core!… Why don't you answer, when your mother is talking to you???!!!" And her exhausted son was looking at the window with a dull expression on his face being only able to nod listlessly…

How can the behavior of this "mommy", who sincerely loved her child, be characterized?

Was it violent? — Yes, it was. Was it tactless? — Yes, it was. One could name some more of her traits… But what is important to stress now is that her love lacked peace.

The ability to feel deep inner peace, especially when there is no need to perform energetic actions is a very important and valuable quality. It is a fundamental prerequisite of true love.

Attempts to love without this inner peace sometimes turn into what I have just described. Such "love" can only cripple its victims. It induces in them only an urgent need to escape. If there is a place to escape to…

… The state of God-the-Father in His Abode can be described as Tender Peace. Let us learn this from Him when preparing ourselves to meeting Him.

But true peace is not something opposite to a sound drive and energy, but matches them harmoniously. Let us analyze this postulate — and apply it to our lives!

Karma Yoga (Selfless Service)

The term *Karma Yoga* means "Path to Mergence with God through performing selfless service".

What is *service to God*?

An incompetent reader may start to recall: "I know the term *Divine service*... What is it? Prayers... And what are prayers? 'Lord, give me this! Lord, give me that!'"...

Yes, for the majority of believers who consider themselves Christians, praying means begging something from God. And, paradoxically enough, they see in this their duty and their "service to God"...

But God does not need our panhandling! He does not listen to it! Otherwise it would "make Him sick" to hear all the nonsense that people invented, their addressing Him as a servant who is allegedly supposed to supply whatever He is asked for.

He needs our efforts on self-development and our help to other people in this. He wants us — every one of us! — to take an active part in His Evolution, rather than to whine passively and expect "grace" from Heaven...

Helping other people on this Path — this is what service to God is! He declared this through Jesus Christ, Babaji, and Sathya Sai Baba; the apostle Paul said many wonderful words about this as well [6,11].

But one should not interpret this kind of help too narrowly: only as preaching, conducting religious classes or writing religious books. No. In order to live on the Earth fruitfully and to evolve, people also need housing, food, clothing, fuel, transport, safety, medical help, education and many other things. Therefore, Karma Yoga means helping other people in everything that is good.

144

The most important characteristic of Karma Yoga is the right motivation: that is, one should not act for gain or reward, even in the form of a salary. One has to perform actions for the sake of helping other people, as acts of selfless giving. This does not imply, however, an unpaid work. But it is up to those whom we help and to God to take care of the material welfare of the giver.

In other words, the essence of "mutual settlements" of worthy people who help one another is exchange of gifts. All necessary details of the "theory of giving" are set out by God in chapter 17 of the Bhagavad Gita [6,11].

The essence of it is that God regards only those gifts as sattvic, i.e. true and pure, that one gives to a worthy person at the right time and in the right place.

So, the short definition of the term *Karma Yoga* sounds like this — "selfless help to all worthy people in everything good".

It is very important to emphasize that one develops correctly not through parasitism, panhandling or endless repetition of prayers or making ritual bodily movements — but through creative work and active love for other evolving beings, which is expressed in actions for their good.

Sathya Sai Baba clarifies the idea of Karma Yoga by the following illustrative example. He says that if you are members of one family you do not ask the head of the family for payment for each kind of work you perform around the house — it is outside people that work for money, but not the own ones. So you, if you feel that God is your Father, you must not engage in bargaining with Him, but on the contrary — you must act in the interests of His Plan, for Him, for the Evolution and not for your personal gain [6].

This kind of activity is the background against which God allows us to develop intellectually, in love and in power.

Abandonment of the Lower "I" for the Sake of Merging with the Higher "I"

This is the final part of the Teachings of Babaji. It includes Mergence of the individual consciousness of a person who has reached the highest eon with the Consciousness of the Creator. At that, the person's self-awareness dissolves in the Ocean of the Creator.

Attempts of the leaders of some sects either to destroy fully the self-awareness of their disciples without providing them with a new substrate for self-identification[6] or to convince them that they are already God should be regarded as incompetent and extremely harmful. One's self-awareness must not be destroyed but transferred. And the cognition of God and Mergence with Him are not performed through being convinced or convincing oneself, but by means of stage-by-stage penetration with correctly developing consciousness into more subtle eons, their exploration, establishing in them, mastering Mergence with the Consciousness of the Holy Spirit first and then with the Consciousness of the Creator. All other directions prove to be dead-end and lead to either delays in the person's development or to cultivation of gross vices and turning to the direction opposite from God, which is fraught with diabolization and insanity.

Work on this part of *Babaji's formula* should begin with elementary correction of one's behavior in communicating with other people.

For example, the tendency of many people to dominate over others, to behave as if they are the "boss", to look "important", — looks comical from the standpoint of spiritual growth.

---

[6] Sometimes leaders do this on purpose — to make slaves-zombies from their disciples.

Violence, resentfulness, jealousy, revengefulness, wrathfulness, desire to *own* people and things (except for essential ones), sexual desire, like any intensive wanting of something from people or from God, — all of these are vicious manifestations of the lower "I". They must be eliminated.

Jesus Christ and His Apostles left many invaluable formulas-precepts for us: do not sit at the high place, if you want to grow spiritually — become a servant to other people, never resent or revenge yourself, regard others as higher than yourself, etc. [6,11].

Lao Tse and Juan Matus were saying about exactly the same in a very straightforward and concise way [6,11][7].

It takes deep self-analysis and hard work on repentance in order to get rid forever of manifestations of the "protruding" lower "I".

We have to understand that there is no such phenomenon as "forgiveness of sins" whatsoever: God does not have such a concept.

The purpose of repentance is not obtaining forgiveness for concrete acts that we have done, but getting rid of vices.

"Sins", i.e. our mistakes, are either consequences of our lack of experience and knowledge or specific manifestations of those qualities of our souls that are called vices.

The true mechanisms of deliverance from vices are self-analysis, repentance, and strict self-control.

If it is not possible to eliminate the vice that has been discovered and realized right away, one should recall the entire line of its manifestations — starting from childhood (and sometimes from the previous incarnations).

---

[7] In order to understand correctly the works of Carlos Castaneda, one has to read the book of his wife Margaret Castaneda [23].

And one has to re-experience anew mentally all situations, which one previously resolved incorrectly, but this time in the right way. Moreover, it makes sense to "play over" in advance all possible future situations when this vice can manifest again.

It is also important to try, if possible, "to redress the wrong" to those whom we harmed — be they people, animals or even plants. Even if they are not currently "alive" on the Earth — we should address them as non-embodied souls. And let us remember that God really accepts such efforts on getting rid of our vices.

We need to repent of all the instances when our non-love for other people and for God was manifested, as well as of all our egotistic actions and emotions.

* * *

Many dull-egotistic persons try to push their bodies into a subway train car as soon as the doors open without letting the people get out first.

Or, while waiting for a bus or a tram, they block the sidewalk with their bodies, instead of standing on the side so as not to hinder anyone from passing by, thus showing care for other people.

Or, entering the subway station hall some people hold the spring door behind them to help the following person get in, while others let the door go, crashing their "neighbor" with it.

Even when they get into a sound spiritual school, egotistic primitive people behave in the same manner. As long as the course is conducted, they feel good; they are happy and filled with bliss. But once the course is over — they start to feel bad: they have already gotten used to the situation when someone is making them feel good; and suddenly it stops... And since they do not feel good anymore, they start to experience increasing negative emotions towards the instructor and the school...

Egotistic people know only their selfish interests and resent when an obstacle in the form of someone else's need gets in the way of their satisfaction.

When a person strongly wants something from anyone, it is an indication of the viciously protruding lower "I" of the one who wants. This triggers the mechanism of bio-energetic "vampirism" and becomes the cause of diseases of those, from whom a person wants something [7], and of "aggravation" of destiny of the one who wants.

But loving people are always being attentive and care not to hinder anyone in anything, but, on the contrary, use any possibility to help everybody, giving the interests of other people a higher priority than their own.

Such people are always polite and benevolent, strive never to offend anyone without a reason, even when not in the best states, being sick or tired, for instance.

In sexual relations they never obtrude themselves but wait for the moment when the partner desires the same.

... In this kind of self-analysis, detailed recommendations by Sathya Sai Baba can be of great help [6,11].

* * *

When we have achieved the deliverance from coarse emotional states and the ability to attune to sattvic phenomena of life, this allows us to begin with meditations of "dissolving" ourselves in harmony of the surrounding space. Such meditations can be especially effective in quiet evenings, at dusk — in the forest, prairies, at lakesides, seashores, or near other water bodies. The meditation should be performed using the following formula: "There is only harmony of the surroundings: forest, lake, — but there is no me". At that, the consciousness expands from the anahata chakra and merges with the subtlety and purity of nature.

The next fundamental stage will be mergence with the Holy Spirit in *Pranava* meditation (see below), and then stage-by-stage mastering of the *total reciprocity* (Nirodhi[8]) in the eons of the Holy Spirit and God-the-Father.

This is how man completes the personal evolution forever, becoming a Part of the Primordial Consciousness, a Part of the Creator. After that such a soul continues to live creatively — not as a separate being but as Him.

Completion of the Path

The scheme for studying the structure of the Absolute which can be found in the end of this book (it was first published in the book [10]) depicts the multidimensional nature of the universe as well as positional relationships of the unstructured (akasha) and structured (matter, individual souls as well as forms that the Holy Spirit accepts) Manifestations of the Absolute.

At the same time we should understand that the structure of the human organism is also multidimensional. The words from the Bible that God created man according to His image are about this and nothing else.

In the incarnate state, people in the beginning identify themselves only with the body. But the process of spiritual self-realization implies gradual cognition of the remaining components of the human organism, gaining the ability to move freely with the concentration of the consciousness within them — just like one can learn how to shift the self-awareness within the physical body. In this way one cognizes Atman. And then Atman merges into Paramatman.

This is the task that man should try to accomplish.

At that, when one enters with the concentration of the consciousness into the Abode of the Creator and merg-

---

[8] Another spelling of this word is Nirodha.

es with Him there, he or she becomes an essential part of Him.[9]

Coming out again from the Abode into the world of the Creation, He or She turns into the Holy Spirit.

Embodied on the Earth with a sacrificial mission of helping embodied people, He or She becomes a Messiah.

Practice of the Straight Path

The doctrine of the Straight Path was not invented by people. No, it was suggested by God. This doctrine was set out in detail by Krishna and then repeated by Jesus Christ, Babaji, and Sathya Sai Baba. Quran and Buddhist scriptures contain the same description of it and even use the same term [6,11].

This doctrine may be summarized in short in the following three points:

1. There is God — One Universal Consciousness of the Creator, Who lives in the highest eon of multidimensional space.

2. He is Love.

3. We have to become one with Him through transforming ourselves into Love, into the Universal Spiritual Heart, into the *Heart of the Absolute*. Understanding and accomplishment of this are the only things that make sense to spend the life for.

Now we will describe specific methods of advancing on this Path.

They can be divided into several groups depending on their difficulty: preliminary, intermediate, and highest.

---

[9] One can learn this through a series of meditative techniques. One of the most effective of them is the one that Jesus Christ taught His disciples 2000 years ago. This is the Cross meditation described by Philip the Apostle [11].

Preliminary Methods

Preliminary methods help one develop faith. And faith is essential for emergence of the incentive for making spiritual efforts.

But what is faith? This is a rather multi-level concept.

Some say about their faith: "Well, I know there is something out there...: cosmic intellect, UFO..."

Others will assert with confidence: "Yes, I believe in God!" And they will even make a "sign of the cross". But they do not make even slightest spiritual efforts — even to find out what God wants from them, let alone to transform themselves in accordance with His Will! On the contrary, they will be drinking hard, stealing, hating, killing, and only occasionally thinking: "What if God might not like this? Oh, well — all this is not going to be soon!". Just like I would not be interested to hear about methods of manufacturing golden jewelry or faceting diamonds — they are not interested to hear anything about God.

Once I was talking to a former head of a parish. He was telling me that he was working on his dissertation. I said to him: "But we are already in the age when it is time to think about using the time left to make as much as possible in the monastic pursuit and not in acquiring earthly titles... Will God need your degree?" He replied: "Well, God — it is not known if He exists or not, but the Ph.D. degree is almost mine!"

Faith acquires a real value only when it is characterized by love for God. Because only love can make us want to transform ourselves sincerely, willing to become what our Beloved wants us to be. And later it may even grow into a passion, which will make us give up everything that stands in the Way to the wide-open Embrace of the

Creator... This is when one comes to a true monasticism: to being one-to-one with God...

So, helping people strengthen their faith is the sole purpose of such techniques as making standard ritual bodily movements, repeating prayers, performing ritual dances and worshiping images of God and "saints" on icons or in the form of idols.

But with all the seeming absurdity of playing rites, initiations, common and individual mantras, games, etc. — God "adjusts" to these games that people play and helps sincere seekers overcome the difficult first steps of the great Path against this background.

Although the true baptism in the Holy Spirit (which was described by Philip the Apostle, in particular, [6,11]) in no way resembles the corresponding rite of any Church that is known under the same name, God accepts this act from sincere neophytes if they perform it as a vow to Him that they have an unwavering resolution to seek and to find Him as their Goal.

But when companies of murderers accept baptism before setting off for their bloody crimes, like it was, for example, during the Chechen war, — does it not look like an abominable desecration of the Teachings and the sacrificial death of Jesus Christ for us?

The same can be said about christening of children: does not common everyday experience tell us that it is a completely useless act? One may have seen both christened and-non-christened children get sick, die, become drunkards or criminals when they grow up!

Christening is an oath of devotion to God, and not at all an act of "guard magic". And only experienced and mature people can give such an oath, and they must do it themselves, but not "godparents" for them.

... And strings with crosses that people put on the children's necks sometimes turn out to be slip-knots for little babies. Sometimes they get entangled in those strings that strangle their necks...

Crosses worn around the necks were used by executioners during the compulsory christening of Russians to mark those who had already been christened: so that it would be easier for them to catch and subject to tortures or to kill those people who tried to evade this [9]. But why do people wear crosses now? Do they really think that God needs them to? But it is enough for God if there is a sign of christening in a sincere Christian's soul.

... But on the other hand — prayers before meal, icons in one's house, attendance of churches, participation in rituals, repetition of mantras and feeling a cross on the chest — all of this can strengthen the faith by reminding one about God. And God gives the worthy seekers confirmations of correctness of their initial efforts by affecting their emotional sphere: He grants them an experience of bliss by creating flows of grace.

... But there are no "saving" rituals, nonetheless. And upon acquiring loving faith, one has to start studying the Will of God, as opposed to canons of the organization, in which one started the Path. Also one has to make *real efforts* on self-transformation — transformation of oneself as a soul, as a consciousness.

As we can see, there is nothing wrong in getting involved in ritual forms of religious practice at a certain stage of one's development. This has been typical of all times, countries and religion forms. And it does not make sense to try to figure out which ritual forms are better and which worse. The more peace, harmony, pure and tranquil joy, bliss and love they carry, the better. These are exactly the qualities that religious rites should help believers cultivate.

The main issue is not the form of ritual practices, but the ideology that is preached by the organizations that provide these practices.

* * *

All people differ by their psychogenetic age, i.e. by the age of the soul. The age of the body (the ontogenetic age) is a different thing. In the next incarnation everyone can quite quickly and easily realize what they developed in the previous incarnations. This relates to the intellectual potential, level of development of the chakras, amount of the mass of the consciousness, inclinations in the professional field, intensity of certain psychic traits.

This is why it is perfectly normal that there are adult people who possess dramatically different abilities to comprehend religious issues.

It is also normal that a huge number of believers along with their leaders remain on the preliminary stage of their spiritual advancement until the end of their current incarnations: in their next lives they will have a chance to continue the Path.

But they do need to be informed that this stage is just a preliminary one. This will help those of them, who can go, wake up and move further.

Initial Methods

Ethic Self-Correction

People who are still at the preliminary stage of mastering their religiosity believe that the faith in the ideological concept and rituals of the organization of their choice is a sufficient condition for their "salvation". These people are not yet capable of comprehending words of God, not even those of them that are written in the Holy Scriptures. Opinions and orders of their earthly "pastors" are much dearer and more valuable to them.

For example, despite the fact that God told people not to kill but to love and forgive — "Christians" "became famous" for so many terrifying atrocities throughout the history of Christianity on the Earth! So many wars, murders, tortures and other crimes they have committed!

As for killing of animals — scarcely 0.001% of "Christians" obey the Will of God in this respect. Where is the place for Christian love?! There is no sight of you among "Christians"! This is because these "Christians" are not true ones!

* * *

The initial stage of spiritual advancement implies making real efforts on self-transformation. God expects from us not prayers and kowtowing: He does not need them! He needs us to become better!

And the first thing that the aspirant has to do is to accept the principle of LOVE — accept it not as a nice phrase, acknowledging the beauty of it, but as a strict rule of conduct. And no practical methods — be they exercises of Hatha Yoga, work with the chakras and meridians, winter swimming, etc. — will bring us closer to God (in fact, they can even lead us astray, sometimes) if we do not follow the commandments of God regarding LOVE.

Let us look at the nutrition, for example. If we contaminate our bodies with coarse energies of dead bodies of animals, this will not allow us to attain the required degree of refinement of the consciousness for getting closer to the Abode of the Creator; on the contrary, it will drag us towards hell and create for us bad karma, which will have to be redeemed in our next incarnations.

But health and karma considerations are not a principal issue here. The main point is that God is Love. And He allows us to get close to Him only if we become Love.

Impressions as "Food" for the Soul

But material substances are not the only food that we consume. As "food" we, as souls, also use impressions (Russian religious psychologist George Gurdjieff was among those who talked about it in these terms in the beginning of the 20th century [62]).

And if we want to "turn away from what is evil and cling to what is good", we need to take all opportunities to use "food" of this kind — in nature, art, communicating with spiritual people, etc. and attuning to the subtle and harmonious phenomena. At the same time we need to keep away from coarse impressions, which are primarily created by people of the tamas guna.

Initial Control of Emotions

Avoiding outer coarseness is just one of the methods. But the main task for us is to eliminate inner coarseness, including that which comes out of us. This can be attained by controlling emotions, which are states of us as consciousnesses.

Each emotion emanates beyond the body, affecting surrounding people and other living beings. And the more intensive it is the further from the body it emanates.

Solving the task of controlling the emotions radically will be possible only at the next, higher stages of work. But if we do not set this goal right now and start to accustom ourselves to self-control, we can hardly expect ourselves to achieve any success in the future.

For now, an effective method of struggling with bursts of coarse emotions and various manifestations of egotism is penitential work, which we have discussed in detail.

About Compassion

Let me note that a superficial and shallow attitude towards ethic issues can sometimes produce an opposite effect compared to what is expected.

For example, we discussed acceptance of the COMPASSION principle as one of the first steps towards LOVE. But does everyone clearly realize that compassion does not have anything to do with plunging into unpleasant emotional states of "worrying about" someone?... People who fall into states like that become unbearable for others, especially for those whom they "worry about". The bioenergetic impact of the fields with such characteristics sometimes can be the "final blow" for those wounded or sick people who become the subject to such "worrying". The victims may feel a desperate need to get rid of this "compassionate" monster who overwhelms them with such a state — to get rid by all means, at the level of the deepest instinct of self-preservation, which is beyond the control of the intellect...

Such "compassion", just like bioenergetic vampirism [7], ruins loving relationships between people, destroys families...

No, compassion does not mean "heavy" emotions, but overall pure and careful attitude towards all manifestations of life, avoiding causing any unnecessary harm to anyone, as well as willingness to help everyone in everything good.

Self-Discipline and Energy

The initial stage of spiritual work is not sattva yet. It is rajas. And among the most important factors that determine success at this stage are energy and self-discipline, cultivating the ability to make efforts and super-efforts on the spiritual Path.

One can develop these qualities well by engaging in various dynamic sport activities, of which especially great are those that connect us with living nature (hiking, mountain climbing, etc.). Practicing oriental martial arts would also be very good for that purpose. But it is important to emphasize, that this practice should in no way lead to growth of aggressiveness, brutality and rudeness. Another important thing to understand is that the techniques of martial arts per se cannot conduct the seeker to spiritual heights: this can be achieved only by working with the chakras and through mastering the art of meditation, which are integral parts of the training in the best schools of this orientation.

In any specific kind of classes at this stage — be it karate, hiking, or something else — both instructors and students must pay their principal attention to increasing the level of their morality, which is based on causing no unnecessary harm to any living beings.

It would be appropriate for everyone to start thinking about and to make right decisions regarding their service according to Karma Yoga principles and change professional occupation, if necessary, or start studying in order to acquire a new profession.

Hatha Yoga

People with unstable emotions as well as those who cannot concentrate or have unpleasant obsessive thoughts will benefit from taking a course of Hatha Yoga lessons. Exercises of this stage were developed in ancient India, and their performance teaches one concentration of the consciousness in various parts of the body, as well as relaxation of the body and mind; they also contribute to elimination of many bioenergetic defects within the body and can heal one of some chronic diseases.

The mechanism that is at work here is as follows: maintaining postures of Hatha Yoga for a long time causes accumulation and redistribution of energy in the energy structures of the organism, which results in their development. The following dynamics of sensations is typical when mastering new asanas. For the first few days of practice, one may not feel anything out of the ordinary, only a regular adaptation of the body takes place. During the next few days, there appears absolutely new "mysterious" and pleasant sensation of energies "flowing" inside the body, which "flow" in meridians like streams of liquid; one may even hear a babbling sound at times. But in one or two weeks they suddenly disappear, to one's regret, which in fact means that the asana has fulfilled its role at the current stage. But what was taking place is the following. As a result of doing the asana, the corresponding meridian started to function. While its conductivity was still low, one had interesting murmur-like sensations. When the meridian had opened fully, the energy started to move freely inside it and the "murmuring" stopped.

At the initial stages of mastering the exercises of Hatha Yoga, the necessary condition for doing asanas is performing shavasana after the whole set or after particular asanas, which are performed separately (except for relaxation ones). This is needed for the leveling of energetic strains that may develop due to the low conductivity of meridians. If this condition is not fulfilled, neurotic symptoms (liability of mood, sleep disturbances, and many others) and even visual impairments or disorders of other systems of the organism may develop.

Description of relaxation asanas will be given in the next chapters. Other exercises are described in specialized literature.

Practicing Hatha Yoga without switching to the *killing-free* diet always results in the coarsening of the consciousness of the students. Subjectively it may be perceived as attainment of power. But it turns out to be a terrible trap: by possessing coarse power of the consciousness we program ourselves for living in hell.

Apart from exercises of Indian Hatha Yoga some systems of Chinese dynamic gymnastics can be used for the same purpose. For example, those, where the development of the meridians with images of light (small "sun", etc.) is performed during smooth and slow "rollovers" from one foot to another.

Visualization

Hatha Yoga practice (or other trainings) can be supplemented by exercises, which develop the ability to create visual images. This will prepare one for mastering the highest forms of meditation as well as create prerequisites for attainment of clairvoyance.

We can start with simple things: let us imagine a tomato, an apple, a juicy pear, then let us imagine that we examine them, smell them, bite them, enjoy their flavor and swallow them with great pleasure...

Let us get carried to the morning silence of a lake: in a boat, surrounded by reed... Small tender dewdrops are hanging from every leaflet... Fish splashing, sound of duck's wings... Reed warblers start singing their songs...

Or we may imagine that we are lying on a beach in the morning sunlight... Warm and tender light pervades our bodies and souls, saturating them with bliss...

Or let us visualize ourselves picking mushrooms: cutting and plucking slimy black milk-cups out of wet autumn foliage..., admiring a big and solid cep...

We may visualize numerous similar images. They must attune us to subtlety, beauty and bliss. They must teach us sattva.

Later on we may make the training more complex in the following way: we may imagine ourselves to be some imaginary sattvic object — a sweet juicy pear, a strawberry, a tender fragrant flower, or a caressing sun. We may learn to place these images filled with our own consciousness, with our self-awareness, into the chest — into the anahata chakra.

When this ability is well developed, it will be easy for us to invite into anahata a Divine Teacher, Whose Image we know very well from photographs. And He will "come alive" there: He will start smiling and speaking...

But it will become possible only if we deserve it: if we keep an impeccable life, become established in sattva, study the Teachings of God intensively, and transform ourselves in accordance with them.

Work with images has another name — *visualization*, which was borrowed from Buddhism. But it is important to warn the reader against having a non-critical attitude towards specific recommendations for visualization that one may find in literature or lectures of some ignorant Buddhist specialists.

Some authors recommend surrounding the body with images of "wrathful gods", i.e. devils and demons, for "guard magic" purposes. Such images also "come alive" by getting filled with corresponding hell beings...

A famous mystic and doctor from Saint Petersburg, who was not "overburdened with intellect" and possessed grossest ethic vices while being a good extrasensory diagnostician, started to study these "black magic" methods with a group of his students.

The effect was that people were getting sick having just talked with him.

And when that entire gang visited other esoteric groups to stare at people practicing — students were fainting there.

Coarsening of him as a consciousness reached a tremendous level, and he turned into a devil in the flesh, but he continued to teach extrasensory healing and to "heal". Although it is clear that people like this cannot heal anyone; they can only do harm by "putting an evil eye" on people.

He ended up becoming a knife-victim, murdered in his own bathroom. It was most likely one of the victims of his "healing" or one of a victim's friends.

But hell is not what we need! We prepare ourselves to becoming God, not devils! Therefore, seeing this sad example of spiritual degradation as someone else's tragic experience, let us turn away from it and go to the abodes of Purity, Light, Tenderness, and Love — in order to attune to them and to become one with them.

* * *

If you already possess some skills, which could be of use to other people, — gather some of your friends and teach them what you know. Your knowledge, abilities, and efforts will combine, and you all will grow together, preparing yourselves to the next stages of spiritual growth.

Basic Methods

Basic methods are those which allow one to attain such level of purification and development of energy structures of the organism, which would enable one to feel God, to learn how to attain Samadhi (the emotional states of intense Bliss that occur during contacts of the consciousness with the Holy Spirit).

These preparatory methods ensure further growth of the refined consciousness and develop its power — in order to come at the subsequent highest stages of work to the final Victory — Mergence with the Creator in His Abode.

In Hindu and Buddhist traditions these methods are known as *Raja Yoga*. Their variations were developed in Chinese Taoism and Muslim Sufism. They existed on the territory of Russia before its "christening", which is clear from the high spiritual status of those who developed here spiritually [11, 14]. But the only spiritual practice of this level that is widely known in Christianity is the *Jesus Prayer*[10].

Raja Yoga is based on working with the chakras, main meridians and the *cocoon*. The purpose of this work is to "cleanse" them to transparency and to develop them — in order to connect through them with the Divine level of subtlety.

Hence it becomes obvious that techniques of "coloring" the chakras practiced in some schools are harmful, and using them is a consequence of tremendous spiritual incompetence of the leaders of those schools. For the subtlest color is white with tender goldish hue, and any other color is obviously farther from the level of the subtlety of the Creator.

Another typical mistake that people may make when working with the chakras is placing the emphasis on the development of the ajna chakra and its "window" ("trikutta"), which, ostensibly, results in the attainment of clairvoyance. This tendency has a long history and originates in the incorrect interpretation of Krishna's words

---

[10] Although some individual seekers (including some Greco-Slavic Hesychasts) undoubtedly attained more significant levels of spiritual advancement. But in order to succeed they had to get beyond the limited scope of traditions of their organizations first and to become direct disciples of God.

It is known that Orthodoxy was for a long time intolerant even against the practice of the Jesus Prayer [9]. Opponents of Hesychasm "decreed" then that God is "incognizable". Well, for them He is surely "incognizable"...

in the Bhagavad Gita [11] (8:10), where He recommends channeling energy through the head. But from the next verses of Gita (8:12) it is clear that He meant the energy of Atman. However, in numerous schools, whose leaders have not cognized Atman yet, attempts are made to perform this with regular bioenergies; this results in activation of one of the coarsest (originally) chakras and as a consequence in coarsening of the entire consciousness. Such people develop, in particular, a "piercing", sharp, unpleasant gaze. A tendency like this halts them for a long time in their spiritual development.

But the clairvoyance, which some seekers gain as a result of such practice, is of no real value, because it enables them to see only emotional auras around the heads of other people and is good only for "spying" upon their emotional states.

The truly significant clairvoyance is exercised by the structures of the lower *bubble of perception* (see below). Possessing it enables one to see energies of different levels of *coarseness-subtlety* scale in multidimensional space. As a result of gaining this kind of clairvoyance, one becomes able to observe directly various subtlest Manifestations of the non-incarnate Consciousness of God.

Work on the development of the chakras and other fine structures of the organism is incompatible with taking alcohol (even in the form of kvass or alcohol-containing milk products), since alcohol destroys those subtle structures. Breaking this rule causes serious diseases.

* * *

Work with fine energy structures as well as meditative trainings cannot be effective if the room in which they are performed is illumined with fluorescent lighting, since it produces a coarse energy impact on the organism.

One also must not wear synthetic clothes, because they block a significant part of the spectrum of bioenergies and distort the energy processes inside the body. (The latter instruction does not relate to raincoats, which we put on only in case of rain).

Watches and other metal objects should be taken off during the classes: bioenergetic work makes watches magnetize and go out of order, while all metal objects create energy interference.

We have already talked about the incompatibility of psycho-energetic trainings with eating *"killed"* food. If this rule is not obeyed the energy structures of the organism get constructed of coarse energies.

Practice at this stage of work is better performed in a group. The size of the practice room should correspond to the size of the group. Too big of a hall would be unfavorable, since the group energy will get dissipated in it.

* * *

The first serious information (of that which is known to us) about the role and functioning of the chakras and about the methods of working with them was presented in the books of our School. The fantasies of Aurobindo Ghosh regarding this subject, which were set out in his books, are completely baseless; they deceived many readers, while there was a shortage of written esoteric information in Russia before Perestroika.

Let us get down to specific information about working at this stage of spiritual advancement. The suggested exercises have been published several times. They have been tested by many years of teaching them to great numbers of people and proved to be highly effective.

Cross of Buddha

It is good to start each practice session with emotional attunement and purification of the energy of the surrounding space. For this purpose there exists a wonderful technique known as the *Cross of Buddha*. It is performed in the following way.

For the best performance of this exercise we have to accept the so-called *student posture*: we sit down on the heels holding the spine straight, toes looking backward, and the palms of our hands resting upon the thighs. Then we send waves of our benevolence and love from the chest forward, saying mentally:

"May all beings have peace! May all beings be calm! May all beings feel bliss!"

We produce each of these three states inside the chest first and then radiate them forward. Then we repeat this to the right, to the left, backward, up, and down. This is a powerful technique that allows us to bring harmony to ourselves, to the surrounding space, and to the living beings around us.

Warm-Up

After this, especially at the first few sessions, a very important element of practice would be a physical warm-up, which not only allows us to "cheer up" the energies within the body and to get rid of unnecessary mental dominants, but also teaches us to concentrate the consciousness in the working parts of the body. The latter will come in handy in the future when we will be working with the chakras.

Let us stand up. By making paddy movements with the legs and the trunk, we swing both arms back and forth and then rotate them simultaneously. Concentrate in the shoulder joints. Visualize *light* emerging and growing brighter inside the joints.

Tense the muscles of the arms. Bend and unbend the arms repeatedly in the elbow joints. Watch white *light* gathering from the entire body to the working muscles.

Extend the arms in front of the body. Move the relaxed wrists quickly up and down. Tense the fingers. Bend and unbend them. Move the wrists while tensing the muscles of the forearms and wrists. Then let go of the tension and relax the entire body.

Bend the head from side to side while keeping the neck relaxed. Roll the head over the shoulders making a circle. Turn the head to the right and to the left around a vertical axis. Imagine that the neck segment of the spine is an axle and the cervical vertebras are balls stringed on it. See a beam of white *light* coming up the axle. Tense the muscles of the neck. Repeat the same exercises but this time with the muscles of the neck tensed. Imagine a stream of white *light* diameter-of-the-neck wide rising through it. Again relax the entire body. Shift the head from side to side while keeping it vertical and without moving the shoulders, then rotate the head in the same manner.

Raise the arms over the head. Take the right hand with the left one by the wrist and pull it over the head while bending the body to the same side and stretch the side muscles of the trunk. Repeat this movement with another hand.

While holding the arms up, tilt the trunk to the sides first in the pectoral and then in the lumbar segments of the spine. Tense the muscles of the trunk and make tilts and turns of the body. Imagine that the trunk gets filled with *light*. Relax the body. Turn the trunk around a vertical axis while relaxing the muscles and keeping the feet on the floor, trying to turn the head as far to the back as possible, concentrating in the spine.

Shift the pelvis to the sides without tilting it and bending the legs, keeping the muscles as relaxed as possible. Concentrate in the area of the spine below the navel.

Raise the right leg so that the thigh is parallel to the floor. Rotate the ankle as if drawing a circle on the floor. Concentrate in the ankle joint, seeing white *light* and warmth emerging inside of it. Rotate the shin, concentrating in the knee-joint.

Swing the shin from side to side, keeping the knee in one place and concentrating in both hip joints.

Draw a circle with a straight leg, first in front of the body, then at the right side, and then behind the body.

Repeat these exercises with the left leg.

Relaxation Asanas

After the warm-up we should take some rest in one of the following postures (asanas):

The first of them is the so-called *half-tortoise posture*.

We sit on the heels with the toes looking backward and the knees moved apart. Put the forehead and the extended arms on the floor with the palms pressed against each other. Relax the body and mind completely. Watch the belly sag more and more as the relaxation becomes deeper. This is a wonderful exercise that allows one to get rid of physical and mental tiredness. It should be performed for about ten minutes.

The second asana is called *crocodile posture*. There are two ways of performing it.

We lie on the belly, protruding the elbows forward as far as possible, the chin resting on the palms.

The second option — we put the elbows forward and place one forearm upon the other on the floor, holding the head and the upper part of the body up by tensing the muscles of the back.

In both cases we feel ourselves happy little crocodiles, which have crawled out on a sandy beach to have a sunbath! The sun warms our backs — and we dissolve in pleasure under its tender warmth, which permeates our bodies.

Pranayamas

One has to perform the bioenergetic purification both of the organism as a whole and of its separate segments corresponding with the chakras. There are a lot of purification techniques, and each of them allows one to get rid of the next portion of impurity, which means elimination of diseases, overall improvement of health, and getting closer to the Ultimate Goal.

Now I will describe a few general purifying exercises of pranayama type.

We perform them in standing position. First, bend slightly to the right so that the right arm hangs freely without touching the body. Try to feel the arm thoroughly from the shoulder joint to the wrist. Imagine that a pump chamber, to which "air"-*light* is being fed through the arm like through a hose, expands in the chest with every inhalation and contracts with every exhalation. Special attention should be paid to exhaling. Try to achieve a high clarity of sensations. The "hose" must be as thick as the arm, and nothing should prevent the "air"-*light* from moving freely through it.

Then we perform the same exercise with the left arm, and then with each leg. The "hose" must come down from the chest to each leg through the corresponding side of the body.

Place images of two big barrels under the feet. Let one barrel be empty and the other full of white liquid *light*. Touch this *light* with the foot-hose and pump it through the body-pump into the other barrel. With each inhaling, the pump chamber inside the body and the head is expanding, drawing the *light* from the full barrel through the leg. With each exhaling, the chamber is contracting; the *light* pouring out through the other leg into the empty barrel. Thus we cleanse the whole body from inside.

When the barrel with *light* gets empty — fill it up again and overturn the content of the other barrel into an image of fire, so that all dirt that has streamed out burns. Turn the body around over the barrels — and repeat the exercise with another half of the body.

Then do the same, but this time placing the barrels under the hands.

In this way, we have to attain a feeling that the whole body is filled up with bright white *light*.

After performing pranayamas, we have to rest in one of the relaxation asanas.

Psycho-Physical Exercises

Now let us learn four psycho-physical exercises. They got this name because their psychic component is combined with simultaneously performing physical movements, with the latter contributing to the mastering of the former. The basic idea of these exercises was invented by Peter Dânov, a mystic of the beginning of the 20th century; later it was developed by Omraam Mikhael Aivanhov, and then by us.

The first exercise of this series is called *Awakening*. We awaken from a long sleep of self-isolation from harmony, beauty, and love of the world. (While standing, we raise the hands up and stretch ourselves as if after sleep). We let all the purity, light, and the vitality from outside into us. Feel a waterfall of astonishingly pure, transparent, subtle feelings and morning freshness flowing from above. We fill ourselves with this morning freshness, with these fresh waves, overfill ourselves with them! (Hands move down to the shoulders, assisting this process, then move up again; we repeat these movements several times). We try to reach as high and subtle an emotional state as possible.

The second exercise is called *Giving Away*. We hold the hands against the chest and then make a wide gesture moving them forward and apart: what we have received, we must give away to other people — our level of spiritual advancement is measured by our ability to give. Also, so that a vessel may get filled with fresh water, it needs to be emptied first. They who do not empty themselves by giving away what they have, do not get renewed, do not grow. We repeat this exercise again and again, pouring out, giving away all the good that we have accumulated — generously, without the desire to receive a reward. Send subtlest and intense waves of streaming fresh and pure love far forward. Feel how the chest gets inflated by the energy of love that comes swelling from behind. A flower, exhaling a tender fragrance, starts to blossom out in the middle of the chest. Send these subtle vibrations forward. This is the fragrance of love itself!

The third exercise is *Reconciliation*. Raise the right hand above the head and concentrate in the palm and the space that immediately surrounds it. Then slowly bring the hand down drawing with it a sinusoid with a half-period of about thirty centimeters. The edge of the palm should be facing the direction of the hand's movement. While doing this, try to feel the space, in which the hand moves, as some energy field, to which we assign new characteristics: peace, harmony, and calm. One may "extend" the hand. (One may imagine various ways of performing dancing movements: jerky and quick versus gentle, smooth, and elegant. Each of these ways disposes both the performer and the audience to corresponding emotional states). And this simple but powerful gesture, which symbolizes harmony, will be helping everyone in every situation as they master this exercise (one should feel it deeply through!), even if performed without being accompanied with movements of the body.

The fourth exercise is called *Climbing Up*. We raise the hands up with the palms facing sideward and then bring them down laterally, making sweeps. Repeat this movement several times, with each sweep we hatch out of another coarse envelope, as it were, and become lighter, purer; we rise to the source of the light above — to the sun... It becomes very close to us; a few more swings and we reach it... Flow into space of the purest and subtlest light, and enjoy being in it... Then slowly get down to the earth feeling the sun in the chest. Stand on the ground and shine at people and all other living beings with *sunlight* coming from the chest!

Shavasana

All sessions involving work with the chakras and meridians must be followed by a relaxation exercise called *shavasana*. It allows one to rest from bioenergetic work, which can be very tiring, as well as to get rid of bioenergetic defects that have not been eliminated yet.

Shavasana is the relaxation of the body and the mind in the position of lying on the back.

We lie on the back and make sure that we feel comfortable. Nothing should distract us. Then we begin to relax the body starting with the toes. One may imagine a plane perpendicular to the axis of the body — like a glass wall — and move it through the body from the toes to the head; behind this surface no tension remains. Let us feel that we lose any sensation of those parts of the body behind this plane. We alienate them, saying mentally: "This is not mine! This is not mine!..." If we regain sensation of any part of the body, we move the plane through this section once again. After the plane has passed through the head, we may experience the following states:

The first state: the self-awareness vanishes. We fall into something resembling a deep sleep, but this is not sleep. The self-awareness is regained in about 18-20 minutes. We feel thoroughly rested, as if after a long deep sleep. This is quite a blissful state. One does not have to stand up abruptly, but just enjoy it.

The second state: the self-awareness is retained, but absolute *peace* comes to us. We may scan the entire body with the *inner sight*. We may enter the inner space of the body from below and see light and dark regions. Gray or black colors mean disorders on one of the energy planes, which correspond to the manifest or still latent stages of diseases. We have to try to gather all dark stuff in heaps as if with a rake and throw it away from the body.

When doing shavasana, we may also experience involuntary full exits from the material body: we may suddenly become aware of ourselves being in a usual form but in an unusual position — for example, soaring above the floor or standing on the head and so on. There is nothing to worry about, though: once we feel like getting back into the body — we will find ourselves there right away. But under no circumstances one is encouraged to perform such exits: these are exits into a coarse space dimension — into the so-called *astral plane*. One has to learn to exit immediately into the highest spatial dimensions, but the methods for doing this are different.

Children under the age of 12 must not be taught shavasana: having realized that they are out of the body, they do not always want to return into it.

All these exercises should be practiced regularly: it is impossible to get the full effect from them after only one session.

Latihan. Baptism in the Holy Spirit

When all the previous exercises have been mastered, we can proceed to the exercise called *latihan*.

The term *latihan* was introduced in the beginning of the 20th century by a Sufi named Bapak Mohammad Subuh [20], who used this word to denote one of the ways of communicating with the Holy Spirit. He visited many European countries, where he taught this method to Catholic monks and healed with its help many ill people, including those suffering from cancer.

In this technique, one addresses the Holy Spirit for help and asks Him to concentrate above the head (one has to become aware of Him there) and then to "shower" Himself down through the entire body as through a transparent glass cylinder. This will be a true baptism in the Holy Spirit.

In this way comes the healing of the body.

The body, having surrendered to this Stream flowing through it, starts dancing and performing other smooth and harmonious movements... This phenomenon is a variation of laya yoga — a set of methods of "dissolving" oneself in Divine Streams as well as in static states of the Divine Consciousness.

In fact, this is very simple if we really believe, if we really love Him and are willing to surrender to Him. And the Holy Spirit is always present everywhere as a sea of *Light*, including the space above our bodies — watching, loving, teaching, and... waiting for when we finally pay attention to Him with love and ask Him for help...

If we have prepared ourselves with the help of all the previous exercises, including *Awakening* — we will succeed in doing this one right away. If not — we may try to imagine ourselves… in paradise, under a heavenly waterfall, immersed in the tender sunlight, aroma of flowers, singing of birds… A cascade of heavenly water is falling down through the body, purifying the soul and making it worthy of paradise…

In order for the laya dance (the dance of "dissolution") to start, being guided by the Holy Spirit, we should stand on tip-toes and raise the hands; the clothes must be light and loose — so that we almost do not feel them…

After the dance, it will be good to have a rest in a relaxation posture.

Cleansing of the Chakras. Opening of the Spiritual Heart

Upon achieving the mastery of the above said, we can get down to the cleansing of the chakras.

The condition of the chakras is closely interrelated with the condition of the physical organs located in the corresponding parts of the body. The chakras play an important role in supplying the organs with energy, while diseases of the organs negatively affect the condition of the chakras.

For example, the following chakras are responsible for the following organs:

— anahata: heart, lungs, arms, and mammary glands;

— manipura: among other organs — stomach and other structures of the digestive system;

— svadhisthana: the organs of reproduction, urinary bladder, legs, and others;

— sahasrara: forebrain hemispheres;

— ajna: the rest of the brain, as well as eyes, ears, nose, and nasopharynx;

— vishuddha: the entire neck, thyroid, both jaws, including teeth, and others. (The border between the "spheres of influence" of ajna and vishuddha coincides with the palate).

* * *

Let us get down to work with the chakras. There exist certain combinations of sounds (a sort of mantras), singing of which contributes to the development of the chakras by producing resonant vibrations. Mantras will also help us attain clear sensation of our chakras. Here are these mantras:

for sahasrara — AM (a-a-am),
for ajna — VOM (vo-o-om),
for vishuddha — HAM (ha-a-am),
for anahata — YAM (ya-a-am),
for manipura — RAM (ra-a-am),
for svadhisthana — VAM (va-a-am),
for muladhara — LAM (la-a-am).

One has to sing these mantras gently, producing high frequency sounds (taking female voices as a pattern for the pitch), but not in a loud voice, at the same time concentrating in the corresponding chakras. When moving the concentration of the consciousness into the next chakra, one should enter it from behind the back or the nape of the neck, as if getting into a cell or a niche.

One has to repeat the whole set of mantras several times, trying to achieve clear perception of vibrations in all chakras.

This exercise must be practiced every day. When there is no possibility to sing the mantras aloud, one may sing them mentally to oneself but only after mastering singing them aloud.

Let us pay maximum attention both at this and the next stages to work with the anahata chakra — just doing this makes life brighter and more joyous.

If the very subtle and gentle singing of the mantras for chakras has not been mastered — no further work can be successful. Men usually are the ones who have this difficulty especially frequently, since subtlety is often unknown to them. The following recommendation may help them. Take some water in the mouth and start gargling so that a gurgling sound can be heard. Bring the water lower down the throat. The sound must become higher. Let it reach as high of a pitch as possible. Those are the notes, at which one has to sing the mantras for chakras.

Let us learn another method of cleansing and development of the chakras. Visualize behind the anahata a white shining 3-dimensional figure formed by four equilateral triangles with joined sides. This figure is called a tetrahedron. Insert this figure into each chakra (one chakra at a time) from behind, with one of the tetrahedron vertices looking forward, while rotating it rapidly counterclockwise (looking from behind) around a horizontal axis coming from back to front. For the two outermost chakras the rotation of the tetrahedron must be performed around a vertical axis; in case of sahasrara the vertex of the tetrahedron must look upward, while in case of muladhara — downward. The direction of the rotation of the tetrahedron for these two chakras must be counterclockwise (looking from inside the body). Performance of this exercise will be easier if we combine it with "blowing" of the corresponding mantra into each chakra.

All exercises with the chakras described above (as well as with meridians, which will be described later) are more efficiently performed while standing.

But there is a simple exercise with the spiritual heart that everyone may try doing without any pre-conditions. Imagine that your head has moved into the chest. Feel the nose, the forehead, the lips. Move the lips. In order for the head not to rise to its usual position, we may imagine that we put a hat on the head. Then follows the most important thing: we need to open the eyes and to "blink" the eyelids there… From now on, learn to look at the outside world from the chest. The world will look completely different: not as tough and hostile, but as subtle, tender, and responsive to the emotions of love.

This is what is called opening of the spiritual heart. As we can see, this is quite easy to do. The only thing required here is one's will!

Later on, one needs to learn to look from anahata not only forward but also backward.

One has to perform the exercices with the chakras and all further meditative trainings with open eyes. (You may try to find out yourself — why?)

* * *

Having mastered this, we have to do the same with all other chakras. (The "windows" of muladhara and sahasrara look downward and upward respectively. But we can look also forward and backward from these chakras).

Learning to look backward is important not only because it contributes to the development of the chakras, but also because by looking forward we accustom ourselves to seeing the world of material objects, while pure and subtle eons with the Consciousness that lives in them are found behind.

Moreover, by performing this exercise, we prepare ourselves for future conscious exits from the body. And this must be also performed backward from anahata.

Exits from the Body

A great number of mystics of various countries and cultures get deceived by learning to exit from the body forward or upward. This manner of exiting from the body gets them into a certain sub-layer of the *astral plane* (depending on their own status on the *coarseness-subtlety* scale) — a rather dense eon, which is closest to the material world. From the *astral plane* one can very easily see the material world and people with their thoughts. This comes along with the possibility to "spy" upon them, play jokes on them, or influence them in some other way… This turns out to be interesting and exciting…

But when the body of such a person dies, he or she stays attached to material objects. He or she did not get any closer to God, and the incarnation was spent in vain.

But if we have made necessary transformations of our main meridians, especially of chitrini (Brahmanadi) — one of the subtlest structures of the organism, then by passing through chitrini we immediately "fall out" into the eons of the Holy Spirit at the least. And there we can see Him as *Light-Love* and feel Him as Tenderness. There we learn to merge with Him and to become one with Him.

… Do not these prospects, so easily attainable, spur you to reject your old dogmas and vices and to dash "with all your heart, and with all the soul, and with all your mind, and with all your strength" towards the Embrace of God?

Development of the Chakras. Dantians

In the mean time, we may practice filling and "inflating" the chakras with an image of pure shining and sparkling white *light*, which we may "blow" into each chakra from an imaginary hose that comes from a powerful pump.

Images that we create in the subtle eons become a reality in them. Not only can we cleanse our energy structures with the help of these images but also heal other people by eliminating black areas of diseases and even by performing "surgeries" using images of various surgical instruments.

Starting from this stage of work, one can become a good healer. Healing is one of the ways we can give our love to people. This is why the Holy Spirit is always happy to help us when we heal, especially if we ask Him for it!

If we possess the skills of communication with the Holy Spirit, then during a healing session He may flow through our chakras if we ask Him. This facilitates development of the chakras and makes them more refined (see details about healing in [7]).

* * *

Now let us learn another exercise with the tetrahedron:

1. Rotate an image of the tetrahedron behind each chakra as a dentist's drill.

2. Then insert it into the chakra like in a cavity of a decayed tooth. Dirt flies out in all directions; wash it down with an image of a shower.

3. Increase the size of the imaginary tetrahedron; this allows enlarging the chakra.

4. Upon working all the chakras through, take a "shower" and perform shavasana.

... The next technique of the development of the chakras is the following: get inside each chakra, one at a time, starting with anahata and feel the whole of oneself there like in a cave filled with *light*. Then by pressing against each wall of the chakra with the hands push them away to infinity...

And here is one more wonderful exercise: we imagine ourselves a powerful light bulb as big as the body, which is turned on; the bulb's filament is in anahata. And then illumine the surrounding space with the light from anahata.

In the future, we may move the filament from anahata into each of the remaining chakras and "burn" the arms, the legs, and all those parts of the body where any ailments are present. In this manner we get coarse energies "burned away" from the body; we cleanse, lighten, and heal ourselves, accustoming ourselves to being one with this *light*. For "God is *Light*, and in Him there is no darkness at all" (1 John, 1:5). In this way — gradually — we begin getting closer to the state of God.

* * *

The developed chakras can be combined into functional groups, called *dantians* in Chinese. The upper dantian is made up of the three upper chakras; the middle dantian is represented by anahata; and the lower one — by the three lower chakras.

Out of the three, the most important is the middle dantian, since it is by employing this structure that we can transform ourselves into Love and to infuse into God. The other two play auxiliary roles. The upper dantian helps to develop the middle one with its intellectual and esthetic appraisal functions. And the lower one, being the main power center of the organism, provides energy for this process.

All dantians (as well as all chakras) have to be developed harmoniously, although the middle one must always be given priority over the other two during the training. In the face of God, the main function of the organism is love. But love cannot become full-fledged unless it is supported intellectually, ethically, and energetically. This is why one has to pay attention to the development of each of these functions, while always remembering about the necessity to strictly adhere to the policy of constantly increasing the level of the subtlety of the consciousness: setbacks to coarse states of the consciousness would constitute a crash of all efforts and a halt in the development at best, and even a complete failure at worst.

The correct development of the lower dantian (also denoted by the term *hara*) can be achieved optimally by practicing special meditative techniques at special *places of power*. One of the secrets here is reviving the functions of the "embryonal" meridians, which used to connect the energy systems of the fetus and the mother together. It is upon this "revival" that hara starts functioning as a whole, as a united power-center.

Work with Meridians. Sushumna, Chitrini, Zhen-Mo, the *Microcosmic Orbit*, and the Middle Meridian

Upon mastering all exercises described above, it would be appropriate to put the main meridians of the body to rights.

The whole human body, as well as the bodies of animals and even plants, is being run through by numerous canals, invisible with regular eyesight, which channel energies of various levels of refinement around the organism. These canals, called meridians (or *nadi*) were discovered and utilized in ancient Chinese medicine (Zhen Tsyu therapy).

The meridians can be discovered, in particular, because of their increased — compared to adjacent body tissues — electroconductivity (but one should keep in mind that electric current, even the weakest one, is inadequate for them; therefore the methods of punctate electrodiagnostics and electropuncture can be used in the extraordinary cases only).

The meridians can be seen by people whose range of perception was expanded through a system of training similar to ours.

As a result of inflammatory processes in the body tissues, a contaminating type of nutrition, or external negative energetic influences, the meridians can lose their conductivity. In this case, lingering disorders of the organs, deprived of proper energy supply, may develop. Such diseases usually cannot be completely cured by using drug therapy. In cases like this, acupunctural methods and similar healing techniques (laser, vibration, and other kinds of influence through "biologically active points" of the integument) turn out to be efficient. These methods work, because they restore conductivity of the meridians by means of sending currents of energy through them.

But it is more effective to cleanse the meridians on one's own using the methods described in this book.

Let us talk about several meridians that can be successfully used in psychic self-regulation.

All the chakras are connected with one another by large meridians that run along the spine, as well as the front and the middle part of the body.

A wide canal called sushumna (tu-mo or du-mo in Chinese) runs along the spine from muladhara to sahasrara. One of its functions is to distribute the energy extracted from food to the chakras. Within sushumna — in its back section — there is a significantly narrower canal (its diameter is about 2 centimeters), called vajrini, through which the energy of svadhisthana (called *udana*) flows to other chakras.

The third of the spinal canals — chitrini (Brahmanadi) — is located behind sushumna. It begins at the end section of sahasrara, passes under the occipital bone, and runs down the back part of the neck and then — down the backmost part of the spinal column, coinciding with the spinous processes of vertebras and the skin.

Chitrini is an extremely important structure. It will serve us as a standard for one of the subtlest states, to which we can attune the emotional sphere.

On the G.Gurdjieff's *scale of hydrogens* [62], the state of chitrini is assessed as H-3. This is the Holy Spirit's level of subtlety. Upon learning to concentrate in chitrini, one can easily "dive" as a consciousness through this canal into the eons of the Holy Spirit and directly communicate, embrace, and then merge with Him there. This is how religious truths turn from abstractions into reality.

The system of the chakras is also communicated by the front channel (zhen-mo). It begins from the upper end of sushumna, forks into two branches that turn around sahasrara and join in the forehead area to split into several small canals that run down the face and join again in the vishuddha region. One more branch of this canal goes through the middle of the head, reaches the chin coming through the palate and joins the other branches at the neck. After that the canal runs down the front side of the trunk, branching off to every chakra, passes the share bone, and heads for the coccyx.

We should pay special attention to the upper part of this canal, which unites the four chakras of the so-called *emotional center* [62] — anahata, vishuddha, manipura, and ajna — into one functional block.

Anahata and vishuddha play the leading role in this complex. The intensity of emotions depends to a certain extent on the manipura chakra, while the ajna chakra serves as a liaison for interaction with hypothalamic-pituitary complex, which plays an important role in coordination of the emotional and behavioral reactions of the entire organism through the endocrine system.

Only those people whose front canal is well developed and who know how to use it are able to experience truly exalted positive emotions in communicating with other people and with nature. But such people are extremely few: only a handful per thousands. Most people do not have a developed front canal, and it takes special efforts to develop it.

In Chinese tradition, the system of the spine and the front canals is called *microcosmic orbit*[11]. By means of circulating energy around the *microcosmic orbit*, one can perform transformation of energies within the organism. The aim of this work is to produce and accumulate *Golden Elixir* within the organism; the subtlest energy obtained as a result of such transformation was called by this term in ancient alchemy.

Performance of exercises with the *microcosmic orbit* produces a strong emotional effect.

On one of the subtlest planes, the system of the chakras is communicated by one more canal — the middle meridian. This wide meridian connects the developed chakras, running vertically through the middle of the entire body. It forms along with the development of the chakras: it cannot be found in people whose chakras are undeveloped. Its width corresponds to the diameter of the chakras. This is also a very important energy structure of the organism.

* * *

Let us begin with sushumna. The easiest way to cleanse it is to use an image of a "bottle brush". In order to do this, we need to imagine ourselves moving back from the body out of anahata and becoming a little bigger then the body. Then we start to scrub sushumna with this "bottle brush". An important detail to keep in mind while doing this is that we need to cleanse also the passage from sushumna to muladhara, which goes not just down from the sacrum in a straight line, but down and forward.

---

[11] In buddhi yoga there are exercises with macrocosmic orbit.

186

The next in turn for cleansing is the middle meridian. It is convenient to work with this structure at special *places of power*, which are auspicious for moving the concentration of the consciousness below the body. This implies that by this time the consciousness of the practitioner must be developed by performing the previous exercises to such an extent that allows moving as a consciousness below the body without losing the subtle state.

Upon entering the middle meridian from below, we have to "wash" its walls with an image of a wet rag with soapy foam for example, or in any other appropriate manner.

After that, it is quite important to cleanse the partition between sushumna and the middle meridian. In order to do this, one has to be in both meridians at the same time, coming into sushumna from above and to the middle meridian — from below. In this case, the partition between these meridians and possible dark spots on it become visible. Elimination of these spots brings the next stage of purification of the body.

When sushumna is cleansed, we may start working with the *microcosmic orbit*. For this purpose, we enter the two lower chakras and bring their energy up the sushumna, move it over the head, and bring it down through the front canal back to the two lower chakras. We repeat this exercise several times. During this process, coarse energies, including those causing diseases, get transformed into subtle ones in the zhen-mo meridian.

After the first few times of working with the *microcosmic orbit*, one must perform a deep relaxation in shavasana.

In the future, we may learn to change the trajectory of the energy moving around the *microcosmic orbit* — so that the energy flow will pass through the diseased regions of the body (if there are any). This will enable us to heal them.

We begin to learn to rotate energy around the orbit which includes the sushumna meridian. But then we have to learn to do the same through chitrini and within the energy *cocoon* that surrounds the body. All this will bring yet other levels of health improvement and refinement of the consciousness. In the practice of our School, this is usually performed quite easily at the corresponding *places of power* — areas that have a special energetic significance for a human being. You may well find them somewhere around the place you live in.

In conclusion of this chapter I want to mention that there are methods of Chinese Qi Gong that got into Europe, which involve work with the *microcosmic orbit* without preceding thorough cleansing and development of the chakras and meridians. In such cases the entire work is performed only at the level of visual images, while purifying, healing, and refining effects are not obtained.

The *Cocoon*

The energy *cocoons* mentioned above surround the bodies of all incarnate living beings. (They are also called *etheric bodies*. But one should take into account that the meaning of the latter term is unclear: some authors may denote with it other structures and states, when they simply do not know what to call them). The *cocoons* form of the aggregate biofields of all cells of the body. There can be multi-layer *cocoons*, i.e. they can consist of several layers of energies of different densities located at different distances from the body.

The *cocoons* of healthy people are more or less egg-shaped. But their borders can have either protuberances or dents against the diseased regions, which corresponds to either increased or decreased activity of the cells in the affected parts of the body. This is significant for performing extrasensory diagnostics and can be determined by palpating the boundaries of the *cocoons* with the palm of one's hand. But it is preferable to learn to see the *cocoons* as well.

It is easier to learn to see one's own *cocoon* first, and then cocoons of other people with the help of the following method. One has to place the concentration of the consciousness (the *assemblage point*, in Juan Matus' terms) in the area about 50 centimeters behinds one's own heels. From there one may watch the volume inside the *cocoon* and begin cleansing it.

Cleansing of the *cocoon* is an important healing method, because pathogenic energies may reside not in the body but in the *cocoon* as well.

Bubbles of Perception

The concluding knowledge of this chapter would be that the *cocoons* consist of two unequal parts, which Juan Matus [6,11] called *bubbles of perception*.

The division of the *cocoon* into two *bubbles of perception* takes place at the collarbone level. The upper *bubble* includes the head and the neck, while the lower one encloses the rest of the body.

In other words, the upper *bubble* includes the upper dantian, and the lower — the other two and the legs.

The upper *bubble* is very important for communicating with the material world, while we use the lower *bubble* for communicating with the non-material one. A practitioner can perceive from them separately either material world or other eons.

The quantitative growth of the consciousness and meditative work are performed primarily by the lower *bubble of perception*.

The main part of it is the middle dantian, refining in and expanding from which we get closer to Perfection. I emphasize this point again, because this is the most fundamental postulate of the entire psycho-energetical work, and any deviation from this mainstream results in prolonged straggling and in wasting of very precious time of our short stay in bodies here.

Harmonious development of the lower dantian (hara), which is the second important component of the lower *bubble of perception*, is also absolutely essential for meditative achievements. But regarding this structure as the basis for spiritual growth, which is typical of many schools of martial arts, is a gross mistake.

The overall energy structure of the body can also be considered as consisting of 4 vertical segments. But talking about it in practical terms makes sense only at significantly more advanced stages of spiritual development.

* * *

Such exercises not only change us in the needed direction, but the attitude of other people towards us also changes. We become pleasant to communicate with as well as just to be around. People start coming to us for spiritual advice too. I have witnessed a great number of such transformations.

… Two interesting cases come to my mind.

Once, after a class that I conducted, a woman came up to me and complained: well, you are saying right things about love, but what can I do with my flatmate: he is always irritated; we have not talked together or said hello to each other for years! I answered her: look, why don't you start pouring your love at him tonight — right through the wall — like in the exercise *Cross of Buddha*. When she came to the next class, she told this: I did as you recommended and the next morning when I met my flatmate in the kitchen, he smiled to me and said: "Why haven't we said hello to each other for so many years? Let's start greeting each other!"

There was another case. A young woman came to take part in a class in tears. I asked her what had happened? She said that she had been on the beach, taking sunbathes and doing the *Cross of Buddha*. A child had suddenly come up to her and said: 'Don't go there; there is a snake!'. 'Why are you crying then', I asked. She said, 'It was the first time in my life that a child came up to me on his own!'

The realization of the functions of the spiritual heart is the first serious step towards God that man can take. It may become the beginning of the Straight Path towards the complete spiritual self-realization, towards Perfection, towards Mergence with God in the aspect of the Creator.

* * *

It is most convenient to perform the exercises with the chakras and the following meditative training in standing position or even when walking.

Development of *Power in Subtlety* (Correct Crystallization of Consciousness)

After completion of the courses that we have just described, only a few of the total number of students are able to move immediately to the next — the higher — stage of spiritual ascent. The only ones that can go that fast are the ones who were mastering these stages in their previous incarnations and now are only reviewing what they studied before. Other people have to stop for a while in order to establish themselves in the states they have learned to attain.

But this does not mean the latter have nothing to do. There must be a lot of reading, thinking, discussing, helping others, and listening to how God assesses one's actions... It is necessary to seek harmony with nature, especially in the early morning. It would also be good to learn to identify the voices of best singers among birds, to know them by names and how to attune to their subtlety. Among them are song thrushes, blackbirds, starlings, blackcaps, whitethroats, robins, skylarks, large curlews, woodcocks, black grouses, and snipes...

One can use also special esthetical classes that include analysis of works of various kinds of art and creative activity of the participants.

And development of the *power in subtlety* (or *crystallization of the consciousness* in G.Gurdjieff's terms [62] — by analogy with the growth of a crystal) can be best attained at this stage through meditations at special *places of power*, winter swimming, and *meditative running*. Other methods of *crystallization* include special exercises of athletic gymnastics and Sufi whirling: both should be performed while being in special meditations, but it does not make sense to write about this in this book.

It is important to emphasize that *crystallization* can be correct only if performed by consciousness concentrated in the spiritual heart. At the same time, it can be successful only when the structures of all dantians, including the lower one, are developed and working properly.

Correct *crystallization* is performed by a consciousness that grows in the subtlest eons: in this way we can cultivate Divinity in ourselves. But coarse *crystallization*, i.e. performed by people who eat bodies of killed animals, live in coarse emotions, and are devoid of correct spiritual aspiration, can form devils out of them. The same psychic techniques will produce either the former or the latter effect, depending on the inner state of the one who practices them.

This is one of the reasons why it is so dangerous to reveal secret esoteric knowledge to those who are not ready to apply it correctly.

Winter Swimming

Winter swimming, i.e. swimming in ice-cold water, is a wonderful method not only of tempering the body, but also of increasing the energy might of the organism.

Statistics holds that among those practicing winter swimming the sickness rate decreases for cold-type diseases 60 (!) times, and for other diseases — 30 times. As a therapeutic method winter swimming can heal many diseases, including radiculitis, both high and low blood-pressure, pulmonary tuberculosis, pancreatic diabetes, chronic gastrointestinal diseases, inflammations in genitals, menstrual cycle abnormalities, dermatoses, and so on [32,65].

One should not begin to swim in cold water necessarily in autumn, as some people think: one may start right during the hardest frost, if one likes. But it is recommended to master first the psychic self-regulation techniques that we described above. In this case, winter swimming will directly contribute to strengthening the ability to preserve the subtlest psychic states. Coming out into the frost naked and submerging into ice-cold water become not only an act of volition, but also a controlled experiment on oneself in order to maintain the subtlest states of the consciousness in the conditionally adverse environment. It is beneficial to disidentify oneself from bodily sensations and to merely observe them from the depths of the subtle planes.

The organism responds to the cold shock with energy stress, which may be colored with positive or negative emotions — depending on the mood, with which one set about winter swimming in the first place and one's psychic self-regulation skills. The activity of the energy system of the organism increases and initiates an intensive heat generation process. The right mood and disidentification from bodily sensations allow one not to feel the coldness of the air and water even during a hard frost. After staying in ice-cold water, a person also does not feel cold for some time, while when the frost is not too hard, one may even start to feel hot due to the continuing process of intensive heat generation in the organism. But after 10-20 minutes, the resources of the organism get depleted, and one starts chilling and shivering. As one proceeds with training, the intensity of such sensations decreases. At such moments one may warm oneself by performing active movements, indoors, or coming near a fire. These kinds of stress and depletion of the energy system of the organism train this system, increase its mobility and capacity.

One has to submerge into water together with the head. Upon entering water, one should immerse oneself into it completely, then wait until the breath calms down, and then immerse oneself again together with the head. During this procedure, one may notice lumps of dark energy flowing out from the body; this has a healing effect on the body.

One of the most eminent popularizers of cold tempering in Russia was Porfiriy Ivanov, who with his life example demonstrated the possibility of merging harmoniously with nature in all its manifestations. He walked barefooted even during sharp frost wearing only pants, swam in natural water reservoirs many times a day or showered himself with water from wells during winter, as well as slept in the snow without clothes.

Although swimming in ice-cold water is undoubtedly the most effective tempering procedure, do not get too upset if there is no suitable water reservoir where you live. You may, for example, run barefooted in the snow and, if there is the possibility, lay in the snow for a while without clothes. You may pour well-water on your body. As a last resort you may lay in the bath-tub filled with cold water or pour it on your body from a bucket or basin.

But one should keep in mind that water with temperature over 8 degrees centigrade (about 46° Fahrenheit) does not induce the launch of the described energy processes in the organism and swimming in it is less effective, while it may even cause untrained individuals to catch cold.

Cold procedures can be performed both as a part of a special training and every day in the morning or in the evening after work in order to relieve fatigue, as well as in all those cases when for various reasons we have lost inner harmony or do not see *light* in ourselves anymore.

All cold procedures must be performed using psychic self-regulation methods and not merely through an act of volition. Attempts to increase their effect by creating sharp temperature contrasts also do not make too much sense. For example, if you plan to pour cold water on your body, it would be appropriate to submerge the wrists into it first and imagine streams of blissful freshness and joy rising up the hands. Then you may wash your face and feel the freshness and joy entering your body through your face. Spill a few handfuls of water on your head imagining that this is the water from melted snow in a spring puddle on a meadow, that this is spring itself. And then you may really feel the sincere desire to get united with this water with your entire body!

After swimming or showering, you should observe the energy processes inside the body. You may see there the bright white *light-fire* blazing up, which you should distribute evenly over the entire space inside the body. This *fire* heals the body and rids us of coarse energies.

In conclusion of this chapter, I want to say the following. Even without prior studying the techniques of psychic self-regulation, winter swimming saved many people of severe diseases that were considered terminal, including cancer. There are many well-known cases of quick healing of respiratory diseases in the acute stage using this method. Enthusiasts of winter swimming accumulated certain experience of healing children, and this issue deserves a thorough in-depth study.

But it is not a panacea (the cure of all diseases). For example, in case of chronic diseases, which are accompanied with slightly increased body temperature, it does not always produce the positive effect. The organism apparently does not have the resources that could be activated by submerging the body into ice-cold water. Such patients should rather get hyperthermal (high temperature) bath treatment [64].

There may be no constraining to winter swimming, even for therapeutic purposes, since it is being mentally ready that to a large extent predetermines the effectiveness of this method.

Meditative Running

Meditative running is a powerful method of increasing the energy potential of the organism and of development of its energy system as a whole. This method was created by Tibetan spiritual seekers (it was called *Lung Gom* running). In Russia, the group version of this technique became popular thanks to efforts of Yan Koltunov (Moscow).

The method consists in performing pranayamas and meditations during a long group running, which is done at a slow pace. Performed in this manner, the meditations and pranayamas help students: a) distract their attention from bodily sensations, allowing them not to concentrate on being tired, b) create and maintain positive emotional state, c) train their concentration, visualization, and meditation abilities, d) develop *personal power* (power of the consciousness), e) harmonize loads on muscle, cardiovascular, respiratory, and other systems of the organism, etc.

Running sessions of groups consisting from 5 to 50 people should be led by an instructor who uninterruptedly (this is important!) suggests exercises to the group.

Compared to the static variant of psychic self-regulation classes, the exercises of meditative running are performed at an incommensurably higher energy level, which increases their efficiency dramatically.

The condition of psychic attunement of all participants of the running and the monotonous background of the working muscle system contributes to better concentration.

It is advisable that this method is used after all participants have mastered the basics of psychic self-regulation. Unprepared beginners must not be included in the group, since those unable to participate in meditative work synchronously with the rest of the group make this work more difficult for the group as a whole.

Below we are going to set out our modification of this method as a program for a two-hours running (without taking the warm-up time into consideration). As we will see, this program is an intermediate stage to the higher methods of spiritual work, which will be explained in the following chapters.

First sessions must be limited to 30 minutes or less. Then one can gradually increase the load.

Because of certain adjustments that take place in the muscular system during the time of the trainings, one should increase the quantity of protein in one's diet (milk products, eggs, nuts, mushrooms, etc.). Drinking milk afterwards will also be very good.

I also want to mention that women may experience menstruation delays during intensive running trainings (this is a well-known phenomenon in sports medicine); this must not be considered as a dangerous indication.

If you decide to run in the morning, you may do it on an empty stomach or have just a glass of water with a teaspoonful of honey or jam. In case the running sessions are held during the day or in the evening, the last intake of food should be several hours before them. It is very difficult to run with a full stomach.

Clothes should be light. So, if the air temperature is above 0 Centigrade (32 Fahrenheit) just a regular tracksuit will be enough. When it is below -10 Centigrade (12 Fahrenheit), you may put additional training pants, light sweater, and a cap. But you may also dress lighter — overheating of the body should be avoided while performing this type of exercises.

During summer heat, it makes sense to make the route go near natural water reservoirs and to make stops for swimming. It would be still better to run in the morning and to stay near the water during the day. This time may be used for discussions and studying food resources of the forest. In winter, the running session can be followed by swimming in an ice-hole (but it is absolutely necessary that near the ice-hole there is a warm room or a big fire made in advance). If these conditions cannot be found, a hot shower would also do just fine. The running session must be followed by the washing of the body.

Before running, one has to perform an intensive warm-up of the body that would involve all muscles and joints (its description can be found above). In winter, it is better to warm up indoors, so that one comes out to the frost in the already warm condition attained due to muscular activity.

Then the running itself begins. The instructor has to run behind the group so that everyone can hear him or her. The first thing the instructor does is giving the command to maintain the correct posture:

"Attention to the posture. The body is straight. We may even slightly bend it backward. The body should be in such a position so that the muscles of the back are not strained. Relax the muscles of the back. Throw the head slightly back. Relax the back muscles of the neck.

"Attention to the feet. Place them on the ground straight with toes looking forward. Feet are relaxed. They touch the ground smoothly and gently. Relax the muscles of the shins and the thighs. Feel that legs are relaxed all the time, so that we cannot feel the moment we are touching the ground.

"Attention to the chest. It is slightly raised. Imagine that the collarbones are like small boards lying on it, feel them. The chest remains expanded during the entire running session.

"Raise the chest and let it stay in this expanded position while breathing. The belly is relaxed, but it does not hang down as long as the chest is expanded.

"Make sure that the body does not bend forward — otherwise it will get tired very soon. Fix it in the correct position. Attention to the wrists: they are relaxed and hang loosely.

"Imagine that we are suspended on a long wire attached to some distant cosmic object. The body is suspended; it hardly touches the ground and is relaxed.

"Move with the concentration of the consciousness to muladhara. Then look to the center of the Earth from it and see a sea of *Fiery Light* there. Let us send a beam from muladhara towards this sea. Here, it reaches the abode of this Power... A powerful reciprocal impulse of energy rushes up that beam and fills our chakras and our entire body. Let us repeat this exercise. Concentration is in muladhara. We are sending a signal beam to the center of the Earth..., and receiving a reciprocal impulse of Power!... Feel energy inside the chakras. The entire body is filled with power and *light*; it expanded; the density of energy inside it increases... We repeat this over and over...

"Let us imagine a giant vacuum-cleaner 30 meters below the Earth surface with its nozzle facing upward.

We are going to turn it on, and it will start sucking all dark energies inside and around us and sending them to the center of the Earth. Here, we turned the engine on, it started grumbling, the sucking power increases... We observe the space around the group and see the dark energies fly away, sucked down by this vacuum cleaner. Track their way... They rush at enormous speed towards the center of the Earth — and vanish there...

"Let everyone examine the space within one meter of the body. We click the switch, and the engine power doubles. Watch dark pieces rip off and fly away. Scan thoroughly the space around the head..., the neck..., the chest..., the belly..., the pelvis..., the hips..., the knees..., the feet...

"And now let us turn the attention into the space inside our bodies. Click the switch once more. The power quadruples! The vacuum cleaner starts shaking. Incredible sucking power tears off all dark stuff that remained inside the bodies. Everyone scans the head, the neck, the chest, the belly, the pelvis, the hips, the legs... The body gets filled with the purest *light* that comes from above to replace what has been gone...

"Let us turn the palms of the hands upward. Imagine a tennis ball made of white-goldish *light* lying on each of them. We toss them from one hand to another. They grow brighter. Superpose them into one ball on the left palm. Let us inflate this ball with energy from our anahatas...

"Muladhara — 'inhale' from below, anahata — 'exhale' into the ball. Muladhara — 'inhale', anahata — 'exhale'. (Repeat this ten times). The ball is as large as a large watermelon... (Some more 'exhales' into the ball). It is already one meter in diameter... All balls merge into one common ball... Look at its surface from inside. It separates us from the surrounding space securely. There is a subtlest transparent environment filled with lucid *light* inside the ball. It is incredibly easy to breathe in it; we feel amazingly light and weightless... It seems that all bodies merge into one organism inside the ball... We continue running inside the ball.

"Let us do a series of pranayamas. 'Inhale' the *light* through the legs and 'exhale' it through muladhara forward, pushing out everything that hinders its flow. This is the *light* that we may see in abundance below the Earth's surface. The left leg — 'inhale', muladhara — 'exhale' (3-4 times). The right leg — 'inhale', muladhara — 'exhale' (3-4 times). The left leg — 'inhale', svadhisthana — 'exhale'. (And so on — going through all the chakras). Muladhara — 'inhale', anahata — 'exhale' (3-4 times). The spine — 'inhale' from below, ajna — 'exhale' (3-4 times). The left leg — 'inhale', the entire right side of the body — 'exhale' (3-4 times). The right leg — 'inhale', the entire left side of the body — 'exhale' (3-4 times). The left arm — 'inhale' — through anahata — the right arm — 'exhale' (3-4 times). (And then the other way around). Muladhara — 'inhale' from below, sahasrara — 'exhale' up. (Repeat this several times; then it should become the uninterrupted flow of *light*). Make this flow stop and watch a cloud of *light* forming above us. It wants to pour into our bodies; let us open ourselves up and let it in, let it fill us with its tenderness and purity...

"Feel a small sun between the palms. Look at its goldish *light*, feel its caress... The sun dissolves in our hands..., we soak its warmth and *light* through our arms into anahata and sense a pleasant expansion inside the chakra. And now we will emanate the *light* and the warmth of the sun from anahata at all living beings around us...

"Let us shift the concentration of the consciousness into the rightmost part of anahata. Find the subtlest plane of *light* there and cast out all coarse layers from the chakra. (Repeat the same from the rightmost part of vishuddha, then ajna and sahasrara, then from the leftmost part of sahasrara, ajna, and so on in a circle).

"Let everyone imagine that we are foxes. A red fox with a large fluffy tail runs smoothly in the forest. Running is a natural state for a fox. We run upon soft green moss among trees, bushes, and stones. We run, ignoring everything that surrounds us. The fox has a goal. The fox has to see the sunrise. A pointed gently sloping woodless hill is ahead. We run up its slope and freeze at the top. We stand on the top, watch the disk of the rising sun go up from the horizon. Anxious expectation, readiness... The sun rises and touches the hill with its *light*. Here, it is up. We look at its disk. The streamy *light* flows out of the sun and fills the body. Let the body get filled with *light*, let the *light* grow thick and liquid. We fill the entire body from the tail to the eyes with this *light*... Density of the liquefied *light* inside the body increases...

"... And now each of us is a fallow deer. A jump — and we soar upward, enjoying the freedom. The bodies get filled with happiness, exultation of flying over the woods and fields, immersed in the tenderness of the clear morning and golden *sunlight*. We get overfilled with happiness, ecstasy, and bliss. We breathe in the freshness of the warm wind, mixed with *sunlight*. Down below is a forest river and hills covered with grass and bushes. A small wave of wind touched the leaves. We get close to the ground. Aroma of flowers reaches our senses. We touch the ground and shoot upward again into the space of *light*, towards infinite joy of flying!... Feel the warmth of rays of the sun with our soft and gentle fells; we smile at the sun, at the whole world, at all living beings that surround us: birds, flowers, grass, trees, beetles, butterflies, animals, and people! We want to fill them all with the *light* of joy, to melt hardened and rude souls!... What a happiness it is — to live in harmony with everybody and everything, to live in love!

"Now let us get back into our human bodies, which keep on running, and start to form an 'envelope' of *light* around them. We 'bandage' the body, starting from below, at the distance of 50 centimeters of the body, with wide bandage clockwise if looking from below. Form an envelope around the feet..., the shins..., the hips..., the pelvis..., the belly..., the chest..., the neck..., the head... Then let us touch its walls from inside with the hands of the consciousness... Let every one of us imagine the mirror image above ourselves, the double, running upside down. Now let us continue making an 'envelope' to include the double's body: the head..., the neck..., the chest..., the belly..., the pelvis..., the hips..., the shins..., the feet. Then detach ourselves from this 'envelope' and fly about 5 meters up. Do not look down... Enjoy the coolness of the wind, the expanse and the freedom..., then get above the park (the forest, boulevard, the stadium). Birds fly around us, let us greet them. Now rise close to the cloud layer (if there are clouds), and look at them from below... We get ready to break through the clouds where the sun shines (if we run during the day). We turn into a rocket for a second and skyrocket there — into the world of exultation and *light*! The sunlight reflects in the dazzling white clouds beneath us. The shine and sparkling of joy in the bright sunshine! Let us feast on this *light* and fill ourselves with its joy!

"And now let us head for the outer space and leave the Solar system... We glide in the expanse of the boundless cosmic space... Stars are all around us... Silence... Let us feel the eternity and the endlessness of the universe in all their entirety... Stars are shimmering... This is the cosmic pulse. Let us feel this rhythm. Stars are shimmering rhythmically. Silence. Calm. Eternity and Infinity... Wisdom of the boundless space...

"Let us start returning. Now, we approach the Sun. It grows larger; we immerse ourselves in its familiar tender *light*, fill ourselves up with its rays again, and get ecstatic! We suspend ourselves over white dazzling clouds and dive down through them. Underneath is the surface of our home planet, forests, rivers, fields, villages, and cities... Let us start descending. We fly over the Earth surface and shine at all living beings with the *sunlight* that we accumulated in our bodies... Send our care and tenderness to trees, birds, animals, people... Let us wish all people to live in peace and harmony with everyone and everything... Let us pour the *light* of love into all emptied and hardened hearts. Let them get rid of coarseness, hate, violence, selfishness, lie, and addiction to alcohol! Let the whole world become filled with the bliss of peace and love! Let all living beings' hearts become filled with *sunlight*!

"We descend to our city, to the park, then even lower and look at the group of people running down below. These are our bodies; we approach them, get into them, move immediately to muladhara and send a beam of *light* to the center of the Earth from there, receive a reciprocal impulse of Power, that starts filling the chakras, the entire bodies... (We repeat the latter element 3-4 times).

"Now let us work with the *microcosmic orbit* for some time. Then let us feel ourselves in anahatas..., in manipuras..., in svadhisthanas, in muladharas, in svadhisthanas again..., in manipuras..., in anahatas..., in vishuddhas..., in ajnas..., in sahasraras..., then above the head... We swim in the *light*, fly freely, feel joy, tenderness, purity, subtlety of the *sunlight*!

"Then we start to condense our flying forms, draw the *light* of the subtlest space into them as if with some magnets... The flying form of everyone accepts the anthropomorphic shape, grows dense and filled with *light*, starts shining like a morning sun and then becomes our 'sunny double'. We slowly superimpose the physical body on this 'sunny double'. We feel dense *sunlight* inside ourselves, this precious load of *Golden Elixir*, making sure it gets distributed evenly inside the bodies.

"Now let us place a ball that consists of goldish white *light* between the palms of the hands. We place it in front of manipura. Then we connect a tube to the back part of manipura, through which a stream of *light* starts rushing into the chakra and then into the ball. The density of *light* in the ball increases (but its size remains the same). Now that we have filled the ball to the limit, we disconnect the tube and dissolve it. Attention — into the ball. Internal processes that produce the colossal rise of pressure begin inside it! A subtlest goldish-white *fire* rages inside the ball! We insert the ball into manipuras with our hands. The chakras is bursting with power. The whole bodies get filled with incredible strength!... We can hardly control the bodies, it wants to make giant leaps, to tear at full speed... A red triangle starts moving forward slowly out of manipura... It drags every body by the center of the belly. (In 1-2 minutes we stop accelerating our pace with the command:) Dissolve the triangle!... The front runners — run on the spot! Get closer to one another. Manipura — 'inhale', vishuddha — 'exhale'. (Repeat several times).

"Everyone imagine a fragrant whitish-pink rose in front of anahata. Rays of the rising sun are sparkling and playing in the dewdrops on its delicate petals. We insert the flower into anahatas. The chakras gets filled with a delicate aroma. (Let us insert images of flowers into all the chakras).

"Immerse ourselves into the blue of the clear morning sky. We let the *light* of the sky into the bodies and fill the inner space of the bodies with it...

"(If it is winter and there is a pure snow — we may take off our shoes and run in the snow barefooted for some time).

"We continue running. Concentration — in the center of the palms. In the center of the palms, pulsating warmth emerges. Feel the pulse in the palms! Feel the pulse! Feel it! Concentration — in the thumb-cushions. Pulse and warmth emerge there! Feel the pulse! Feel it! (And so on, repeating this for all intervals between fingers and the cushions of all fingers' end phalanges).

"Feel the wrists. There is pulsating warmth in them. The pulse! Feel the entire arms, the arms along with the chest, then with the head, feel the pulse in the whole upper part of the body! The entire body turns into a pulsating heart! Imagine ourselves to be a pulsating heart! It grows in size — two times, ten times... A huge pulsating heart, tireless and powerful organ filled with hot blood, with immense inexhaustible power in it!... We keep on pulsating!... Feel ourselves like pulsating hearts!... Gradually shrink and condense ourselves, sense the body again and realize the concentrated power of this gigantic organ inside the body...

"Expand, as consciousnesses, in the surrounding space. Let us concentrate on the plants around us: grass, flowers, bushes, and trees. (Or in case of winter we make corresponding exceptions). We feel their state and send our tenderness to them... Let us attune to the emotional state of the birds singing, and then send our love to them.

"A wall of wind-*light* approaches us from behind. The subtlest *light* blows through our bodies on the subtlest plane, washing and carrying away all coarse layers. Body shells got deflated, we realize that we are incorporeal beings floating in the space of *light*, driven by the wind-*light*. We merge into one big ball of *light* and continue floating...

"Everyone reclaims their individuality again by condensing into forms of white swans. We fly up in the rays of the morning *light*. Above is the blue of the sky with bright white clouds floating. We enjoy the flight, feel the warmth of tender *sunlight*. Feathers vibrate gently in the currents of warm air. We move our wings slightly. We enjoy the flight. We look down. A river winding about in the forest carries its waters to a big lake with small islands. We get down to the water, approach its mirror-like surface. We touch the water with our paws, splash a line, stop, look around... All swans are talking tenderly with one another in their musical swan language. We swim up to one another, fluff our feathers and gently place our heads onto the backs of our friends from the flock. Vishuddhas get overfilled with the bliss of this moment.

"We swim up together to the green patch of reeds and admire its reflection in the water. Well, it is time to fly again! We take off softly and head to the sun effortlessly. We get higher and higher... Let the *sunlight* flow into the bodies, let it condense inside them, filling them from the tail to the eyes. We fly towards the sun and get filled with thick golden *light*... The entire body gets filled with thick, heavy, and blissful *light*-power, the unshakable power of love...

"We get down — and fall into our human bodies. A golden fuel of life spreads all over them. We create an increased density of this fuel in the lower chakras. Next portions of the same kind of *light* pour into the bodies from above; the bodies get filled up with it...

"(The exercises for climbing up steep slopes on the route:) A strong current of white *light* blows at us out of the Earth through muladhara. It inflates every body like a balloon. The body gets blown up and grows weightless... It becomes difficult to keep it from taking off; we can hardly touch the ground with our feet... It takes tremendous efforts to reach the ground with our feet...

"We enter into anahata with the concentration of the consciousness, look at the world out of it..., then enter into manipuras, look out of manipuras, enter into svadhisthanas..., into muladharas..., again into svadhistha-

nas..., into manipuras..., into anahatas..., into vishuddhas..., into ajnas..., into sahasraras.... Imagine ourselves
above sahasraras in the form of a small disk-shaped
clouds... We draw in *light*, become brighter and brighter... All of us merge into one large disk. The disk starts
drawing in the subtlest *light* from the surrounding space
and gets filled with it... The *light* inside the disk grows
brighter... The higher the density of the *light* inside the
disk, the more intensively it draws in the energy from
space... We accumulate tremendous power in ourselves...
Now the disk is able to move in space instantaneously,
at the speed of a thought...

"We imagine ourselves beyond the clouds — in the
bright sunshine... We are behind our running bodies...
Now we are far ahead of them... We extend ribbons that
consist of *light* to our bodies. Each ribbon is attached to
the center of the belly of the running body. Start towing
the bodies. The disk accelerates slowly; the ribbons get
strained... Tow the body by the center of the belly, the
speed increases gradually... The ribbons turn into navel-
strings. The energy of the disk transfuses into the bodies through them. The bodies get filled with the power
that was pertinent to the disk and with the qualities that
were pertinent to it...

"Everyone imagines themselves to be a small cloud
above the running body. Draw in the *light* from the surrounding space. By drawing this *light*, we condense ourselves to the human form, becoming our 'sunny double',
who runs as it were on the first floor — above the head of
the body, which runs on the ground floor. Imagine ourselves totally to be running on the 'first floor'. We run in
the space of goldish *light*, draw in this *light*, and thicken
it inside ourselves... The *light* inside the bodies of our
'sunny double' grows thicker, more dense... (we may
perform the *Cross of Buddha*, a series of pranayamas, and
other exercises while running on the 'first floor').

"Get down to the ground to the right of the running bodies. Let us take it with the left hand by its right hand. Now we run together holding hands with our bodies. Let us transfuse ourselves into the running body, superimpose ourselves on it and feel the blissful power of *Golden Elixir* inside...

"Attention — into muladharas. We perceive them as firm foundations. A house built on such foundation will never suffer from any storms... We feel the power of the *Golden Elixir* in muladharas. Connect muladharas with the *Fiery Light* in the center of the Earth with a beam of *light* and fill these chakras with that power. Muladharas are filled up with dense *light*, energy, power."

We slow down to walking, surprised at how unusual it is for us to walk. Running has become a natural state of the organism, hasn't it? We watch our breath and pulse. They are the same as those during regular walking.

After the running, one should swim or have a shower, perform a deep relaxation and other exercises.

It should be noted that the impressive lightness and the sense of being filled with positive emotions that appear during group meditative running cannot be achieved when running individually.

Here are examples of the meditations that can also be included in the program of running:

The *Cross of Buddha* performed from the dictation of the instructor.

While running on the "first floor" we may deviate from the previous trajectory and far aside from it perform actions that the instructor suggests.

When running in the forest or a park, we may "extend" the arms that come out from the anahata and gently touch or caress tree-tops with our hands.

Run forward from the body, then run near the body holding hands with it, then hurry the body by pushing it on the back. (This meditation can be easily turned into a merry game, filled with jokes; casual witnesses of such moments get amazed at seeing a group of laughing runners compared to the usual sight of exasperated and exhausted sportsmen).

When running on the "second floor", "connect" "cosmic hoses" to the chakras and fill them up with "cosmic fuel": fill muladharas with the "fuel of eternal life", svadhisthanas — with transparent subtlety and purity, manipuras — with energy of powerful and harmonious motion, anahatas — with white *light* of all-embracing love, vishuddhas — with subtle blueness of the morning sky and first golden rays of the Sun as well as with morning dew and aroma of flowers, ajnas — with active and mobile "intellectual fuel", and sahasraras — with the subtlest all-pervading and all-embracing cosmic *light*. Feel the wholeness and conformity of the entire system of the chakras, of the entire organism, as well as its imperishability and ability to withstand all difficulties that may emerge on our path. Perfection can be found primarily in Love. Let us feel love for all living beings. Perfection is also in Wisdom. Let us get filled with understanding of everyone and everything and unite this quality with Love. Perfection is also in Power. Let us feel perfect and unconquerable power, merged into one with Love and Wisdom, as well as readiness for great selfless service. Let us realize in ourselves the qualities of Those Who have already attained Perfection. Let us feel one with Them. Let us feel Them in ourselves, the simplicity and clarity of Their perfect Love..., deep, universal, and powerful Wisdom, as well as boundless courage and impregnability of Their perfect Power!... Let us imprint all these qualities into ourselves forever!

Imagine ourselves to be running behind the bodies and cleanse them inside and out of all that is different from *light*. Then wash them from a hose and fill them with *light*.

While running on the "second floor", let us feel the energy structures of our organisms... Perform exercises with the *microcosmic orbit*. Then concentrate in chitrinis behind anahatas. From this point, rush forward through anahatas into the space of the purest *light*. Expand in it and merge with it... Then condense ourselves again to human bodies dimensions... Feel the power distributing all over the bodies that keep running on the "second floor": every body becomes solid and resilient. Tense the muscles of the legs..., those of the lumbar segment of the body..., of the arms..., of the chest... Feel clearly that all muscles of the back are tensed... Jump on the ground of the "second floor" with our strong and resilient bodies, make a somersault... Run on the "second floor" raising the knees high in the air..., then touching the buttocks with the heels...

Concentration — in the center of the belly. From there, extend a "tentacles" and attach them to a distant cloud. Transfer attention to the "tentacle" completely. Then everyone contracts the "tentacle" and pulls the body forward with it. No additional muscle efforts should be made! Just contract the "tentacle" (the speed, at which we run, accelerates dramatically, we do not feel any additional load on the muscles).

Slow down to walking. With the "tentacles" snatch at various objects and pull ourselves to them. Tense and relax the "tentacles". No energy of the body is being spent for these actions, thus the body does not get tired.

Imagine that we run behind the bodies. Then with a wand made of *light* cleanse the middle meridian from the bottom up to the head chakras.

We may allow ourselves to play and to frolic. While running far ahead of the body, turn a somersault in the air, jerking the legs in a funny way intentionally: we must not feel shy — nobody sees it anyway, except for us. Watch friends doing this (everybody laughs).

Running on the "second floor", feel it as our home — familiar and cozy... Before getting down to the "first floor", each of us attaches one end of a rubber string to the "second floor". The strings will stretch without hindering our movements, but we will always be able to pull ourselves back to the "second floor"... Attach the strings to the "second floor" and get down to the "first floor". Everyone attaches the other end of the string to the center of the belly. We may touch the strings with our hands. We stretch them — and find ourselves on the "second floor" at once.

(While climbing uphill:) we imagine that we are in a rapid stream of water. It drags us forward at enormous speed...

Immerse into the space of *light* inside the body. Then scan it through and cleanse it, then turn all attention to the *Light* that exists inside the Earth, look at the Earth as a living planet, which loves us. Let us comprehend the nature of the *Light* that fills the Earth — and there will be no doubts that the Earth is a living being and that she loves us as her children! Let us send an emotion of our gratitude to her...

Let us immerse into the *Light* of the Earth. Let us feel its tenderness and our close relation to it. Let us submerge in it completely and expand as consciousnesses from anahatas across the entire inner space of the Earth. Now we are one with our dear planet. Everyone is now aware of oneself as being in the space of the mother-Earth filled with tender *Light*. There is the inner space of the Earth and a small jut on its surface — the inner space of the body... From the inner space of the Earth, we watch this jut of *light* moving on Earth's surface.

Let us move the concentration of the consciousness back into our bodies and feel the *Light* of the Earth inside them.

Let us imagine a rising sun, wash our faces with its *light*... Let the subtle *light* of the early spring morning — into the body through the face and fill the entire body with it!

Let us look up through sahasraras and see clouds of *Light* that gathered above us — sparkling goldish *Light*! Let us raise our hands and bring a wave of this *Light* down into our bodies!

We watch the *light* of the Earth and *light* of the Sun merge inside our bodies...

Higher Methods

The higher spiritual practices provide one's further development — as the spiritual heart — far beyond the body and *cocoon*. We have to try to transform ourselves into universal spiritual hearts!

This Path — if everything is done correctly — represents the realization of Jesus Christ's precept: "God is Spirit, and those who worship Him must worship in Spirit and Truth!" (John 4:24)

That is we have to come to meet Him — the Universal Consciousness of the Creator — being free from material bondage, pure, refined up to His level and developed to "decent" sizes for a meeting like this.

At this stage worthy adepts can master a large number of methods that allow them:

— to cognize the Holy Spirit in all His manifestations within one's own expanded spiritual heart and to learn how to become Him;

— to "raise" Kundalini and to merge this individual Atmic energy with Paramatman — the Universal Consciousness of God-the-Father;

— to cognize all major eons of the universe;

— to learn how to get into the Abode of the Creator and to merge with Him there;

— upon successfully establishing in this state, one may receive from God-the-Father the right to control the matter, including dematerialization and materialization of one's own body.

Pranava. "Birth" and "Maturing" in the Holy Spirit

Speaking in the terms that Jesus Christ used when teaching His disciples-apostles, the baptism in the Holy Spirit is the *latihan* meditation that we described above.

But the next, deeper, stage of cognizing Him — "birth" and "maturing" in Him — is performed in another meditation called *Pranava*. This was exactly what Jesus tried to talk about with Nicodemus (John 3:1-21). Philip the Apostle spoke in detail about the same in the parable manner [6,11].

To perform this meditation, we need to find a place auspicious from the energetic standpoint, which would be open, without houses and trees (it can be a beach or sandbank, steppe, mountains, etc.). At this place, we exit from anahata through chitrini as far back as possible, expand as a consciousness there, feel the Living *Light* of Love of the Holy Spirit — and, having infused ourselves into Him, start moving forward together with Him as one Flow passing by and through the body. The body is as if in a huge river. Let it get washed through and become absolutely transparent.

This meditation can be repeated many times: the Holy Spirit is always happy to help the worthy ones. Performing the meditation will be easier if it is accompanied by the wonderful Orthodox prayer-meditation *Heavenly Tsar* or the mantra AUM.

This meditation can be translated from the Church Slavonic language like this:

"Heavenly Tsar, the Consoler, the Spirit of Truth!

"Omnipresent and All-pervading!

"Treasury of all good and Source of all life!

"Come and abide in us!

"And cleanse us of all impurity!

"And save our souls, oh Blissful One!"

We sing this meditation while moving in *Pranava*.

The mantra AUM (or OM) in reality sounds like AOUM. One should sing it delicately, in a prolonged manner and in a high-pitched voice (just like the mantra for anahata), also while moving in *Pranava*. (Growling of the OM sound in coarse voices, which is practiced in some ignorant pseudo-religious companies — is a "singing for the devil" but not for the Holy Spirit).

In the future we have to learn to stop in the *Pranava* meditation being merged with the Holy Spirit and being aware of ourselves as a part of Him.

The Holy Spirit can be cognized in His more subtle manifestation. One does it also in the *Pranava* meditation, but performed in a slightly different way.

This time we exit back from anahata not horizontally but down at an angle of approximately forty degrees. In other words, we find ourselves below the Earth surface — and discover there a layer of more subtle Living *Light*. And then, just as we did while performing the first variant of the *Pranava* meditation, we start moving as a Flow in the forward-upward direction around and through the body.

As we master Mergence with this *Light* of the Holy Spirit, we may discover that He prevails inside our planet except its core.

One has to explore Him by filling Him with oneself as anahata — both in front and behind the vertical plane, which coincides with the back of the standing body.

The next levels of "birth" and "maturing" are to be performed in the Divine *Fire*, which we will talk about a little later.

About Self-Healing

If one learns, while performing the *Pranava* meditation, to stop and concentrate oneself behind the body — one may insert a hand of the consciousness in it and eliminate all energetic disharmonies.

Also, if you are merged with the Holy Spirit and concentrate at about 2 meters behind your body — then from this position you may become capable of seeing and controlling demons (non-incarnate people or animals with evil character traits) that may be living in human bodies. If you look in this manner through your own body at the body of a possessed person, it becomes possible to talk to these demons, which cannot ignore the Holy Spirit's questions and must respond. They will tell why God sent them into the body of this person: what are his or her faults and karmic liabilities. If the patient realizes his or her problems, repents and improves — you may ask the spirits (in a kind way!) to move to some other place, where they would feel good. For example, you may ask a fish which the patient killed a long time ago, to go live in a lake, if it is a bird — you may talk it into moving to the forest, in case of a pig or a dog you may describe in glowing terms how great it would be for them to incarnate again in auspicious conditions, etc.

All spirits are under the control of the Holy Spirit and obey Him. But in order to succeed in doing this type of healing, one has to never leave the state of the Holy Spirit.

This kind of healing is an opposite of the attempts to drive out demons by hating and cursing them during special sessions (these methods are called exorcism). This is not only ineffective from the standpoint of healing, but it also results in coarsening of those exorcists and thus determines hell to be their abode after they leave their bodies. Such "demons exhorting sessions" belong to the realm of black magic; they are anti-Christian in essence: for Jesus Christ taught love, not hate.

Total Reciprocity (Nirodhi)

But the complete mergence with the Holy Spirit can be achieved only through mastering the meditation of *total reciprocity* (*Nirodhi*, in Buddhist terms). While performing this meditation, the consciousness enters the state of "non-I" and becomes *All*; as a result, the individual lower self vanishes.

There is absolutely no way to explain this in words. But this state can be easily attained at special *places of power*.

Mastering of the above said means attainment of Nirvana in Brahman, which Krishna called upon us to do in the Bhagavad Gita [6,11].

Baptism in the Divine Fire

The next stage of cognition of the depth of the multidimensional Absolute implies cognition of the subtlest Divine *Fiery* Manifestation.

Thus God-the-Father manifests Himself to His worthy disciples who attained proper refinement of the consciousness — in a gigantic anthropomorphic (resembling human body) *Flaming* form, which does not burn them.

In this *Fiery* Form, Ishvara is also described in the Bhagavad Gita [11] by Arjuna who saw Him like that: "I behold You... like a blazing flame or a dazzling Sun, You radiate the rays of light hard to look at!" (chapter 11:17) and "If the shining of a thousand Suns blazed forth in the sky, it would be comparable to the Glory of this Great Soul!" (chapter 11:12).

Chaitanya told us about this *Fire*: "*Fire* is a functional state of the Consciousness that lives in the Abode of the Creator".

Sathya Sai Baba told us the same: "*Fire* is not an independently existing state, but that State of Mine, which those Who have cognized Me can see when I enter the world of the Creation".

The total and steady submerging of the consciousness of a spiritual aspirant into the Divine Fire and mergence with It result in "burning" of all remnants of karma. And "burning" the body throughout with this Fire brings about the complete healing of the body.

We have to learn to merge with this state of God, by filling His entire form with ourselves as spiritual hearts.

Yet, God does not help everyone in doing this but only His worthy disciples whom He selects.

The *Root*

The Divine *Fire* can be also cognized in another way: It is always present in that part of our planet from which its creation began — its core.

The *baptism in the Divine Fire* can be accepted there as well. And by moving deeper in the multidimensionality scale — under the Fiery component of the planet's core — one can get into the highest spatial dimension and cognize the Primordial Consciousness there for the first time.

For everyone of us, the passage to the Abode of the Creator is the energy *root* that connects the anahata chakra with the highest spatial dimension. By passing along this *root*, those who accumulated proper amount of power in subtlety and learned to enter the highest lokas can cognize God-the-Father.

Krishna was talking about the *root* in the Bhagavad Gita.

Chinese Taoists work with this structure, calling it "the stem of the golden flower".

Through this *root* Tibetan yogis using tummo methods raise Divine *Fire* to the body [22,27].

One may also find mentioning of the same structure in Agni Yoga (*Leaves of the Morya's Garden. Call* [40]).

God suggested a meditative image for working with the *root* through the apostle Paul for us (Romans 11:18).

But the majority of people are sure that deep inside the Earth there is... hell and that God is... "up there" (relative to our round-shaped planet)...

... I see that for a materialist it is hard to imagine that someone can get to the center of the Earth: since the Earth is associated with something "solid" in the mind.

But the one who has advanced on the spiritual Path and mastered entering the highest — the subtlest — eons, sees our planet as a multi-layer sphere of Living *Light-Love* where one can move from one layer (eon) to another, dissolve oneself in each of them, collect oneself into an individual consciousness again, accept various forms of different sizes, as well as flow beyond the "islet" of our planet into the Universal *Ocean of the Infinity* and dissolve in It...

But in order to make this happen, one has to become free from the tamas guna, to move through rajas and sattva, and then to come to the direct communication with God — as an immortal consciousness free from the chains of the body, full of zeal for mergence with the Main Beloved.

In reality, this religious Path, which God calls Straight Path (Vajrayana), does not even slightly resemble any ritual religious form where people fear death of their bodies and mourn over those who left their bodies already, where they love themselves and are enslaved by their gluttony so much that they consider killing animals and eating their bodies their inherent right...

... It does not matter where we cognize God in His *Fiery* form for the first time: be it through the *Fiery* core of our planet or in a *Fiery Mahadouble*. But it is necessary to go through both.

"Raising" of Kundalini

Before we can enter the Abode of the Creator, we have to complete another significant stage of work — "raising" of Kundalini.

Kundalini is Atmic (of Divine level of subtlety) energy of consciousness that everyone accumulated in all the best moments of all their previous incarnations. It is produced and accumulated when we are in the states of tender and refined love. But this energy does not get embodied every time the incarnating part of the soul (jiva) enters into its new body, but is "stored" in a sort of "money-box", whose shape resembles an elongated balloon.

The size of this structure, when it is developed, is measured by kilometers; it is located in the corresponding subtlest eon inside our planet at the level of its mantle. The size of Kundalini correlates with the level of evolutionary maturity of the soul.

Kundalini and jiva of each man represent an integrated system, being connected together by a special energy canal, which is attached to the lower front part of muladhara.

Only those people can "raise Kundalini" up to their bodies and use it in spiritual work who have accumulated a sufficient amount of this energy, i.e. mature and worthy of entering the Abode of God-the-Father and Merging with Him.

So, as it must have become clear for the reader by now, Kundalini is not located in the muladhara chakra and all the more it does not have anything to do with the coccyx, as some authors write in their books. And the "raising of Kundalini" can be attained neither by beating the coccyx against the floor nor by jerky dancing. Exercises on "raising Kundalini" that Rajneesh was teaching his admirers were nothing but jokes.

The true "raising of Kundalini" can be performed only after completing the preparatory stages of work, which were described in this book, at special *places of power* (or without them) with the help of a competent spiritual Master or directly by a non-incarnated Divine Teacher.

The purpose of the "raising of Kundalini" is: first — to merge this accumulated individual Atmic energy with the Creator (Paramatman), second — to perform "burning through" of the body cells with the Atmic energy that heals and transforms them, and third — to learn to identify oneself with Atman. The latter becomes possible when Kundalini has come through the body (this must be performed in horizontal position; the body lying on the back) and formed a new energy accumulation behind sahasrara.

It follows from the above said that before starting to "raise Kundalini" one has to think twice.

If the energy of Kundalini is transferred into Paramatman, the person (as an individuality) loses it. And the only correct way out of this situation for such an adept is to merge the jiva with the Creator in the current incarnation. If this does not happen (for example, if the adept, who has not become well established in subtlety, reverts to coarse emotional states because of a certain reason) — the next time he or she incarnates, it will be without this invaluable energy potential and the person will have to accumulate it again starting from scratch.

Entering the Abode of the Creator

The Universal Abode of the Creator is saturated with the sate of His Great Tender *Peace*. The shine in the Abode resembles the state of calm and warm delicate morning sunlight.

This state is opposite to the "black world" of the devil eon saturated with "sticky" coarseness and spite; getting stuck in it gives one a false sensation of rude and violent might... This can tempt someone... But we do not need this!

The Abode of the Creator is not a *Void* in the literal sense of this word. *Void* (*Vacuum*) is just an incorrect translation of the Buddhist term that reflected the Reality somewhere in the past. And this incorrect translation led many people into temptation — both non-Buddhists and those who consider themselves Buddhists.

It does look absurd for a sound religious person: to aspire not to God but to the Void... Therefore, numerous followers of Buddhist tradition get lost in the "Buddhistic" terminological labyrinths, and having no correct understanding of the Truth, lose an incentive to strive for the Primordial Consciousness.

As a result, the "house" of Buddhism collapsed with time into numerous sects, the majority of which do not have the highest knowledge.

But the term *Void* should be translated in a different way — in this case everything becomes easy to understand for a warrior who stands on a Threshold of the Abode of Adibuddha.

... The Abode of the Creator is on the other side of a miraculous barrier, which can be compared to a mirror. His Abode is truly in the *Transmirror Realm*[12]. In order to take worthy disciples in there, a Divine Teacher gives them His or Her Mahadouble as a Yidam. And there, where the Mahadouble comes out from, the disciples can

---

[12] It can be translated from Russian also as Looking Glass World (translator's note).

Some authors use this term incorrectly, denoting by it all non-material worlds (eons or lokas).

merge in Love with the Father of the Universe and gradually cognize His Total Cosmic Universal Greatness...

... This state is quite reversible. The only distinct feature of the body of the person who become established in the Abode is that the *Light* of Love constantly shines out of it and it carries a field of *Calm* around itself.

Spiritual warriors feel themselves guests in the Abode first. But then the next phase begins — the phase of serving as the Holy Spirit, as a Representative of God-the-Father.

The Meaning of Our Lives (lecture)

Cosmic space is multidimensional. The dimensions of space are not just mathematical symbols but actually existing layers that resemble stories of a multi-story building. But there are some specific features concerning them:

1. One can enter the most valuable parts of this "building" only as a developed spiritual heart,

2. Each of the basic "halls-stories" is unlimited in size.

3. The "halls-stories" differ not by height but by the *depth* of their location (by the state of energies in them): the "stories" of the most subtle energy state are the deepest, while the grossest "stories" — are on the periphery of this structure. The *deepest* "hall-story" is the Abode of the Creator.

In most cases, when we say or hear the word *God*, we have to understand it as the Primordial Universal Consciousness, that is the Creator.

The purpose of our evolution is to seek to cognize the Creator in His Abode and to merge as a consciousness (soul) with Him.

The main part of everyone of us, the part which is capable of fulfilling this task is the spiritual heart. It has to burn with love for the Creator, be refined to the Divine level of subtlety, and be grown to Divine sizes.

The mind of such a spiritual seeker has to be developed enough to avoid false ways and illusions of pseudo-achievements on this Path.

He Who has reached the Abode, settled in it, and then comes out from it with a part of Himself to help incarnate beings is called the Holy Spirit (Brahman).

And He Who having merged with the Creator lives also in a human body is called Christ, Messiah, Avatar (these words are synonyms).

From the above said, it is clear that God-the-Father, Christ, and the Holy Spirit are indeed consubstantial. This is where the idea of the Trinity comes from, which was reduced afterwards to the level of folk tales.

Let me repeat again that the primary meaning of the word *God* is the Creator dwelling in His Abode. And from the above said it must be clear that a Christ is also God; and the Holy Spirit is God as well.

Sometimes this word is used to denote everything that exists in the universe including the Creator, all aspects of His Creation, and the "construction material" for it. In this case, this One Universal Organism is denoted by the term *the Absolute* (i.e. God in the aspect of the Absolute).

In this Universal Multidimensional Superorganism — in the Absolute — everything is correlated, controlled, and nothing happens "by chance".

It is really ONE — and in this aspect It resembles the human organism, which is also multidimensional. From this we can understand the biblical idea that man was made in the image of God.

That is, the multidimensional structure of the human organism is similar to God in the aspect of the Absolute. But it does not mean that God-the-Father looks like an old man on a cloud!

Inside the Universal Organism of the Absolute, vital processes of transformation of the constituents go on — as it is the case with the human organism. This constitutes the Universal Evolution.

The creation of new "islets" of matter within the Ocean of the Absolute (followed by the decay, dematerialization of them) serves the purpose of settling there units of life incarnated in material bodies, which have to develop themselves and merge with their Creator, enriching Him by this.

The food for such growing souls is the matter of our usual food.

So, some souls having achieved Perfection during the incarnation merge with the Creator. Others who did not have time to accomplish this "get stuck" at a certain stage of their personal evolution. They will have to get embodied again. Another group of souls is a "waste" of the Organism of the Absolute — they get cast into the *outer darkness*, i.e. into hell.

By using our free will, i.e. the freedom to choose the direction of our development, we can form our destinies.

Let every one of us think: where do we want to go?

… Some people do all kinds of silly things for the sake of spiritual development or "for the sake of God" — as they believe.

Some torture and kill people and animals, bluntly and violently obtrude "their" *rules of conduct* upon others, some people in modern Russia drink urine, some learn to plug up the lower foramens of the body in order to avoid dropping out into hell through them (some Buddhist "masters" teach this practice).

There are also fools who, instead of making efforts, hope that they will get to heaven by having "priests" pray for them.

Only when we know the true need of God and His plan for us, we can understand the absurdity of all those things and understand what we have to do in reality.

... Now, how can one attain Perfection? And what is Perfection specifically?

There are three main aspects of the Perfection of God: Love, Wisdom, and Power. Let us list what we have to do in order to either progress in the direction of His Perfection or, on the contrary, degrade to the state of demonic beings.

So in order to get to hell, if we want to:

1. Instead of fostering love we need to cultivate irritability, aggressiveness, as well as to seek to defile everything and everyone.

Let our egocentrism triumph. And if other people do not satisfy our egocentrism, we will react with an outburst of rude emotions, revenge, will lose peace and sleep, will live in constant stress of negative emotions, will get sick because of this and it will create even more reasons for us to hate other people: they are happy while we are sick!

It is not enough to learn to hate everyone around and concentrate on disgust and contempt towards them — we will have to learn to pick concrete objects of these emotions. And if people and animals become hostile to us in return, then it will only help us in acquiring mastery of malice: their hostility will make our aggressive feelings stronger!

In order to develop further such features, we need to eat dead bodies (meat and fish dishes) — then the souls of killed animals will move into our bodies and will avenge themselves upon us for their sufferings. This will cause chronic diseases of our digestive systems and later — psychic disorders of schizophrenia type (obsessive-compulsive disorder, hallucinations, delusion of influence, as well as "voices" that condemn others and provoke us to take absurd actions).

Also we have to attune to the most coarse kinds of music and songs with violent and defiling content (using obscene language, preferably). By the way, if we use obscene language as a means of defiling other people and intensifying negative emotions, it will help us in making faster progress in this direction.

As for esoteric techniques — concentrating in the ajna and manipura chakras can be of great help for this purpose. Practicing all these methods will make us devils in the course of our lives in the physical bodies, and we will retain this devilish status after death, thus our going to hell will be guaranteed.

2. Our intellectual activity has to be directed at devising special programs of further self-development in this direction. For this purpose it would be helpful to study the experience of other people who succeeded in this. For example, we can practice self-identification and attuning to the most prominent fascist politicians and black magicians-devils, who make a living by "healing" practice.

3. In order to become even more powerful devils, we may use special kind of training on negative *places of power*. There we can accustom ourselves with different types of hellish states: powerful aggressive emotions, paralyzing anger, hopeless despair, and depression.

Near Saint Petersburg there are *places of power* of that kind. Some monsters in human bodies carried out "training" there, and even arranged special benches!

Having mastered these states, we can be sure that even the death of the body will not interrupt them! All this will be ours almost forever — until the complete decay of the soul occurs in the "outer darkness where there is weeping and gnashing of teeth"!

And before the decay of the soul takes place, we will have time to enjoy by harassing less powerful demons and various dweebs among embodied creatures using the most sophisticated ways!

... Now let us have a break from attuning with this nightmare and look at how we can develop ourselves in the opposite direction.

The best way to start going the opposite direction — not to the *outer darkness* but to the Creator — is to step aside from the human filth and begin to attune to pure and beautiful phenomena, and to make every effort to activate the spiritual heart.

The development of the spiritual heart starts from the center of the chest, then it gradually fills up the entire chest volume, grows bigger and bigger in the surrounding space, penetrating deeper into the layers of the Absolute — until it merges with the Creator.

But no attunement and no psychic techniques can help if one does not do deeds of love, does not control emotions, does not refrain from exiting the state of love, as well as does not focus the attention on the Creator as on the main Beloved.

Of course, it is not possible to know and to love the Creator if one does not know what the Creator is and where we have to seek Him.

And it is impossible to bridle emotions without mastering the control over the organs that produce emotions. That is, one needs to learn the methods of psychic self-regulation based on work with the chakras and main meridians.

Also we cannot succeed if under the "deeds of love" we understand only sex.

... Yes, a positive sexual experience is highly important for spiritual self-realization. Sexual love enriches one's emotional sphere with the ability to experience very subtle, sexually colored tenderness. Having mastered this step, we have to come to know even more subtle love, even more subtle states of the consciousness in order to be able to merge with the Holy Spirit and the Creator.

Let me note that woman's mammary glands have a direct topographic and bioenergetic connection with the spiritual heart. And their erogeneity contributes to stimulation and natural development of the spiritual heart.

Men do not have such a natural and direct opportunity; their chance to begin the spiritual Path is to attune to the most subtle states of women or to use special psycho-techniques, which develop and refine the emotional sphere.

This is why many more women than men achieve success in spiritual self-realization.

But in order to be called really spiritual, sexual relations must include a tender love-giving of oneself to the partner rather than a rude and egoistic behavior. Also they must not become a kind of entertainment in the form of group sex.

Sex must not become an end in itself and an obstruction to a much more important thing — building one's loving relationships with God!

Let me stress that the ability to love emotionally can be developed not only through practicing its sexual aspect. Caring attention, respect and esteem for those who deserve respect, the ability to forgive errors of others, to help others even if it requires to sacrifice one's own interests or even life — these are the most important and essential aspects of love that we have to cultivate in every possible way.

We also need to understand that recommendations of some "psychologists" to focus the attention *on love for oneself* are the opposite of spirituality. True love implies *self-forgetting* for the sake of others! And this becomes possible only if one (sensibly) abandons attachments to earthly welfare and even to life in the body.

Let us start learning to love, helping even plants. If we see a dry bough hanging on a living branch of a tree — let us remove it. If someone drops a piece of tinplate, plywood, or board on the grass — deprived of light plants are doomed to death — let us save them. When we see that someone defiled a tree by putting a dirty rag or an empty bottle on it — let us remove it, so that this living evolving being can continue perfecting in its natural beauty.

It is not compatible with love to make a fire (without an absolute necessity) if it injures living plants, to cut flowers for bouquets, to participate in killing spruces and pines for Christmas for the sake of watching how they die slowly...

It is necessary to understand that in the bodies of animals and plants the same process of evolution of units of consciousness goes on just as in our bodies. And we must not cease it on our will unless it is absolutely necessary. An example of such absolute necessity is using plants for food, for construction, and so on.

We may kill animals only if we are defending ourselves or others.

Let us recall one of the commandments that God gave to us through Moses: "You shall not kill!". But neither Moses himself nor almost all Jews kept this commandment. Jesus Christ also declared this principle[13], but all mass movements that call themselves Christians did not pay any attention to this commandment of God.

Yet without accepting fully the aspect of LOVE called COMPASSION, one cannot approach the Creator! And compassion must include all living beings, not only embodied ones...

"God is Love" — taught Jesus. And if we want to become Divine and fulfill the Will of our Creator, we have to transform ourselves into perfect Love.

---

[13] [6,11].

... If we only have learned to live in the permanent state of subtle love — we are guaranteed to live in paradise.

If with the help of special meditative techniques we have attained Mergence with the Holy Spirit and have mastered living in Mergence with Him, then we become Him and remain in Him even after the death of the physical body.

And the Ultimate Goal is to cognize the Creator in His Abode and to merge as a consciousness with Him.

... Let us keep in mind: it is the emotional status to which we accustomed ourselves while living in the body on the Earth that we continue to live in for a very long time after the death of the physical body.

The emotional status is a state of consciousness. It is our dominating emotions, the emotions which we got used to during our living on the Earth.

And after the death of the body we find ourselves in the corresponding layer of the multidimensional space — according to our level of *coarseness-subtlety*. There we find ourselves among other beings similar to us: inhabitants of hell or those of paradise, or in the Holy Spirit, or even in the Abode of the Creator.

And after this happens nothing can change the situation: neither relatives and friends drinking on the grave nor any kind of rituals or praying performed by anyone.

So, where do we want to go?

* * *

God is cognizable, though the majority of the followers of the modern "Christian" movements believe the opposite.

The founder of Christianity — Jesus Christ — taught that God can be cognized [6,11].

And God is indeed very easily cognizable: both in the aspect of the Holy Spirit and of Jesus Christ, Who lives now (though not in a physical body). It is much more difficult but also possible to cognize Him also in the aspect of God-the-Father.

But in order to accomplish this, one must not be a pseudo-Christian who keeps talking about Christ yet lives in total contradiction with His Teachings; one must be a true Christian who lives not for oneself but for God, who lives in love and seeks to serve Him, to know Him, and to merge with Him in love!

As for "Christians" who believe that God is incognizable, who drink, kill, damn, and hate — He is incognizable indeed. For they are not Christians at all!

About "The Tree of Knowledge of Good and Evil" (lecture)

The scheme for studying the structure of the Absolute[14] shows, among other things, as if windows, doors, and gates, which are entrances to "other worlds".

Also on this scheme one can see that the souls are conceived by the Creator in paradise, though they cannot be called human souls yet but rather a kind of embryos which will be embodied first in vegetal and animal bodies. (This truth is reflected in the biblical story about Eden).

Some souls, incarnating and evolving in the world of matter thanks to the freedom of will that they were given (for the purpose of better development of the Evolutionary Process) — preserve their purity from the filth of negative emotions.

---

[14] See it at the end of this book.

Others get "attached" to material objects including their own bodies. These attachments give rise to egocentrism and hostility towards other creatures, considering them rivals with whom one has to compete for possession of food, luxury, and objects of sexual lust. Some people even assume the right to kill animals for the sake of satisfaction of their gluttony.

Such a choice between good and evil can be represented schematically as a fork, like that on a branch of a tree. The choice of the way of evil is what the Bible calls the *Fall of Man*.

God continues to offer each soul an opportunity to make a choice in ethically important situations: to act for the sake of oneself at the detriment of others — or to sacrifice something of oneself for the sake of others. That is, to do evil — or good.

In this way each soul draws a graph of its development — many branchings where one always has to choose only one direction. It is from this picture that the image of a *tree* originates.

As a result of moving along these trajectories of choice, some souls come to the Abode of the Creator, others — to the hell, which they have chosen.

... There is another interpretation of the story about the "tree of knowledge of good and evil" — it is also correct and supplements the first one.

The error of people consisted in forgetting that God controls everything that enters our lives; and in that respect good and evil that come to us are equal. For they both are manifestations of the pedagogical measures of our loving and wise Parent. Therefore, we should regard everything as a blessing coming from Him.

So, when evil comes to us we should try to see the intention of God behind it. And having realized it, having discovered its reason in ourselves, we have to strive to improve.

One can react in a wrong way by trying, for example, to *revenge* oneself upon the offender having forgotten about the Master of our destinies — God.

Or sometimes in some originally primitive or degraded religious movements in order to explain the roots of evil, people create a "rival" to God who is almost equal to Him. They call him Satan, Lucifer, and by other names. Such primitive religious conceptions can appear when people reduce Boundless Universal God to a flying old man sitting on a cloud...

... Correct understanding in the situations of encounters with evil is extremely important! There is a mechanism of self-transformation that consists in the ATTUNEMENT of the consciousness to the state of a certain object.

If we attune to the beauty of the rising sun in the quiet tender morning or to the singing of morning birds, then we fill ourselves with subtlety and harmony of nature!

If we seek the Creator and try to attune to Him — we approach Him. And He helps us in this!

If we fix our indriyas of the consciousness at some embodied or unembodied filth, we automatically attune to its hellish state and become similar to it by our emotional status. And if we leave the body before we have improved, then we will go to hell along with it...

This is why Jesus Christ taught not to revenge oneself, not to damn the offenders, but to forgive them sincerely and feel compassion for them. And not to demand back what we were bereft of — it is better to give to the robber even more than what he wants to take from us — so as not to exit from the state of love!

I was deceived and betrayed many times. I was even killed by such human filth and was painfully dying for many months. But I remained a Christian — I neither revenged myself, nor did I attune to them. I continued to seek the Union with God — and I won! Also I have helped many others in this and will help more!

You can do the same — and win as well!

Stages of the Spiritual Path (lecture)

A person who starts walking confidently the religious Path can go through the following seven stages of it:

1. Acquiring the correct understanding of our highest Goal and the ways of its attainment.

2. Initial ethic self-correction in accordance with the intention of God through elimination of ethic imperfections as well as through the development of required qualities, of which love is the principal one.

3. Refinement of oneself as a consciousness in order to get into the highest planes (eons or lokas) of the multidimensional space, of which the Abode of the Primordial Universal Consciousness — God-the-Father, the Creator — is the subtlest.

4. Quantitative development of the refined consciousness.

5. Mastering the methods of merging with God.

6. Consolidation of Mergence with God.

7. Acquiring Divine powers — and providing help to other incarnate beings from the state of the Holy Spirit.

For the majority of the readers, deceived by the atheistic and sectarian propaganda, this may sound surprising and even implausible. But this is exactly what God has been teaching people throughout the entire history of mankind — through prophets or Himself, appearing before people in human bodies of Messiahs, Avatars, and Christs (all these words mean the same in different languages).

The meaning of our lives consists in the development of ourselves as consciousnesses, first within our temporary abodes — our bodies, and then beyond them — in the boundless multidimensional universe.

This development has two major directions: qualitative and quantitative.

The former consists of the following three components: intellectual and ethic perfection and refinement of the consciousness.

The quantitative aspect implies a direct increase of the amount of the energy of the individual consciousness, which subsequently — using special meditative techniques — infuses into the Ocean of the Universal Consciousness, Who may be called differently in different languages: the Creator, God-the-Father, Jehovah, Allah, Tao, Ishvara, Primordial Consciousness, Adibuddha, etc.

... The universe is multidimensional. This is not just a mathematical reasoning but reality, which can be experienced by man. Spatial dimensions have been known to religious practicians from time immemorial. They were called *eons* in Greek and *lokas* in Sanskrit; in Agni Yoga the term *layers* was used to refer to them.

The highest, primary spatial dimension is the Abode of the Primordial Universal Consciousness, Which, as it was described in the Bhagavad Gita, creates the "manifested" world by condensing diffused cosmic energy (protoprakriti) to the material state. These "islets" of solid matter get inhabited by small parts of another kind of previously diffused energy — protopurusha — which will have to evolve up to the Divine state by means of multiple incarnations into organic bodies and then to infuse themselves into the Primordial Consciousness, thus enriching It with themselves.

This process of soul development starts with initial forming of lumps of energy on crystalline lattices. Then follow incarnations into vegetable, animal, and finally into human bodies.

The task of every one of us — at the final stage of the development of the soul — is to make efforts on bringing ourselves as soon as possible to the Divinity and to Merge with the Creator.

* * *

Creation of the world is not a phenomenon of the all-universal scale. Astronomers periodically observe birth of new stars and planets. Other star systems get destroyed. This constitutes their *end of the world*.

All souls who have not attained Divinity by that moment get disintegrated down to the protopurusha state. The material component of the "islets" of matter and material bodies of people, animals, plants turn into proto-prakriti and become thus the construction material for new worlds.

Protoprakriti and protopurusha are collectively called *akasha*. (In some publication this word is sometimes translated as *ether*, which is absolutely inadequate).

We have described already the multidimensional structure of the universe. Here I can only say that this phenomenon can be likened to radio waves of different frequencies that coexist within the same volume of space with little or no interaction with one another. And all of them are in the multidimensional *depth* beneath the material world, including the matter of our bodies; we are being unable to perceive them under regular conditions.

In the same manner spirits that inhabit coarser eons cannot see what is going on in *deeper*, subtler eons, although they are supervised from there.

… One can move into subtler eons only in the incarnate state — by making spiritual efforts. The transformation ("transmutation") of the energy of the consciousness can take place only in a human body — a specialized "transmutation factory" capable of assimilating the energy derived from ordinary food and using it, among other purposes, for growth of the "lump" of the energy of the consciousness.

From this, it becomes clear that neither someone's prayers nor "solicitations" have the power to resettle souls from hell eons to those of paradise. The legend about Jesus Christ releasing sinners from hell contains distorted information: He was not saving non-embodied sinners, but embodied ones — by giving them the Teachings of God; by following these Teachings they could free themselves from suffering through the refinement of the consciousness — through love-tenderness, forgiveness, compassion, elimination of anger and all kinds of rudeness, as well as egocentrism.

* * *

In esoteric literature one may encounter inadequate usage of the term *fourth dimension*. This is the case even with *The Book of Jesus*[15], in which Jesus used this term when talking to Ben Cullen "in his own language", i.e. using the words which His interlocutor uses and whose meaning he knows. In this book the term *fourth dimension* was used even in two inadequate interpretations: as the Abode of God-the-Father and as the aggregate of non-material eons.

But in reality, by the logic of the term *fourth dimension* itself — it should denote the material world, existence of which is determined not by three but by four "dimensions": length, width, height, and time.

* * *

Let us continue talking about the universal Evolution.

---

[15] [25].

The process of settlement of every new "islet" of the Creation begins with the Spirits Who achieved the state of the Holy Spirit (Brahman) in the course of Their evolution on other "islets". They become *Constructors* and *Supervisors* of the evolution of life on the newly created planets.

The whole space inside and around our planet is also pervaded with Their huge Consciousnesses, Which are called collectively the Holy Spirit or Brahman.

In other words, as it must already be clear, the Holy Spirit is not at all a "radiation" of God-the-Father (or of God-the-Father and of God-the-Son). No! The Holy Spirit is Living Divine Consciousnesses — subtle and loving, Who teach us and are constantly present inside and outside our bodies. They are extremely glad when we lovingly direct our attention towards Them, willing to accept Their help in order to get closer to Them — to Their state.

The same is true for the Consciousness of the Creator. It is even deeper in the multidimensional space and incomparably larger — It is boundless.

The Consciousness of the Creator, as the Consciousness of the Holy Spirit, is present inside (in the multidimensional *depth*) beneath every cell of our bodies. The distance between us and It is not greater… than the thickness of finest paper, as Jesus Christ perfectly formulated[16].

And one should not fly anywhere or travel too far in search of God: He is present right here and now — inside us, but in another eon. And the only thing separating us from Him is our coarseness, which is a consequence of our religious ignorance and lack of the development of the consciousness.

We have to find God *inside*, in the depth of our own spiritual hearts. This well-known postulate is not just a

---

[16] [25].

nice metaphor but a quite concrete instruction on where we have to direct our efforts.

… Apart from the Abode of the Creator, there exist many other eons that differ by the level *of coarseness-subtlety*. The subtlest of them are called paradisiacal. The coarsest ones are called hellish.

If we want to save ourselves from going to hell after the death of the body, then we have to learn to live steadfastly in a light, pure, and subtle state of the consciousness while we are still embodied. Since upon parting with the physical body, we will live in the state, which became habitual for us during our life in the body.

And, according to this, we will find ourselves in the eon inhabited by beings similar to us: either evil, furious, irritated, anxious, and deceitful — or affectionate, calm, tenderly loving and caring…

How Can We Fall
in Love with God?
(lecture)

Our love for God must guide us not towards attainment of paradise but towards reaching even greater spiritual heights — towards Mergence with the Creator in His highest eon. This is what He expects us to accomplish, because this constitutes His Evolution, His very Life! And if we love Him, we have to do this — for His sake, not for our sake!

It is good to fall in love with Him — to such a degree that we long for Him, being unable to find any peace without Him!

Being in love with God must become similar to being passionately in love with another person! It implies longing for the real Mergence — the Mergence of consciousnesses, just like human souls, flaming with love for each other, merge.

In order to fall in love with God like this, one has to know about Him as much as possible.

And He can be cognized in reality, not only intellectually.

But He becomes audible, visible, and tangible only for those who have reached the Godlike state of the soul.

God is Love. And only those who have also become large, refined, and strong Love can perceive Him like this. And Mergence with God for them becomes not just mere words but their own experience.

… Those who attained Mergence with the Creator become integral Parts of Him forever. But, when necessary, in order to accomplish Their Missions on the Earth or on other planets — They can separate a Part of Themselves without losing unity with Him.

Jesus described this, using the image of a vine (John 15): from the "Soil" (that is from the Consciousness of Universal God-the-Father) comes the "Trunk" — the Consciousness of a Divine Teacher, Who supports with the "Hands-Branches" many embodied souls.

In this way Divine Teachers manifest Themselves for embodied people. At that, They can either have physical bodies (be embodied) or not.

Incarnate Divine Teachers work not only where Their physical bodies are present: They can be with Parts of Themselves-Consciousness in any place on our planet and work there. They (as Consciousnesses) are incomparably greater than our planet; They place only very small parts of Themselves in Their bodies.

* * *

Let me dwell on it some more to clarify the difference between pagan "deities" and personal Manifestations of God-the-Father. Confusion regarding this issue is primarily due to the fact that almost all religious people do not know about the multidimensionality of space.

The criterion here is the following: only that One is a Part of the Creator Who lives in the state of Mergence with Him in the highest primordial eon, which is one for the whole boundless universe.

As for pagan "deities" — they are either fictitious folklore characters or real spirits of a certain (but not the highest) level of evolutionary advancement.

God in the aspects of the Creator, the Highest Teacher and the Ultimate Goal for all of us, is *One*, though He consists of a multitude of Perfect Consciousnesses merged together. What They have in common is that all of Them live in the Abode of the Subtlest Consciousness and act on various "islets" of the Creation by coming out from this Abode.

It is clear now, is it not?

All that we have to do is to get into *There* and to establish ourselves *There* in Mergence with the Creator.

* * *

The most fundamental landmark in the beginning of this Path is realization of the functions of the spiritual heart (the energy of the anahata chakra or the middle dantian). This energy structure of the human organism is the organ responsible for generation of the emotions of love.

Very few people have a developed spiritual heart "from birth" (i.e. from the previous incarnation).

Some women can easily succeed in developing the functions of this organ in a harmonious marriage, since the female organism with its typical hormones and erogenous mammary glands directly connected to anahata, and which also provides an opportunity to perfect one's love by taking care of children, gives the souls embodied into female bodies a matchless advantage over the "stronger" (in coarseness and violence) sex.

For the rest of people, the use of special psychic techniques, which have been developed by spiritual schools of Taoism, Hinduism, Buddhism, Islam, Christianity, and other religious traditions, remains the only possibility to change themselves dramatically.

... God is Love. He asserts this Himself. Everyone who has really cognized God can also confirm this.

And in order to become Godlike, we have to become Love in the literal sense of this word.

One begins to accomplish this with accustoming oneself to living permanently with the concentration of the consciousness in the anahata chakra.

That brings the energy of the consciousness to the state of emotional love.

After that, with the help of meditative training, one gradually expands in this state to become significantly larger than the body and then to encompass the whole Earth with the spiritual heart, and later to embrace God with oneself turned into Love.

In this way we can become "universal spiritual hearts" and infuse ourselves into the Ocean of the Universal Creator.

But in order to realize this simple scheme, one has to perform an enormous amount of work. The problem is that God does not let in Himself the unworthy.

Now let us talk about realization of this scheme — gradually, from the very beginning, — so that the unworthy may become worthy of complete spiritual self-realization even in the current incarnation.

* * *

One has to begin spiritual work with studying and accepting the concept of the Path. Then follows initial ethic self-transformation, and only then one enters on the spiritual Path and starts walking it.

The word *spirituality* originates from the expression of Jesus Christ: "God is Spirit". That is, *spirituality* stands for association with or likeness to God-Spirit. And the spiritual Path is the Path of gradual transformation of oneself into Him. This transformation is realized through growth and qualitative change of the spiritual heart first of all. In other words, the spiritual growth is one's growth as a spiritual heart.

I have described already how one can become a spiritual heart and transmute oneself further. Now I want to note that the criterion of the first success is the ability to look at the outer world from within the chest with the "eyes" of the soul (not in a figurative but in the very literal sense!).

When we begin to experience ourselves not as bodies but as free consciousnesses, then we begin to see with the eyesight of the soul.

It is with this eyesight that unembodied spirits see. And with this eyesight God sees what happens to us in His Creation.

One can say also that the Creator is the Heart of God — God in the aspect of the Absolute.

This is why one can know Him and merge with Him only after having become a perfect spiritual heart.

* * *

In one of the greatest spiritual scriptures — the Bhagavad Gita — there is an omission that resulted in a multitude of errors of people who tried in vain to attain Perfection without love, not through love.

Namely, in a talk with Arjuna, Krishna, pointing to His chest, said that between these "eyebrows" one has to open an exit of the Atmic Energy (it was a joke: He pointed to the hair on His male chest)...

But His gesture was not mentioned in the Bhagavad Gita, and the joke was not understood by the readers and later many people were trying to "open the third eye" — the eye of the soul — not from the spiritual heart but from the one of the most coarse chakras — ajna.

But the results were always sad: dramatic coarsening of the consciousness and sometimes stresses and health disorders. (In some cases people acquired the ability to see the colors corresponding to various emotional states of other people, but it had no value for the spiritual Path; it only "strengthened" this vicious tradition).

That is, one has to open the "third eye" (trikutta) not on the forehead but in the center of the chest.

If you do not believe me now — you may ask Krishna, as I did. But first you have to get close to His state and, having become a developed spiritual heart, learn to see Him as a Divine Consciousness. (Otherwise you will hear anything from a demon who calls himself as Krishna).

Practice
of the Modern Hesychasm
(lecture)

The spiritual direction known as HESYCHASM originated among Christian adepts. Therefore, before discussing Hesychasm let us discuss first what Christianity is.

Christianity is, first of all, the Teachings about God and about the Path to Him that were given to people by the incarnate Messenger of the Creator — Jesus Christ.

Let us consider the main postulates of His Teachings:

1. Be perfect, as your Father in Heaven is perfect! (Matt 5:48)

2. I and the Father are One! (John 10:30)

3. I am the Vine! (John 15:1-5)

4. Even as the Father knows Me, I also know the Father! (John 10:15)

5. I love the Father! (John 14:31)

6. O righteous Father! I have known You! (John 17:25)

7. And learn of Me! (Matt 11:29)

8. God is Love! (1 John 4:16)

9. You shall love the Lord your God with all the heart, and with all your soul, and with all your mind, and with all your strength! (Mark 12:29-30)

10. You shall love your neighbor as yourself! (Mark 12:31)

These are the main principles of Christianity. In them Jesus calls people to BECOME LIKE HIM, and to cognize the Heavenly Father and become One with Him.

In the New Testament, there are many precepts that can help realize this appeal of Jesus if one follows them. They call us:

— to be absolutely honest in relationships with other people, to have no debts, not to misappropriate,

— to take care about well-being of others more than about one's own,

— to be peacemakers,

— to be affectionate and tender with each other,

— to help others in everything good,

— to forgive, not to avenge, not to damn,

— not to hate, not to get involved emotionally in judging others,

— not to seek accumulating earthly wealth: otherwise one can miss the opportunity to accumulate spiritual wealth,

— not to be afraid of attacks of aggressive primitives, who can harm only the body, but cannot harm that with which we appear in front of the Heavenly Father after death of the body, i.e. the soul,

— not to drink alcohol,

— not to be arrogant, but to be humble and respect others,

— to strive to do all that we can for helping other people spiritually,

— not being obsessed with sexuality so much that it, instead of God, becomes the center of one's attention; the personal search for God and service to Him must always be of the primary importance in one's life.

I will give just several excerpts:

I give you a new commandment, that you love one another! As I have loved you, you should also love one another! (John 13:34)

Above all things have fervent love for each other, for love covers a multitude of sins! (1 Pet 4:8)

Whoever claims to love God yet hates a brother or sister is a liar. For they who do not love brothers and sisters, whom they have seen, cannot love God, whom they have not seen. (1 John 4:20)

Beloved! Let us love one another! For love is of God!

The one who does not love has not known God, for God is Love! (1 John 4:7-8)

If we love one another, God dwells in us!... (1 John 4:12)

Owe no one anything, except... love! (Rom 13:8)

There is no fear in love, but perfect love casts out fear. ... Those who fear have not been perfected in love! (1 John 4:18)

Though I speak with the tongues of men and of angels, and have not love, I have become as sounding brass...

And though I have prophecies, and understand all mysteries and all knowledge; and though I have all faith, so as to move mountains, and have not love, I am nothing.

And though I give out all my goods to feed the poor, and though I deliver my body to be burned, and have not love, I am profited nothing.

Love has patience, is kind,
love is not envious, is not vain, is not puffed up,
does not behave indecently,
does not seek its own,
does not get angry,
thinks no evil.

Love does not rejoice in unrighteousness, but rejoices in the truth...

Love never fails, even if prophecies will be abolished and tongues will cease... (1 Cor 13:1-8)

Love your enemies! Bless those who curse you! Do good to those who hate you!... (Matt 5:44).

Blessed are the peacemakers!... (Matt 5:9)

Judge not!... (Luke 6:37)

Whatever you desire others do to you, do even so to them!... (Matt 7:12)

Give to everyone who asks of you, and from those, who take away your goods, do not ask them back! (Luke 6:30)

If you forgive men their trespasses, your Heavenly Father will also forgive you; but if you do not forgive men their trespasses, neither will your Father forgive your trespasses! (Matt 6:14-15)

Who are wise and understanding among you? Let them show it by good life, by deeds done in the humility that comes from wisdom. But if you harbor bitter envy and selfish ambition in your hearts, do not boast about it or deny the truth. Such "wisdom" does not come down from Heaven, but is earthly, unspiritual, of the devil!... (James 3:13-15)

For such is the Will of God, doing good to silence the ignorance of foolish men! (1 Pet 2:15)

They who claim to be in the light but hate their brothers or sisters are in the darkness! (1 John 2:9).

Let love be without hypocrisy!

Shrink from evil, cleave to good!

Be in brotherly love one to another!

In honour prefer one another! (Rom 12:9-10)

Bless those who persecute you! Bless, and do not curse! (Rom 12:14)

Repay no one evil for evil! (Rom 12:17)

Do not avenge yourselves! (Rom 12:19)

If your enemy hungers, feed him. If he thirsts, give him drink! (Rom 12:20)

Do not be overcome by evil, but overcome evil with good! (Rom 12:21)

Why do you judge your brother? Or also why do you despise your brother?...

Each one of us will give account on oneself to God!

Then let us not judge one another any more!

But rather judge this, not to put a stumbling block or an offense towards a brother. (Rom 14:10-13)

Brothers, if man is overtaken in a fault, you the spiritual ones restore such a one in the spirit of meekness, considering yourself, lest you also be tempted! (Gal 6:1)

Let not any filthy word go out of your mouth! But only good, so that it may give grace to the ones hearing! (Eph 4:29)

When you are invited by anyone... do not recline in the chief seat... For whoever exalts themselves shall be abased, and whoever humbles themselves shall be exalted! (Luke 14:8-11)

Do not lay up treasures on earth for yourselves, where moth and rust corrupt, and where thieves break through and steal! But lay up treasures in Heaven!...

For where your treasure is, there will your heart be also! (Matt 6:19-21)

All things are lawful to me, but not all things profit... (1 Cor 10:23)

You cannot serve God and Mammon[17]! (Matt 6:24)

What benefit is it to the one who gains the entire world but does harm to one's own soul? (Matt 16:26)

Again, you have heard that it has been said to the ancients, "You shall not swear falsely, but you shall perform your oaths to the Lord". But I say to you, "Do not swear at all!... But let your word be, Yes, yes; No, no!" (Matt 5:33-37)

And do not be drunk with wine, in which is excess! But be filled with the Spirit!... (Eph 5:18)

It is good neither to eat flesh, nor to drink wine, nor anything by which your brother stumbles, or is offended, or is made weak! (Rom 14:21)

Let us walk becomingly, as in the day; not in carousings and drinking; not in cohabitation and lustful acts; not in strife and envy!... (Rom 13:13)

Let no one seek one's own profit, but each one another's! (1 Cor 10:24)

In lowliness of mind let each esteem others better than themselves! (Phil 2:3)

The one who does not gather with Me scatters! (Matt 12:30)

Do not fear those who kill the body but are not able to kill the soul!... (Matt 10:28)

Put off... anger, wrath, malice, blasphemy, shameful speech out of your mouth! (Col 3:8)

Let My joy remain in you and your joy be full!

This is My Commandment, that you love one another as I have loved you! (John 15:11-12)

---

[17] Pagan "god" of wealth.

These things I command you, that you love one another! (John 15:17)

* * *

Let every one of us test oneself: does my understanding of Christianity conform to these excerpts?

For Christianity is exactly this! This is what Jesus taught and teaches! All the rest is perversion, sectarianism.

Let me stress again that Jesus, in His earthly life known to us, also taught His disciples the meditative methods that are essential for cognition of the Heavenly Father.[18]

In the New Testament there is the following statement of Jesus: "God is Spirit, and they who worship Him must worship in spirit and in truth!" (John 4:24). The meaning here is that one has to go to God with correct understanding of the essence of God and the evolutionary tasks of man. And one has to worship Him not by bodies, not by "religious" bodily movements, but by souls, which gradually get liberated from the dependence on their material bodies with the help of meditative methods of self-development.

* * *

The established practice of many Christian Churches includes public worships, ritualism. However, it was not present in the Teachings of Jesus. One may ask, is it good or bad?

On the one hand, it must be clear to any reasonable person that God is present in temples not more than outside of them, and that one has to seek Him in the *depths*

---

[18] Rich experience of meditative work performed under the guidance of Jesus can be seen in the Epistles of the Apostles John, Philip, Thomas, also Paul. One can read about this in the books [6,11].

of the universe, not in the material ritual objects or buildings.

On the other hand, worshipping practice emerged as a natural need of people with common spiritual interests to come together just for the sake of emotional communication with like-minded persons, exchange of ideas and experience, for the sake of helping one another, learning.

Ritualism may be useful: it contributes to calming of the mind when assembled people attune to perceiving of the Divinity. Against this background, many of them for the first time receive proof of the reality of the mystical: they feel touches of invisible hands, energy flows emanating from icons, thoughts and even voices of invisible interlocutors...

For some people these are manifestations of God, for others manifestations of demons... It depends on the level of ethical purity of each particular person.

The ethical purity of the "flock" largely depends on the level of ethical advancement of the "pastors". This is the main problem... Because under the guise of Christianity, they often preach something directly opposite of it...

When we discuss differences between the established religious directions, we should put the emphasis not on ritualism! Ritualism is not the point! Let the ritualism of various directions remain as it is! The problem is that they lack the complete picture in the understanding of the Beingness of the Universal Consciousness, in the understanding of Its evolutionary aspect, in particular!

The universal space is really (and not only mathematically) multidimensional and consists of 7 main layers of multidimensionality.

The layers of multidimensionality of space differ, first of all, by the degree of the subtlety of the energies that fill them.

The deepest and the most subtle layer of the universal multidimensional *Ocean of emanations* (i.e. the Absolute) is the loka of the Primordial Consciousness, Which in different languages may have different names: God-the-Father, the Creator, the Heavenly Father, Allah, Tao, Ishvara, Odin etc.

The eon of the opposite end of the *scale of multidimensionality* is hell — "the cesspool of the Evolution". It is the abode of the energetically coarsest beings. They are those who accustomed themselves during life in the embodied state to be in coarse emotional states.

Now, is it clear to us why God advises us to live in the emotions of tender love rather than anger, condemnation, irritation, malice, hatred?...

... It is not always easy to change one's own character to better. One simply does not know how to do this. In this situation one can get some help from the system of psychical self-regulation based on mastering the functions of the chakras, which are the organs responsible (among other things) for production of emotions.

The main chakra of every one of us is anahata, located in the chest. It is in this chakra that the emotions of heart love are born — the very state that makes us really closer to God and that was so pronouncedly preached for us by Jesus Christ and His Apostles.

Above the anahata — in the neck — there is the vishuddha chakra responsible for esthetic perception.

Higher — in the head — there are two "thinking" chakras.

And below anahata — in the belly and the region of the pelvis — there is a system of three chakras called the lower dantian or hara. It is a power block that supplies the organism with bioenergy.

It is anahata with its precious content — the spiritual heart — that is the main part of everyone of us, which we have to keep pure and to develop, to grow... — or, to be more precise, to grow ourselves having became the spiritual heart, having placed *oneself as a soul* in the spiritual heart, having "settled" in the spiritual heart.

* * *

God is Love. And to become closer to Him, we have to transform ourselves into Love.

The only way to realize this goal is conscious volitional control of one's own emotions: avoiding coarse emotional states and cultivating subtle ones.

This can be accomplished only through the methods of spiritual work described above.

If we transform ourselves ethically according to the principles of the Divine ethics listed above, then we merit active help from the Divine Teachers — Representatives of God-the-Father, Who are called in the aggregate sense the Holy Spirit.

… The Creator is directly interested in our positive development. It was He who sent us to develop in the conditions of Earth's incarnations! What for? So that we grow to the Divine level and infuse into Him, thus enriching Him with ourselves.

It is clear that not everyone is able to infuse with the consciousness into Him right now. But He sends us to incarnate not only once, but many times. The age of the souls is different among people, because someone incarnates into a human body for the first time, while others have incarnated hundreds of times.

Moreover, before Earth's human lives, all of us — as souls — evolved first in bodies of plants, then in bodies of animals. And they who are incarnate now in such bodies are… people to be.

Having understood all this, can every one of us treat all living beings embodied on the Earth into physical bodies with compassion and respect?

... God gave to Moses the Commandment: "You shall not kill!" Moses, however, was the first to break it... Since that time, this Commandment was never followed in mass by Jews, neither by those who considered themselves Christians, nor by Muslims.

God commanded through Moses not "Do not kill humans!" He engraved on a tablet a formula with more extensive meaning: do not kill anyone! At that, He explained: "... I have given you every herb seeding seed which is upon the face of all the earth, and every tree in which is the fruit of a tree seeding seed; to you it shall be for food" (Bible, Genesis, 1:29).

Then He specified (Bible, Genesis, 9:1-4): it is forbidden to eat creatures that have blood! And these include all mammals, reptiles, amphibians, fishes, mollusks... — almost all beings except for plants.

And even for those who deny the Bible, is it not appropriate to ponder: whether it is acceptable to kill for the sake of gluttony those creatures who can suffer of pain? Is it compatible with love for them, with the very principle of LOVE?

This is why there are people who — out of ethic reasons! — switch to nutrition based on plants, milk products, and bird eggs.

And let me assure you: without this, God will never acknowledge someone's love as perfect!

* * *

Learning to love the Creation starting from its particular manifestations we gradually develop in ourselves the ability to love as the Creator Himself loves.

In this way we become closer to Him — in the state of souls.

In this way we develop ourselves as Love.

And we gain — as a result — the ability to fall in love with the Creator.

Having become the perfect Love, we merge with the Creator, become His Integral Parts.

This constitutes the main essence of the Teachings of God, which He tries to impart to people.

Spiritual warriors, who achieve ethical impeccability, receive comprehensive help from Divine Teachers with developing themselves — as souls, consciousnesses — to Perfection. And then such people come to Mergence with the Creator in His Abode.

In the Abode of the Creator, all formerly individual Consciousnesses of the Perfect Ones are merged into *One*.

This is why one can say that God is *One*.

But They are capable of assuming partial individuality when They come out from the Abode of the Creator as His Integral Parts. It is They Who are called the Divine Teachers, Holy Spirits or — in aggregate sense — the Holy Spirit.

Among Them there are Those Who have male or female appearances — according to the last incarnation.

Each one of Them is absolutely free in moving around and can appear in any part of space. Sometimes one can observe several of Them gathered as a group in one place.

Most often They appear in giant human-like forms (Mahadoubles) which have sizes from tens of meters up to many kilometers. On the top of a Mahadouble one can see a Divine Countenance. They come out from the Abode of the Creator, yet remain connected to Him, and freely permeate with Themselves — as a transparent Divine Flame — the Earth's matter and all material objects.

Some of Them have "areas of responsibility" on the Earth's surface, where They try to help incarnate people to become better, create educational situations for them — with the purpose of learning ethics, first of all.

They also teach there people who perceive themselves as disciples of God and communicate directly with their unembodied Divine Teachers.

For example, over Saint Petersburg one can always see the Divine Countenance of the Apostle Andrew. But there are also smaller local areas where one can always converse with Jesus, Sathya Sai Baba, Philip the Apostle, and with Others.

Sometimes They are wrongly considered as "Patrons" of a city or of some other region. No: They are not Patrons, but our Tutors — harsh or tender when necessary, but anyway — Wise. They are Coordinators of our destinies: the destinies that each of us deserves.

In communication with incarnate disciples, each of Them tries, first of all, to give the knowledge and the methods which were the basis of Their own personal Path to Perfection. But very often it happens that the personal experience of several of Them gets combined — as it was in our case. This speeds up the growth of the students and makes it possible to perfect further the methodology of spiritual development — in application to the concrete ecological and cultural conditions of teaching.

* * *

The human fantasy created a fairy-tale image of a devil: necessarily with horns, hoofs, tail, of male sex, and... — with traits of a sex maniac.

Yet, this is a very harmful lie. Harmful — because the people who follow the path of very real diabolization of themselves do not understand their desperate situation: why, I have neither tail, nor horns — it's okay!

In the conditions of dominating religious ignorance, it is quite easy — for many people! — to become devils. I observed such persons among political leaders, among officials of "spiritual" organizations, among alcoholics.

They can be of any sex.

Who are they? How to recognize them?

Their distinctive feature is constant stay in intensive coarse emotional states (anger, irritation, hatred). Falsity, meanness, aggressiveness are their characteristic features as well.

They will remain the same after disembodiment. Hell will be their abode, where they will live in the thick of beings like them, torturing each other.

But some of them will be able to continue for some time to harm incarnate people — even as they did it during their embodied life.

Incarnate devils can make physical harm — by killing, maiming, raping, damaging, robbing, blackmailing, setting up other devilish people against the victims...

But both incarnate and non-incarnate devils are capable of creating so powerful coarse energy fields and energetic influence that they drive their victims to psychotic states. Physicians diagnose the latter with schizophrenia with symptoms of delusion of influence. Yet, this is not delusion but reality. I knew personally two men who fell under such influence of devils and found the way out of this situation only in suicide — they jumped out of the window to death...

Why do I tell about all these nightmares? Not for the sake of frightening the readers! On the contrary, for the sake of helping people who will find themselves in such situations.

First of all, one has to remember — in such cases of calamities, disasters, and afflictions — that everything happens in God's sight. And is permitted by Him.

Moreover, it is He Who creates these situations!

It is important just to understand: what for? What do You, Lord, want to say by this, what do You want to teach me, what do You want to correct in me?

God does not live on some other planet! He is not a flying invisible person who cannot keep an eye on everyone of us! God is a Universal Ocean of Consciousness existing *everywhere,* in every point of space — but as if under a thinnest *cover* which separate the Creator from His Creation.

And nothing significant happens to any one of us without bringing some good to us!

Pain, for example, can be given to teach us to be compassionate to pain of other beings and not to inflict pain on them anymore.

And various evil deeds of other people allow us to learn in practice the human psychology.

Or it may mean that it is time for us "to change company"...

And so on. All is for our good!

In my published autobiography[19], I gave examples of how God used various human filth for changing my life situations radically — to my own good!

Once, deadly maimed, I cried to Him, asking for explanation of the incident. He started with the words, "You will be grateful to Me for this!"...

Later, He turned to be right!

And further more: in all difficult situations, one has to snuggle close to Him! Often He creates problems for us exactly with this purpose.

... As for those two who jumped out of the window... — one of them developed vanity up to grotesque repugnance; the second one... suffered because he engaged into a quarrel with a diabolic person — his former companion in business who did not give him back his money...

Jesus Christ taught: "If somebody took away your goods, do not ask them back!" (Luke 6:30). And that man forgot this Commandment though he read it... But one has to follow the Teachings of God, not just read them!

---

[19] [7,14].

His second mistake — he focused his whole attention on a devil, instead of going to the embrace of God. And, indeed, he had *lost* God in the very direct sense!...

In general, he did not stand the test on ethics...

I, too, got into such situations. But I used them for consolidation of my Mergence with the Creator: I felt bad in the body, but in the Creator's Abode — it was very good!

These devils helped me a lot.

... But the worst thing is not to undergo attacks of a devil but to become a devil. This dooms one to a really awful fate!

Once God proclaimed through a prophet the following principle: "Everything is a boon!"[20] Let us try to remember it so good that we do not forget it when the time comes for "taking an examination" with God on the subject of "practical ethics".

He also teaches us to regard evil controlled by Him as a catalyst of the development of good. In this principle, too, there is something to ponder over and to remember.

... Many times I heard the objection, "No! God, if He exists, is kind! He can't cause to us so much suffering! All evil is from the devil!"...

This statement is caused by typical misunderstanding of the principles of the relationships between people and God. People thinking this way have so "deep" an egocentrism that they consider God as their "omnipotent servant" who has to arrange life for them according to their desires! And if this is not the case, then they do not want to recognize God! Or they start to believe that there is no God at all!...

But there is God. And He is indeed omnipotent. Yet, the nature of relationships between Him and incarnate beings is quite different.

---

[20] [6].

260

In fact, He and we are not fundamentally different beings. We are only His particles (particles of Him in the aspect of the Absolute) sent by Him to "Earth's pastures" for maturing!

And only our predetermination consists in maturing on these "Earth's pastures"!

He — our Good Shepherd — "pastures" us with this only purpose: that we, having reached a certain stage of perfection, infuse as souls into Him, become Him, enrich Him with ourselves!

This constitutes His Life, His Evolution!

There is no other meaning of our Earth's existence!

And those of us who, using the freedom of will, mature successfully — receive the most favorable conditions from Him. And evil people are culled out and find themselves in the "cesspool of the Evolution", in hell, in the *outer darkness*.

This is why the only correct principle of relationships with Him — from our side — is full OBEDIENCE to His Will and taking heed of His directions and lessons!

Our egocentrism has to be substituted with Godcentrism!

"Your Will be done on Earth as it is in Heaven!" — this has to be not only read, said aloud, and even sung! This has to be really accepted — by everyone! — as a formula of my relationships with Him!

Let Your Will be done, my Lord!

I recognize You as my Omnipotent and Infinitely Great Universal Father!

You are Everything!

And I — Your humble child — love You and learn from You! And want to cognize You completely and merge with You in love!

Pasture me on the pastures of Your Earth!

And lead me to Your Home by the Straight Path!

* * *

So many times I was not paid back large amount of money! So much awful slander was spread about me! At that, slanderers attributed to me qualities directly opposite to those I possess! There was a murder resulted in two clinical deaths, there were constant threats of slaying from fascists during these last years...

Also, I came to know that some author stole a chapter (*Teachings of Juan Matus*) from my book: he simply republished it under his name...

I considered all this as tests of my devotion to God. Do not become distracted! And I... simply continued to go further, hating no one, taking revenge on no one, asking no compensations "for caused physical and moral damage"...

It was enough for me to engage in one of these conflicts — and I would fail in the main work, for the sake of which we were sent to the Earth, and would not be able to help all those people who have received help from me and will receive it later — help in healing souls and in spiritual advancement!

Having violated the Commandments of Christ, I would be no more a Christian...

... "Dogs bark, yet the elephant goes", this is what Sathya Sai Baba said about such situations.

So, every one of us who is pure in soul in front of God and people and who goes the spiritual Path may also accept this slogan for oneself.

"I control everyone. Thus, get angry with no one!" God taught me[21]. These words from Him helped me a lot. Let them help you as well!

---

[21] [7].

* * *

The only way for us to avoid Earth's troubles — now and in the future — is active spiritual self-development. In particular, it results in the correct growth of the consciousness in a quantitative aspect, ensuring a so-called *crystallization* (by the analogy of growth of crystals in the conditions suitable for it). And this gives one the power for opposing evil more effectively.

And let us remember the following Commandment: "Do not be overcome by evil, but overcome evil with good" (Rom 12:21).

* * *

The term *hesychasm* originated from the Greek word *hesychia* — *inner quietness*.

Without this *inner quietness*, meditation is not possible. And meditation — after the stage of learning and encompassing the ethical principles of life suggested for us by God — is the basis of further development of the consciousness on the spiritual Path.

It swas striving to achieve hesychia and to advance then to cognition of God that formed this direction of the "Christian Raja Yoga" known as Hesychasm.

The most important feature and the highest value of this direction consisted in the fact that Hesychasts from the very beginning accepted the correct guiding line — realization of Jesus Christ's instructions that one can develop love in oneself only through the work with the spiritual heart.

In particular, they discovered that if one moves the concentration of the consciousness from the head into the spiritual heart, this stops the *inner dialog*, which prevented meditation.

And at full success — i.e. when the consciousness is fully placed in the spiritual heart, one could understand — all of a sudden! — on one's own experience what Jesus meant by speaking about the spiritual love!

The life of such people changed and they could really love each other and everything around themselves with truly Christian love: "as they love themselves" and even more than themselves!

And with further development of the spiritual heart, they got the ability to fall in love with God.

God supported them in this, providing them with the possibility to experience Him as Love. It resulted — in the end — in Merging of the two loving in the Embrace of Love.

Hesychasts invented the method of development of the spiritual heart which was called *Jesus prayer*. Its formulas may be different: from "Jesus Christ, the Son of God, have a mercy on me!" to the most simple and perfect version: simply an appeal-entreaty to beloved Jesus to enter into my spiritual heart with the humble repetition of His name: "Jesus! Jesus!…"

… But in later times, very few were able to achieve positive fruits from using the *Jesus prayer*. Many people even believed that "its secrets are lost"…

But this is not true: in reality, mass of "believers" lost Christianity in general — with the refusal by them of ethics given by Christ. And this resulted in a failure to form — up to the last years — a comprehensive and scientifically correct approach to human spiritual development. In other words, there was not such scientific-religious direction until now, which has been created by us and called the *Methodology of Spiritual Development*.

… I want to stress once more that one has to start the spiritual development not by practicing meditation but by getting acquainted in detail with general theoretical knowledge on religious philosophy and by accepting the ethical Teachings of God considered above.

Otherwise, the state of the practitioner cannot be stable. Such a person cannot withstand the ethical tests, which God necessarily offers to spiritual seekers. And this may result in mental disorders, among other things.

* * *

Now let us get acquainted with some important ideas from the book of early Christians which is called *Philokalia*[22]:

From Spiritual Directions of Diadochus of Photiki

The acme of faith is... immersion of the mind in God.

The acme of freedom from wealth is to desire to be possessionless even as others desire to possess.

The acme of humbleness is to forget unfalteringly good deeds of oneself.

The acme of love is to enhance your friendly attitude to those who insult and revile you.

From Spiritual Directions of Ephrem the Syrian

Monk, neither desire meat, nor drink wine, lest your mind coarsen...

Be not addictive to meat and wine-drinking, lest you make your mind incapable of receiving spiritual gifts.

God created man *free*, therefore for man are praise and punishment.

The wandering eye causes much suffering to the one who follows it. Keep your eyes from wandering, lest you find no straight way to chastity.

---

[22] [57].

Wisely avoid adverse meetings to keep yourself in goodness.

If you want to conquer lust for wealth, love selflessness and sparing way of life.

If you want to conquer anger, develop meekness and generosity.

Grieve only if you have committed a sin, but even in this case do not grieve too much, otherwise you may become desperate.

If you want to conquer conceit, do not desire praise, laurels, nice garments, respect, favor, but like to be blamed and slandered by people...

If you want to conquer pride, do not say that your deed was done by your hands and might; say that with God's help and guidance it was done, not by your power and efforts.

From Spiritual Directions of Abba Dorotheus

I heard about a brother who, when visiting someone of the community and seeing his cell non-swept and non-cleaned, thought to himself: blessed this brother is, for he set aside the earthly concerns and is so immersed in the highest matters that he has no time to tidy the cell. And if he came to a brother whose cell was tidy, swept, clean, he thought: as the soul of this brother is pure, so is his cell, and the order in his cell is in accordance with the state of the soul.

Do not desire the outcome that you want, but desire it to happen as it will happen: thus will you be at peace with everyone.

Believe that dishonor and reproach are the medicine for curing the pride of your soul. And pray for those reproaching you as for the true healers of your soul...

In response to false accusations say: forgive me and pray for me! When people ask you whether it is true, tell the truth and then bow humbly and say again: forgive me and pray for me!

Never prefer your will to the will of your brother.

About Spiritual Struggle —
John Cassian

(There is) the state that consists in contemplating One God and in ardent love for Him; in this state the mind, permeated with that love, converses with God in the most direct way.

From Ascetic Directions
of Nilus of Sinai

If disgrace befell over you, be glad: for if it is unjust, then your reward will be large; and if it is just, then, having learned from it, you can avoid the retribution.

There is the highest prayer of the perfect ones... — when by unsaid aspirations of spirit they approach God, Who sees their open hearts.

From Spiritual Directions
of Isaac of Syria

Those of lowly mind never stay to look at the crowd, gathering of people, disorder, turmoil; pay no attention to words, talks, clamors, disturbance of senses: they seek not to have much and be constantly busy, but to be free, without cares.

They are never in a hurry or confusion; they have no hot and superficial thoughts; but they always stay in peace. There is nothing that can make them amazed, confused, terrified... All their joys are in what is pleasing to the Lord.

When they touch the forehead to the ground and direct the sight of the heart to the Holiest of the Holy,... they dare to pray only thus: whatever is going to happen to me let it happen by Your will!

The desert soothes passions. Yet man has not only to soothe the passions but also to root them out, i.e. overcome them... The soothed passions wake up once there is a reason for them to become active again.

The one who wants to love God has to take care about the purity of the soul, first of all.

This purity is attained through conquering the passions.

(The one who has not conquered the passions cannot enter) the chaste and pure region of the heart.

Do not hate a sinner, for we all are to be responsible.

From Spiritual Directions
of Theodore of Edessa

Only when we rid ourselves of passions and lust and put the desires of the flesh under the control of Spirit, only then can we accept the cross and follow Christ.

And "withdrawal from the world" is nothing but the destruction of passions and manifestation of the innermost life in Christ.

* * *

The stages of the spiritual Path can be subdivided into three groups:

1. Preliminary (getting acquainted with the theory and accepting it, beginning of the ethical work on oneself, introducing into one's own life the basic hygienic procedures, such as washing the body every day (if possible),

taking sunbathes in summer, or using a quartz lamp in winter etc.).

2. Basic methods, which include mastering relaxation of the body and the mind, cleansing bioenergy structures of the organism with the help of special methods, and — what is more important — mastering the ability to "live" with the concentration of the consciousness in the chakra anahata and to look from it at the outer world,

3. Further development of oneself as a spiritual heart — up to merging with the *Heart of the Absolute* — the Primordial Universal Consciousness, God-the-Father, the Heavenly Father.

* * *

Growth of an individual soul transformed into a spiritual heart is virtually unlimited.

The monastic way of life full of service to God through serving people in their spiritual advancement plus constant meditative training on *places of power* specially selected for this purpose allows spiritual warriors to grow (as a spiritual heart) up to the sizes comparable to the size of our planet, and then — much larger. In addition, spiritual warriors practically master the methods of moving in the basic eons of the Absolute, learn to dissolve with the consciousness in the highest (subtlest) eons.

And then follows Mergence with the Heavenly Father, which becomes more and more firm in the following years of unceasing spiritual efforts.

Upon achieving the first real success on this Path, the practitioner gets rid of diseases, which may have lasted for years. And continuing achievements of new spiritual heights allows the practitioner to cleanse the body up to *transparency*, which can be perceived by clairvoyance. And the Divine Light begins to flow though it into the material world! And the Consciousness developed to Divinity, right now — during existence of the healthy and active physical body — lives in Mergence with the Creator and comes out from His Abode at those parts of the Creation where it is necessary.

... But this is not all to it. There are much more interesting prospects...

Sun of God
or
How to Become
the Ocean of Pure Love
(lecture)

The term *Sun of God* was introduced by Jesus Christ through B.Cullen — a prophet of the past century, who lived in the USA. A book with his Revelations was published in the USA in 1992 and then republished in Russian[23] (unfortunately with many grammar errors).

The main message that Jesus wanted to impart to people through this book is the following.

God is always a Living God! Jesus was on the Earth 2000 years ago, and He exists today among embodied people (though He is not embodied now).

But many believers are engrossed in absolutely meaningless activity: performing endless ritual bodily

---

[23] [25]. The language and the content of this book correspond to the worldview of the person who received the information: God always talks to people using the language and terms they can understand. (Due to this the book describes images of a spaceship and Christ leaving the Earth on it). But this book contains also very valuable information.

Main quotations from this book can be found in [10].

movements, repeating prayers that sometimes are not only useless but also harmful. They do this instead of making efforts on real spiritual self-transformation through realization of God's program for them — which consists in cognition of God and merging by the consciousness with Him in Love.

Jesus says that He walks in churches among believers who appeal to Him in their prayers... — yet they do not see Him, do not feel Him, do not listen to and do not hear Him!...

Instead of doing this silly exercise, Jesus suggests that His followers serve God by serving people, as well as make personal efforts on cognizing the Creator.

It is also foolish to seek God in the sky: one should seek the spiritual Heavens not above the surface of our round planet but in the *depth* of the multidimensional space. And the Abode of the Creator is very close to us! The distance to it is less than the thickness of finest paper! The way to this Abode begins inside one's developed spiritual heart.

The entrance into the Abode of the Creator can be seen by successful spiritual seekers, who approached it, as a giant and tender *Sun of God* that resembles a tender morning sun, only infinitely bigger.

To cognize all this and to enter the *Heart of God*, merge there with the Creator is the ultimate purpose of our lives, of the personal evolution of everyone of us.

On the Path of our self-perfecting and in our efforts to help other spiritual seekers, the Holy Spirit is always willing to help us. Jesus describes Him as a Power of Love of unlimited capabilities that comes out from the Abode of the Creator and is always ready to help worthy people.

But we have to make our state close enough to the state of the Holy Spirit to see, feel, and hear Him, to merge with Him in Love and become like Him, and then to cognize God-the-Father with His help.

* * *

Let us discuss now how can one find the *Sun of God*?

First we have to understand that man is not a body. Man is a consciousness (soul) embodied into a material body for a certain period of time.

The incarnation is important, because the growth of an individual consciousness is possible only in the embodied state, since it is the material body that is the "factory" of transformation of the energy of ordinary food into the energy of the consciousness.

The organism of an embodied man is multidimensional (but not the body).

I should note that the scheme of "seven bodies", invented a long time ago by occultists, is methodologically wrong. It would be more correct to consider a potential presence of man in all the main layers of the multidimensional Absolute; it is this potential that one has to realize.

This concept, by the way, is described in the Bible as likeness between man and God — God in the aspect of the multidimensional Absolute.

It may become easier to understand the above said if you look at the scheme for studying the structure of the Absolute.[24]

This scheme is not so easy to understand, since it is impossible to fully represent the multidimensionality of space in graphical form. In order to understand it, one should keep in mind that each layer of multidimensionality shown lower on this scheme — in reality is located *deeper* on the multidimensional scale. And each *deeper* layer is subtler as compared to the previous one.

---

[24] See it in the end of this book.

The Abode of the Creator is located in the *deepest*, that is, the most subtle energy layer of the multidimensional structure of the Absolute. Thus, we must seek Him there. In terms of methodological direction, this work must consist in refinement of the consciousness, which starts with mastering regulations of one's own emotional sphere.

The whole process of such training of ours (including, in particular, studying of theory, practical classes, and exams) is conducted by the Holy Spirit; He leaves no one without His help and attention, and nothing happens without His knowing and controlling it.

So what do we have to do in relation to everything said above? — Apparently we have to start changing ourselves immediately: right today!

How One Should Understand the Word *God* (lecture)

By the word *God* we have to mean, first of all, the Creator.

There is also the word *Absolute*, that is multidimensional *Absolutely Everything* except for "cesspool"-hell.

In Christianity there is also the concept of Trinity — God-the-Father, Christ (God-the-Son), and the Holy Spirit.

God-the-Father is not an old man sitting on a cloud, as He is depicted on some icons. And He is not a powerful male-ruler sitting on a throne on some planet. He is not a woman, nor a bisexual being. He is impersonal.

He is an aggregate of all Those who formerly achieved the Abode of the Creator — the subtlest layer of the multidimensional Absolute — and settled there forever.

God-the-Father is an aggregate of many Perfect Subtlest Consciousnesses merged into one and abiding in the state of eternal Highest Bliss.

Their main feature is the Highest Subtlety.

Those dwelling in the Abode of the Creator can come out from it with a part of Oneself with the purpose of helping the embodied people, first of all. Such personal Manifestations of the Creator are called, in the aggregate sense, the Holy Spirit (Brahman).

Holy Spirit and *God-the-Father* are words denoting the collective (not individual) states of God.

But in every particular case of communication with the Holy Spirit, we interact with Divine Personalities, with our non-incarnate Divine Teachers.

Divine Teachers, when They come to this "manifest" world, initially retain Their level of subtlety. When They enter paradise, They slightly densify Themselves, so that paradisiacal beings could perceive Them. For the purpose of conversations with beginner embodied disciples, They densify a Part of Themselves even more — to the level of subtlety of those souls: to be perceivable to the disciples.

Divine Teachers can be seen with the eyes of the heart by spiritually advanced people — as giant anthropomorphic Manifestations (Mahadoubles) consisting of soft, tender, subtle white-goldish Divine Light, sometimes fiery-like but never burning for true disciples of God.

Disciples of Divine Teachers have to make every effort in order to approach the Abode of the Creator with the help of the methods of purification of oneself from energetical coarseness and with the help of meditative trainings, which include attunement of the consciousness with a Divine Teacher.

Those successful disciples who have learned to stay in Mergence with the Consciousness of the Teacher (though they have not been admitted into the Abode of the Creator yet) — they have an experience of being the Holy Spirit.

Sometime Divine Teachers incarnate in human bodies. They do this as a sacrificial service to embodied people — for the sake of helping them spiritually, saving deluded souls. (Yet these deluded people very often torture and kill such Saviors).

Messiah, Christ, Avatar — by these words people call Them in different languages.

Every One of Them, having incarnated in a human body, continues to live with the Giant Subtlest Consciousness in the Abode of the Creator, remaining an integral Part of the Creator. But this Consciousness is connected also with the physical body through which God tries to bring to embodied people the truth about the meaning of their lives on the Earth and about how one has to realize this meaning.

... For a successful disciple of God, entering the Abode of the Creator is not an instant and irrevocable act but a long and hard yet very joyful process of direct interaction with God, of accustoming oneself to a new state, which is principally different from the life in other eons. This is gradual settling in the "new home", mastering it, and gaining the qualities of a Messiah.

One can realize this only in monasticism.

... There are cases when some people proclaim themselves (or others proclaimed them) a "new Christ" or "Avatar". Such situations can be created, in particular, by swindlers with the purpose of gaining money or enjoying making mock of the followers; they can be created also by people ill with paranoia or schizophrenia.

On the other hand, it is primitive people that often try to defile true Divine Teachers.

Therefore it is appropriate to define the criteria by which one can distinguish the former from the latter.

Such criteria are three:

First is the subtlety of the Consciousness of a true Divine Teacher, which exists in the form of a giant Spiritual Heart, incapable of entering coarse emotional states.

Second is that such a Divine Person has an understanding of everything that we are discussing here, and possesses a set of methods which are needed to the disciples for achieving God-realization.

Third is an absence of egocentrism in a Divine Teacher; it is replaced with Godcenteredness, which implies, in particular, living and acting for the sake of the Divine Evolution and not for the sake of oneself or of a small group of people.

* * *

The essence of everything taking place in the universe is the Evolution of the Absolute.

This process is guided by the Creator. At His commands, in different parts of the boundless universal space, lumps of primeval matter (prakriti) begin to form of protoprakriti. Then for a long time processes go in them, which result in creating conditions suitable for life of organic bodies. Then begins the stage of incarnation of tiny particles of protopurusha into tiny particles of matter... Unicellular organisms get formed, then — multicellular...

Controlling the process of genetic mutations, the Creator creates organisms of higher complexity. There appear plants, animals, humans...

The developing lumps of purusha are embodied by God in more and more complex organic bodies capable of reproduction... Thanks to this, they grow in size, the forms of their life activity become more complex, including behavior. Animals develop the emotional sphere, memory, the ability to think creatively... Some birds, for example, manifest remarkable esthetical abilities and imagination in creating their nests, paragons of caring and self-sacrifice when protecting their young — it would be good for some people to learn from them!... The intellectual level of the representatives of mammals is higher than that of many people... including those who deny that animals have an intellect and are capable of loving and suffering...

Every one of us, people, was in the past plants, animals of many biological species...

And now we have to behave carefully towards plants and animals — as towards people to be, without harming them but, on the contrary, helping...

We must not kill or maim them in vain; animals live here not for the sake of being killed by us for food...

They live like we, people, for the sake of the process of development of souls incarnate in physical bodies, in the common with us process of the Evolution of the Absolute; they are Its particles — as we are...

... The highest stage of the evolution of organic bodies on the Earth is human body...

And the next stage of the development of human beings (not as a body but as a soul, consciousness) is God in the aspect of the Creator.

... We incarnate in human bodies many times. The most difficult thing for us is to develop the intellectual function of the consciousness to that level when one becomes able to understand completely and realize in life everything that we are discussing here. The majority of people turn out to be incapable even of thinking about this... and if they try — they immediately get stuck in sects where the salvation is promised as a reward for repeating certain prayers, for participation in certain rituals...

... What contributes to the development of the intellect? — It is the study in educational institutions, various industrial and scientific work, self-education in all areas of knowledge which are most significant for spiritual growth; it is also help provided to others in mastering all this.

What prevents the development of the intellect? A lazy way of life, use of alcohol and other drugs that destroy the soul, life in coarse emotional states which makes people "attached" to hell...

Having grown in a series of many past incarnations to the human state, many people go further not to the Creator but in the opposite direction. And they end up in the *outer darkness* — hell; then they "fall back" to the protopurusha — being destroyed as souls... It is from this information that the image of blazing inferno with perishing souls of sinners was formed.

Other people — thee best ones! — gain for themselves the Abode of the Creator. They continue Eternal Life in the Highest Bliss, in most active creative Love directed towards worthy disciples of God — wherever they may be in the whole universe.

Religion — and Religious Movements and Schools (lecture)

The word *religion* is translated from Latin as "Mergence with God" or as "Path to such Mergence".

All religious movements created by God among people were created by Him with that purpose.

Yet with time these movements get perverted by people — up to the completely opposite — because they were led not by true spiritual adepts but by aggressive and selfish primitives, who seized the power in them[25].

---

[25] See [9].

These organizations, conceived and established by God, were converted by people into sects[26].

But in many countries there were also heroes who cognized the Creator and served Him by opposing the evil of religious perversions.

The fanatics of those sects very often persecuted and killed such heroes. Yet many of them managed to create spiritual Schools and to help a number of good souls to approach the Creator.

And now in many countries there exist or appear new religious leaders who create their religious organizations.

These organizations are quite different though. And one cannot say that all of them go in the right direction, although very often their leaders claim that they are guided by God and that they hear His directions and follow them... Why then are they so different? What is the reason?

... We have discussed already that people of the same society, living at the same time may differ much. Among them always:

— the majority are psychogenetically young souls,

— there is a certain fraction of people (depending on the cultural traditions in the present social environment) who indulge in vices; such people prepare themselves for hell; they are the "waste" of the Evolution; as we have discussed already, people prepare themselves for hell primarily by cultivating in themselves coarse emotional states: hostile attitude towards everyone, hatred, anger, irritation; drug addicts including alcoholics also degenerate,

— in every country there are also a number of people who are mentally defective from birth; they can be incarnations of souls who in their past lives were alcohol-

---

[26] Sects are religious associations which deviated in their worldview from the true knowledge suggested to people by God.

ics or other drug addicts; they are born by parents with adverse destinies (which they themselves formed),

— there are people with average and high level of intellectual development, working more or less successfully in various kinds of social activity,

— and there are those who have passed already the stages of the development of the consciousness which allow them in this incarnation to approach the Divinity or even to attain It.

The religiosity of these groups of people depends on all these factors.

For example, I knew a sect whose followers intentionally developed in themselves the ability to hate intensively — for the sake of gaining power over people...

Another similar group of "sorcerers" with the same purpose "charged" themselves on negative *places of power* with devilish energy...

There are also certain sects and groups created by sexual maniacs who disguise their activity as religious work.

There are some schools of "modern psychology" created by diabolic persons, who like to humiliate and mock people. These monsters justify their activity by the necessity of destructing the lower "I" of their victims...

... If we want to consider more "decent" level of sectarianism, then one can mention such typical methodological errors as wrong understanding of the localization, structure, and functions of the chakras; one's focusing attention only on the lower or on the upper chakras; harmful exercises of assigning colors to the chakras according to the colors of the rainbow; wrong opinions about the methods of work with Kundalini, which is allegedly located in the coccyx; worshipping astrological fantasies, taking for "teachers" spirits and "aliens" — instead of the Holy Spirit, etc.

... In order to come from the description of negative phenomena in pseudo-religious environment — to positive ones, let us consider what is really advisable to develop in oneself for the sake of approaching the final Highest Goal:

— We have discussed the necessity of the development of the intellect. It is very important to accumulate as much natural scientific knowledge as possible — in the fields of medicine, bioenergy, fundamental psychology, ethnography, astronomy, on the history of development of religious-philosophical thought. One has to know also the political matters. After all, our spiritual studying is intended for our growth to the Divinity. And one cannot achieve this by meditative exercises alone: one has to strive to approach the Divine competence in everything most important! And this requires a large broadness of outlook!

— It is very important to master harmonious communications with living nature. In order to learn to love the Creator, one has to master first love for His Creation with all its creatures. And this cannot be done in rooms, or museums, or laboratories, or temples. On the contrary, in harmonious natural landscapes with various manifestations of life — if one has a correct (that is loving, careful) attitude towards them — this can be achieved naturally and easily.

— Good health is also important: the purity of the consciousness and its quantitative growth are not possible without good health of the body. Therefore, one necessarily has to study and follow the principles of a healthy way of life — this concerns nutrition, tempering the body, correct ways of clothing the body and curing it from most common illnesses.

— Skills in esthetics with its various aspects — in music, dance, painting, photography, etc. — are important in the work on the refinement of the consciousness.

— The strength of the body, developed through physical labor and sport training, is favorable for accumulating the power by the subtle consciousness. It is also very useful to master the skills of self-defense — in order not to be timorous in contacts with the representatives of the human filth. Yet, excessive keenness on martial arts cannot be considered as a good quality on the spiritual Path: the spiritual Path is the Path of Love rather than aggression!

— Skills of psychic self-regulation including the ability to relax the body and mind, to move the concentration of the consciousness within the body (in particular, in the chakras and main meridians) and then outside the body — are essential for success in spiritual work.

— Everything listed above is necessary. One cannot succeed without this. Yet the most important thing is to develop oneself as a spiritual heart — the organ of spiritual love. After all "God is Love"! Therefore, in order to approach Him, one has to transform oneself into Love. In other words, one has to accustom oneself to living constantly in the state of love — including love for those who attack you, torture and kill your body!

— It is also important to have the correct knowledge about God, about the meaning of our lives and the ways of its realization. The work of any religious organization cannot be effective without forming in its followers the attitude towards God as to a Real, Living Main Teacher, as towards a Goal that we have to cognize, as towards the Main Object of Love.

* * *

... And the last thing: how can one distinguish between true prophecies originating from God — and jokes and mockery of the inhabitants of hell or other spirits?

For highly advanced spiritually disciples of God it is not difficult: they *see* with the eyes of the heart their

Divine Interlocutors and easily converse with Them. Divine Teachers cannot be confused with someone else: They are giant and subtlest Consciousnesses. And even colors of Them as Consciousnesses are also opposite to those of the inhabitants of hell: the color of the former is tender-goldish-white; the color of the latter is coarse-black.

Yet beginner mystics who have not learned to attune to the Divine subtlety get often confused in this matter.

So are there criteria for distinguishing the information of this kind if one cannot see directly its source? The answer is yes.

First, God never suggests to anyone to do anything harmful to others.

Second, God tells about how one can approach Perfection, how to help others in this. Devils and demons say flowery yet meaningless words and provoke one to do ethically inadequate and foolish deeds. God also never makes *forecasts* except for concrete situations: for example, go to that place not sooner than this date, before it the weather will be bad...

Also God never encourages vicious desires like one's striving for wealth.

He helps to perform only that which He needs in His Evolution.

Earthly passions of unwise people are encouraged only by those non-incarnate beings who lived in such desires and are competent in these matters...

Narrow Path
to the Highest Goal
(lecture)

Jesus suggested going to the Creator through the "narrow gate", the "narrow Path", for "wide is the gate, and broad is the way that leads to destruction" (Matt 7:13-14).

What is this *narrow Path*?

This is the path of monasticism.

And monasticism implies complete dedication of oneself to only one goal: cognition of the Creator and helping others in this.

How can one distinguish a monk from other people?

Not by the clothes! And not by foreign or ancient names! Not by the number of kowtows and other bodily movements!

... Let us look: what does a regular person call *work*?

It is, first of all, that for what one receives money!

Yet the true monk by *work* means what has to be done *for God*.

In other words, the former works first of all for oneself. While in the case of the latter, the vector of the direction of the efforts is the opposite: monks work not for the sake of themselves (or for the sake of a small group of people) but for the good of others — in the general process of positive Evolution of the Universal Consciousness.

"Be perfect as your Heavenly Father is perfect" — this is the goal defined by Jesus Christ that every monk has to aspire to!

Of course, for realization of this task one has to have the general methodology of spiritual development and concrete methods, which we describe in these conversations.

... We have discussed already that spiritual work consists of two main stages: exoteric and esoteric ones.

The exoteric part consists of two components:

— studying and accepting fully the concept of the path suggested by God.

— initial ethical self-transformation in accordance with these Teachings.

I talk about *initial* ethical self-transformation because one cannot do all this work at once: the work on ethical self-perfecting continues until the end of the Path to the Abode of the Creator.

... In usual circumstances, people since childhood get often involved in the religious (or atheistic) environment that dominates in the region where they live, or in that which their parents follow. And very often this situation is not good.

And only having become intellectually mature, we start to compare different philosophical and religious concepts, attempt to understand the reasons for their differences, and later in this quest come to understand the Origin.

Only then, walking the true *narrow Path* becomes possible for us.

... Very few people find healthy spiritual schools in the beginning of their quest and avoid a long and sometimes painful search for the true direction of making spiritual efforts...

After this, one usually starts to struggle for the right to be different from the majority of people, who got lost and stuck in vices.

At this point, some give up being unable to withstand conflicts and persecutions. They choose to live a secure life "as others"; they do not really want to go to the Creator.

But others show great heroism and ensure good future destinies for themselves. We can find examples of such heroism among the first Christians, among the victims of the Inquisition, among the first Muslims and later among Baha'is and Sikhs who opposed perversions of Islam.[27]

I, too, had to withstand political persecutions and threats of physical punishment. I underwent an attack of aggressive primitives, which gave me a valuable experience of two clinical deaths.[28] I withstood all these trials and kept on walking — along this *narrow Path*. I helped many worthy people (and hope to help many more).

… On the exoteric stages of the Path, God tests spiritual seekers by various material hardships and oppression from the side of people unable to understand them. On the initial steps of the esoteric stages, they are often suggested to undergo mystical trials: for example, energy attacks of incarnate and non-incarnate devils. Here seekers are tested with mystical fear. If they yield to it and give up; it means they do not have mature love for the Creator, that their love has not become a steadfast and unmovable dominant in their lives yet.

For "there is no fear in love; but perfect love drives out fear. … The one who fears is not made perfect in love!" (1 John 4:18).

We can overcome fear by clinging tighter to our Divine Teachers and by understanding that it is They Who created these difficulties — for the good of Their disciples. And They watch then — how we overcome them.

In this there is a manifestation of Their Divine Love; They just seek to help us to become Perfect.

But without overcoming such difficulties it is impossible.

---

[27] [9,42,58].
[28] [7,14].

* * *

Then seekers longing for the Creator have to develop themselves as spiritual hearts, which cannot be contained within the physical body, have to refine themselves and grow even larger. Then they learn to move as spiritual hearts into the subtlest eons of the multidimensional Absolute and accustom themselves to these eons, one by one — up to the Abode of the Creator.

The Creator is the *Heart of the Absolute*. The process of spiritual advancement can be described as one's becoming gradually *similar to Him*.

Let every one of us think again: what does it consist in?

... Ideally one has to cognize the structure of the Absolute completely. It can be done only by the spiritual heart developed to cosmic sizes. Giant Souls consisting of transparent, flowing energy of Love move easily in the multidimensional space. They do it with the help of the Arms of the Consciousness.

Most easily one can master it practically on corresponding *places of power*. One just has to know how to do this.

Spiritual Warriors Who have cognized and mastered all eons of the Absolute move freely along the entire range of the scale of multidimensionality. They easily pervade all eons: from the boundary with hell — to the Depths of the Abode of the Creator.

The criterion of success in settling in the Abode of the Creator is the ability to shine *from within it* with the *Sun of God*.

Only the full realization of the said above can be considered as completion of the Path of spiritual self-realization, or in other words, — God-realization, full Enlightenment, attainment of the highest Nirvana that brings highest Samadhi.

One cannot describe in more detail these most complex steps of spiritual development in a lecture or in a book. Also they cannot be mastered without the help of a Divine Teacher. It is Divine Teachers that show us the "stairway" of the *narrow Path*. They explain where to step on this "stairway" and how to behave in the universal space that one begins to cognize for the first time.

In this way man becomes God, having merged into the universal Ocean of the Subtlest Love of the Creator. The Kundalini energy of such a person is "unarchived" and merged with the Creator; there are no chakras in the body — in their usual form; there is only the boundless Spiritual Heart in the Abode of the Creator. Everything that is the best, the subtlest is extracted from the upper and lower dantians as well and merged with the Creator. The body, united with Him, continues to live on the Earth, and this allows — in the easiest way! — imparting to people the knowledge about the Path.

... By the way, I was asked to tell about the work with Kundalini. Our next conversation will be dedicated to this.

Atman and Kundalini (lecture)

The word *Atman* (pronounced as *Atma* in Sanskrit) is interpreted as the *Main Essence* of man, man's Higher "I". *A* in this word is a negating particle. *Tma* means *darkness*. The word *tamas* — *ignorance, spiritual darkness* — has the same root. Therefore *A-tma* or *Atman* means *opposite to darkness, shining*.

In essence, Atman is the best, Divine part of one's multidimensional organism.

Atman is the Brahmanic Fire when we become this Fire, and the Atmic energy Kundalini — the precious content of the "money-box", where the best of us, which has been accumulated in all previous incarnations, is stored.

... It turns out that every time man incarnates into the next body, not the entire soul gets embodied, but only that part of it which requires correction and improvement. But God saves the best of it, i.e. something that has been nurtured against the background of the emotion of the most tender love, in this "money-box". Nonetheless, Kundalini still remains a part of the human multidimensional organism and takes part in its life activity.

Ordinary material food that we eat is used by the organism for growth and renewal of the cells of the body, but it also provides: a) the energy for the activity of the muscles, nervous system, glands and for other needs of the body, b) the energy stored in the organism in the form of special bio-chemical links at the molecular level, c) energy for the chakras and other energy structures, and d) energy for the direct growth of the consciousness.

Therefore, both qualitative and quantitative growth of individual consciousness is ensured, on the one hand, by the quality and quantity of material food and on the other hand by intensity and quality of life (that is spiritual or non-spiritual, in the true meaning of these words).

At the *end of the world*, all Kundalinis get infused into the Consciousness of the Creator. But the souls that failed to unite with Atman by that time get disintegrated to the protopurusha state.

Let us get back to the transformation of energy. Our bodies are as factories where transformation of "material" energies into the energy of the consciousness takes place. But the quality of the growing consciousness primarily depends on what emotions we live in: subtle and the subtlest — as opposed to "gray" or "black" (coarse) ones.

As we can see from the above said, God "feeds" and "grows" evolving thanks to the transformation of food in our bodies, which was created by Him from akasha. The energy produced in our bodies from this food transforms ideally into Atmic energy, which He then "infuses" into Himself. From this the role of *creation of the worlds* and the place of all living beings, including us, people, in His Evolution becomes clear once and for all.

So, if we love God — let us take an active part in this process! And, as we can see, it makes sense to express love for God not by begging something in front of the icons but by increasing our Atmic potentials by living actively in emotional love.

... The Kundalini resources of people differ. They depend on the number and quality of lives we have already lived, as well as on how we live in this one.

Our Kundalinis usually exist in akasha inside the body of our planet.

Echoes of the knowledge about Kundalini gave birth to the myths that every person has a sister-soul, meeting with which is what everyone dreams about.

Kundalini is connected to the body of each man with a special energy canal that enters the body at the front part of the muladhara chakra. Kundalini participates in the organism's activity in various ways, including replenishment of the embodied part of the consciousness. The greater Kundalini one has, the richer his or her spiritual potential and spiritual expressions are.

But being Divine (identical to the energy of the Creator by its quality), the energy of Kundalini is still individualized. It is like a drop which is not merged yet with the Ocean of Primordial Consciousness.

When man matures in a series of incarnations up to the stage when the current incarnation can become the last one and when all defects of the incarnate part of the consciousness are eliminated — the time comes when the Kundalini may be brought up to the body, raised through it, and merged with the remaining part of the consciousness. After that, one has to infuse with Kundalini into Paramatman (i.e. into the Highest Atman, into the Ocean of Universal Primordial Consciousness of the Creator in His Abode).

* * *

Accumulation of person's Kundalini takes place only when he or she is in the emotional state of tender love. This is what God wants from people. These are the states that He calls us to live in. For example, Jesus taught: "A new commandment I give to you, that you love one another!" (John 13:34), "And above all things have fervent love among yourselves!..." (1 Peter 4:8), "Beloved, let us love one another!..." (1 John 4:7), "Be brotherly loving one another!" (Romans 12:10).

Where can we experience states like this? First of all — in harmonious sexual relations filled with tenderness, which are inspired by the understanding that subtle and pure harmony of love this is what God wants from us the most, this is an important part of the Path to God, by this we enrich not only ourselves but also Him. We also learn how to love when we take care of our children with joy and tenderness, or when we attune to subtle works of art filled with tenderness.

People, who have become established in these states, later prove capable of experiencing intensive bliss from the direct communication with God.

These states, collectively called *sattva*, are the states that God wants us to live in — for it is in them that we can grow directly (as consciousness), preparing ourselves to the total Mergence with Him, directly participating in His Evolution.

All our opposite states (they are called *tamas*) do not contribute to this and thus are not pleasing Him. And by cultivating them we turn ourselves into the "waste of the Evolution", destine ourselves for living in the "cesspool"

— hell — regardless of our being members of a particular religious organization and our fervor in performing its rites and "sacraments".

... It is significant that aggressiveness and violence are typical of people who belong to the tamas guna; they have a zealous desire to make all other people similar to themselves.

This gives birth to "holy" wars, to propagation of alcoholism and eating bodies of animals, and to desecration of the beauty and value of sexual relations.

Or look at the "religious" rules that demand people to enter the "legitimate" marriage "blindly", without studying sexual compatibility with the partner first.

But people differ dramatically by their sexual features! And successful matches in this respect are rather rare than common! And the majority of spouses in the "religious" marriages suffer and torture each other in sexual disharmony...

But sects prohibit divorces...

And now let us look — is this what God wants?

... Sattva guna (sattvic state) — is the state, which God calls all of us to live in.

Sattva guna is bliss!

And the state of God is also bliss!

Those who got accustomed to bliss on the Earth — easily enter into the Creator's Bliss.

However, the process of entering the Abode of the Creator requires additional efforts. Sattva should not become a "trap" for us; since it can appease us with the earthly kind of bliss and make us give up efforts on active cognition of the Creator in His Abode, on entering it and Merging there with Him.

Yes, if we grow ourselves (as consciousnesses), living in the states of subtlest love and "feeding" the "furnaces" of our bodies with food adequate to the spiritual Path — that is *killing-free*, which does not contain alcohol, drugs and other toxins, is rich in vitamins, microelements, protein — in this case we successfully fulfill our individual *minimum plan* in the Face of God.

But He also has a *maximum plan* for us. It implies that we try to perfect that part of ourselves *(jiva)* that lives in the body apart from Kundalini. Then we will be able to enter into Him with the whole of ourselves, retaining full awareness, and then to help other embodied people from the highest Divine level, like Divine Teachers that are frequently mentioned in this book do.

But let us get back to work with Kundalini.

The term *raising Kundalini*, well known from yogic and occult literature, denotes the method of bringing this energy to and carrying it through the body.

The word *Kundalini* means snake. The origin of this term will become clear as we proceed with this issue.

We have already discussed that bringing Kundalini to the body can be performed only by a Divine Teacher. But subsequent stages of the process are conducted with participation of the aspirant.

Here God encounters a difficulty, about which He says Himself and which consists in the lack of knowledge about work with Kundalini that people have lost due to the ignorance that prevails on the Earth.

This is why the work with Kundalini now can only be performed within few spiritual schools that reached a high level of competence.

I want to note that any attempts to "awaken Kundalini", for example, by knocking the coccyx on the floor, which is recommended by various pseudo-gurus, do not have anything to do with the truth. (They believe that Kundalini is stored in the muladhara chakra, which they think is located in the coccyx. But in reality neither muladhara chakra nor Kundalini has any relation to the coccyx). Attempts like this can result only in bioenergetic or mental disorders.

... So, God brings Kundalini to the body of His worthy disciple first. (I want to mention that developed Kundalini has a size of many kilometers).

Then quite a fine work on carrying Kundalini through the body should begin.

The prerequisites for this kind of work are absolute cleanness and perfect development of all necessary energy structures of the organism: all seven chakras, sushumna, chitrini, the front and the middle meridians, as well as the developed clairvoyance abilities of the aspirant.

The process of *raising Kundalini* usually takes many days, a month or more. (Although the use of special *places of power* can help shorten this process significantly).

The exercise of *raising Kundalini* is performed in the horizontal position of the body and repeated many times.

Every time the passing of Kundalini through the body is initiated by the practitioner: he or she reaches with a hand of the consciousness through the muladhara chakra for the Kundalini, which was brought to the body, and as if he or she stirs the head of the snake that is coiled up there. Then the energy of Kundalini starts flowing through the body, washing and purifying it with the Atmic power, healing its remaining defects. The aspirant, like a hospitable host, has to let the flowing energy through a particular meridian into all the chakras and all the segments of the body.

Upon passing through the body, Kundalini spills out through the sahasrara chakra and concentrates over the head. One should learn how to become one with this energy by merging with it inside this accumulation. In this way we accustom ourselves to living in the state of Atmic subtlety.

The Atmic energy Kundalini, brought in this way through the body, infuses then into Paramatman (Highest Divine Atman, the *Heart of the Absolute*). Thus the practitioner moves There — with a very significant part of oneself.

Serving God
(lecture)

Every child after being born begins inevitably to learn... egoism. This happens because children can do nothing by themselves; everything is done for them by others. This is inevitable...

But then children grow... And at this stage, the correct education must include weaning them of the egocentric dominants and teaching them caring about others...

... One can observe funny examples in behavior of animals, for example, grown-up baby crows.

Baby crows, their bodies are already of the size of the parents, demand again and again food from their parents! The tired parents are desperate:

"We don't have any more food! What can we do?! We flew all over the neighborhood! We are hungry ourselves! You should seek food yourselves: you have grown up!"

Finally the parents manage to find some food. They bring it and put in front of the children. And what do the children do? Eat it? No! They cry even louder, demanding that the parents take the food from the ground and put it into their mouths!

... Another case. People tamed a baby crow. He became large, the size of an adult crow. These people cautiously put pieces of bread into his mouth: he has a large beak and can bite painfully! Sometimes the pieces of food fall out of his beak... The baby crow, instead of taking them from the ground, demands in his crow language: "You have put it bad! Do I have to bow to it?!"

... But as time goes by, his needs will make him seek food himself and bow to it... Then he will have his own children... And these children will become that school where he will learn to care about others, the school of altruism...

... In case of people, it happens in a similar manner. But the correct or wrong education plays here a more important role.

So often one can observe total egocentrism in adult people!... Even in those... who are "believers"...

Yet the true love that God wants to see in us is the opposite of *wanting something for oneself*; love is not one's passion-wanting!

True love, which alone is accepted by God, implies making good to others, helping others in everything good, sacrificing oneself for other's sakes!

Totally egocentric people misunderstand it so much that even in bright altruistic deeds of others they try to see only selfishness, always seeking a reason for irritated condemnation, hatred... Such people cannot understand God. And cannot approach Him...

* * *

How do people understand service to God?

Some think that "to serve God" means simply to belong to the clergy of some religious confession. Others think deeper and seek to serve by participating in common prayers and meditations. And some even dance and sing in honor of God.

But God wants us to do much more.

In particular, Jesus Christ and other Divine Teachers[29] edify us that one has to view the service to God as service to all, to help all in everything good. And one has to help not for the sake of one's own profit, but for the

---

[29] [6,11,13].

sake of those whom one helps; they can be people, animals, or plants. Also, one has to see behind all of them God's interest in this.

In order to be able to understand this and understand also how to discriminate between good deeds and those just seeming to be good, one has to try to look at situations from the point of view of the global strategic Plan of the Creator. Namely, we have to understand the essence of the universal Evolutionary Process and find our place in it.

And then we will be able not only to try practicing the precepts of God but also to see their important role in the global Strategy of the Creator. This will bring us to a deeper understanding of our own tasks and the ways of helping others better. Then we will gradually become active participants of the Evolution of the Universal Consciousness, active assistants to the Creator.

Active participation in the evolutionary process has to be regarded as consisting of two main parts: a) spiritual self-development, b) help to others.

In this process, as the apostle Paul taught (1 Cor 12,14), we should strive to serve with our highest abilities, as well as to seek to acquire even higher skills.

The essence of the Creator's Plan of creating material worlds (including this small "islet" of matter in the universe — our planet) is to transform less perfect constituents of the Absolute into more perfect. In this process, the individual Consciousnesses Who have achieved the full Perfection enrich the Creator with Themselves.

So both personal self-development and help to other evolving souls in their evolution are good from God's point of view.

In particular, if we develop ourselves through meditative work, the quality of our service improves: we become closer to the Creator by the quality of the consciousness and begin to see the world better; we approach His capabilities of seeing and understanding.

We also develop through our activity of helping others, increasing our knowledge about how to help. This knowledge will be useful even after disembodiment.

... Let us feel (or at least imagine) that there is only One Universal Macro-organism — the Absolute. Inside the Absolute, the process of Its development — the Universal Evolution — goes on. Let us feel unity, interrelation of *everything* in Him as a Whole. Let us feel our inseparability from It, from the Process of Its Development. Let us feel the joy of this awareness! And now — with this new understanding — let us direct our efforts to assisting the transformation of all capable "lumps" of consciousness — into the Consciousness of the Creator.

We all are *One* in the Organism of the Absolute. This is the essence of the principle suggested by Jesus Christ: love your neighbor as yourself, and even more than yourself. This principle concerns the aspect of LOVE called CARE. Its highest manifestation is self-sacrifice for the good of others. Jesus Christ demonstrated such a sacrifice: He gave us an example of CARE by the exploit of His life and death on the Earth. Let us become like Him in this respect!

* * *

Quite a few people long for cognition of the Absolute and seek the Creator.

Others, schooled by atheism and perverted religious movements, or those perverted on their own choice are well satisfied with partaking of the "forbidden" (by God) fruits from "the tree of knowledge of good and evil".

Such people risk going to hell, because "earthly" attachments provoke coarse emotions: anxiety, fear, sorrow, despair, jealousy, envy, irritation, hatred, anger, and so on. And those who habituate themselves to such emotional states actually accustom themselves to living in hell and go there after disembodiment.

The fruits of the Kingdom of Heaven are gained by few who find peace of the soul outside of earthly passions and developed selfless Love to such an extent that it enables them to fall in love with the Creator and thus become attracted to Him. And He meets such people with His Highest Love!

But the others…

— "love" themselves,

— call their cravings[30] "love",

— demand more and more love for themselves from others, cherishing thus their egocentrism, and hate other people because they poorly please ME! and, on the whole, do not do what I! want them to do.

* * *

All beings — both embodied and non-embodied — differ by the age of the soul.

It is one of the main features of every person, in particular.

Other important features are such qualitative characteristics as the level of intellectual development, ethical maturity, coarseness or subtlety of the consciousness. The quantitative valuation is based on the size of the soul.

The evolution of a soul goes in a series of many Earth's incarnations. And one cannot expect a high spiritual potential from soul that is incarnated in the human body for the first time; it comes to this soul later, provided that its development is auspicious.

From this, one can understand that not all embodied people — even if they have obtained a certain higher spiritual knowledge — can reach the Abode of the Creator in their current incarnation, no matter how hard they try.

---

[30] Passionate desires of the earthly.

Moreover, when too young souls get involved in meditative work, which is too serious for them, at a certain moment they lose understanding and start to play "religion" like children play their childish games. It may bring to a development of inadequate perception of oneself, just like in the case of boys who play "war", imagine themselves "colonels" and "generals". In the worst case, it may cause mental disorders. The latter is often the case in the religious organizations, where instead of God and Love, frightening mystical factors (devils, demons, sorcerers, vampires, and so on) are brought in the focus.

This is why religious leaders must use esoteric techniques and information very carefully, taking into account their possible harmful effects on those people who are intellectually and ethically immature.

And everyone who seeks spiritual progress should evaluate their own capabilities and not climb those "steps" of the "stairway" of spiritual development where it will be hard for them to stand.

By the way, it is not bad at all — if you have realized that you are a psychogenetically young soul. On the contrary, it means that you have not grown in yourself all these vices that otherwise you would have to get rid of for a long time.

A young soul is the one that has the entire joyful spiritual Path ahead!

Just do not waste time in vain!

* * *

... I have lived my Earth's life very intensively. And when I was making the way to the Creator for me and for my friends, many people got involved into the stream created by me at different stages. At the beginning, it always looked wonderful. But later, starting from a certain stage of the work, many of them would lose understanding of the work, they would get drawn backward or to entertainments. And since I was not interested in playing games, discontent with me, protest, and even hostility towards me would arise.

It took me quite some time to come to understand that one should not give the highest knowledge and methods to anyone asking for them. And this understanding could not come until I accumulated tremendous experience of providing spiritual help to people. Sometimes this experience was very dramatic (for me). (Now I share this experience with you — as I do in my other books — to help you avoid making such errors).

But let these warnings scare no one away from the spiritual quest: one should just choose for oneself the tasks that one is equal to.

One of the really attainable goals for anyone is to ensure oneself of going to paradise after the end of their current incarnation and to predetermine an excellent destiny for the future.

It is very simple to achieve! One has just to know how. And we have discussed this question a lot.

And take into account that this goal can be attained only through one's own spiritual efforts and not through participation in rituals, "prayers of saints", or anyone's prayers altogether.

Also let us not confuse prayer with meditation (sometimes these terms are used in place of each other). The main meaning of these words is the following: prayer is a request to God, which sometimes degrades into begging earthly welfare from God. But the term *meditation* denotes work of the consciousness aimed at cognition of God, which can ensure success on this Path if one is ethically and intellectually mature.

Art
and Spiritual Development
(lecture)

What is spirituality?

Some people believe that spirituality is... going to the cinema, to the theater, attending concerts of classical symphonic music, which was created, by the way, in the epoch of the Inquisition...

But in reality this word originates from the statement of Jesus Christ: "God is Spirit" (John 4:24). It concerns those processes and phenomena which *spiritualize* people, that is contribute to bringing one closer to the Divinity — in the quality of the consciousness, soul. Therefore, only those people can be called spiritual who achieved significant success on this path.

Art can and must play an important role in the process of positive evolution of consciousness. But does it always happen this way?

For example, movies that "savor" violence and killing, where it is presented as a natural way of life and is imprinted by young souls as a *norm of conduct...* — the work of creators and *distributors* of such anti-art should be considered criminal — in the face of God and humanity.

As for the example given above, to reasonable people everything is quite clear about it. But there are cases not so obvious. So the question arises: what can be the objective criteria for judging such cases?

For instance, it happens that insane people try to express themselves by the means of art! They can share their sick experience with other people very vividly! There are plenty of such cases. Let me give just one example — not so grotesque but very illustrative in this respect.

One of my acquaintances, an artist, once showed me the works of his teacher. They were pictures for wall-papers. I looked at them and asked him if his teacher was sick with schizophrenia and committed suicide? The artist was astonished and said to me that it was so indeed!

These pictures were truly awful! Their patterns affected the viewer in a weird way, causing coarse confusion of the consciousness. I hope these pictures have never been used in production. Had they appeared on room walls it would have caused much harm to people!

It also happens quite often that works of art express depressive or aggressive states of their authors! Where do they bring people who listen or view them?

There are also more simple examples, not from psychopathology. Let us recall the battles in the past century regarding abstract art! Was it good or bad? There were also hot discussions regarding rock-n-roll or even the charleston! Was it good or bad?

Always there are people who support something new. And there are others who oppose anything new. Both sides present their arguments. But what is the truth? How can one distinguish subjective factors influencing the evaluation of an innovation or of work of art — from objective ones? How can one discriminate them?

There was a person who, for the first time, spoke about the existence of objective laws of art. He was George Gurdjieff — a bright man well-known in the spiritual field.

He worked in Russia in the beginning of the twentieth century. He was born in the Caucasus, in a Greco-Armenian family. Grown up, he taught in Moscow and Saint Petersburg.

The civil war in Russia made him move abroad together with his school. His students went to different countries: some went to France, others to England, still others to the USA. And there they created branches of the school.

The literary works of Gurdjieff and of his students were published in all main European languages.

Since the early childhood Gurdjieff grew up an uncommon man. From the very beginning he chose a purpose: to learn everything that people can do. And he resolutely lived for this purpose for many years. He learned to dive, to trade, to battle, to darn carpets, to repair all kinds of home appliances existed at that time. For example, when he needed a large amount of money for organizing an expedition, he would come to the city, rent a room, and put an announcement that he repairs everything. At daytime he accepted visitors and at night mended all kinds of things: from gramophones to bicycles, umbrellas, etc. He even collected parts needed for repairing at the city scrap-heap.

Having collected the money needed for the expedition, he hired assistants and went to seek spiritual knowledge.

He visited a lot of spiritual schools, monasteries — Sufi, Christian. He managed to collect much knowledge that allowed him to develop an integral worldview and to establish his own school.

One should not idealize Gurdjieff though. Many things which he did are far from being exemplary. Many ideas of his teachings have only historical interest at present: more perfect knowledge replaced them now. However, there are certain key points in his teachings which are important today as well. And now we can use this knowledge thanks to Gurdjieff.

In particular, Gurdjieff postulated that there are objective laws of art. He did not formulate them though. At least we could not find a list of these laws in many books of his school that we read. There were only some hints. Nevertheless, Gurdjieff contributed a lot even by declaring that there are such laws. Further development of this idea of Gurdjieff allowed formulating these laws. Now we are going to discuss them in detail.

The most important principle (or law, as Gurdjieff put it) is the *necessity of following the path of refinement of the consciousness*. It is the use of this principle that can help us to become competent not only within the material world but also within the whole multidimensional universe. It allows us to achieve the Primordial Consciousness and to merge with It.

For this purpose we must, in the beginning of the learning, undergo the process of refinement on the physical plane, abandon the coarseness in which most people live.

The easiest way to do it is by means of emotional attunement with the subtlest phenomena found in nature. For example, when the morning sun rises and sends its first rays through the mist to the water, to the grass, to the flowers, to the leaves; when the first morning birds begin to sing, when fishes begin to splash in the reed and above this reed illuminated with tender morning sunlight the mist dances and floats about — so wonderfully subtle are the states that nature gives us in such moments!

I should note right away that it is impossible to establish oneself firmly in such states without learning and applying to ourselves the ethical principles suggested to us by God and without mastering the art of psychic self-regulation, which includes the ability to control one's own chakras.

One of the concepts suggested by Gurdjieff is very important for us in this regard. It is the concept of the *scale of hydrogens*. It is one of the most interesting concepts in the history of spiritual search!

What are these "hydrogens"? This term originated from alchemy. At the time of Gurdjieff, there were also schools whose knowledge was not open for everyone.

And the adherents of these schools enciphered their secret knowledge.

Mathematicians use a special language of letters. And at that time there was an alchemical language, which used the names of chemical elements for enciphering.

Probably many of us, affected by ignorant atheistic propaganda, laughed at alchemists who tried to transform lead into gold and to become rich. But in reality, by lead the alchemists called not metal but the basic state of man who has not started the spiritual practice yet. And by gold they called the perfect state of man who had succeeded on the spiritual Path. *Golden Elixir*, by the way, is that goldish Light of the Holy Spirit which we observe in the meditation *latihan* and with which we can fill our bodies.

And all those unusual reactions described by alchemists were but symbols of different stages of the spiritual transformation of man.

These are, for instance, some alchemical symbols: "carbons" are active components of reaction, "oxygens" are passive components, "nitrogens" are the third kind of components — factors like catalysts, which are needed for reaction. And "hydrogens" are those elements or states which are considered outside of the reaction. This is where the term *scale of hydrogens* originates from.

So what does the concept of the *scale of hydrogens* consist in? Its main postulate is that all substances, phenomena, states in the universe can be arranged in order according to their level of *coarseness-subtlety*. On this scale there is a place for minerals, planets, stars, different kinds of food — from corpses of animals that many people eat — to, for example, a wood strawberry. On this scale there is a place for the state of the chakras, for our emotional states, etc. That is — virtually for everything. "Hydrogens" have numerical values; this allows finding some sample states by which we can evaluate our advancement along the *scale of coarseness-subtlety*, that is, along the *scale of hydrogens*.

For example, the morning sun and its light is H-6; it is one of the most subtle phenomena in nature.

Or, take the emotions that occur in harmonious blooming of the reproductive function: sexually tinged tenderness, love for children, those manifestations which we see in plays of young animals, and the energy states peculiar to buds opening in spring — all this is H-12.

There is a very interesting state in our organisms — the energy plane of the *chitrini* meridian (its other name is *Brahmanadi*, the meridian of the Holy Spirit) — it is H-3, one of the main states of the Holy Spirit.

And H-3 is very close to H-1. H-1 corresponds to the plane of the Primordial Consciousness, the Creator.

It is absolutely impossible for a person living in the coarse states pertaining to ordinary people to change immediately to the subtlest state, to "dive" into the *depths* of the multidimensional world, to cognize the primordial plane of the universe, to cognize the Creator! It is not possible!

One can only move gradually along the *scale of hydrogens*. First one has to traverse that part of the path of refinement which exists within the material world — and only then one can "dive" into other spatial dimensions.

In some occult schools, students practice exiting from their material bodies without switching first to ethically and energetically pure nutrition (i.e. *killing-free* nutrition), without getting rid of their initial coarseness (some of them even intentionally strengthen it for the sake of suppressing other people and controlling them; this is the feature of black magic schools). If such students succeed — where do they go? They find themselves in the coarse astral plane, in hell. They find there anger, lie, fear pertain to this plane. They get confused, frightened... Moreover, they develop "friendly relations", so to say, with the representatives of that plane, very obtrusive sometimes. Many such people go mad, as a result...

Therefore, the most important principle of spiritual growth and of the spiritual art, which contributes to spiritual development, is the principle of walking the path of the refinement of the consciousness.

In the art, man can be a creator and a viewer or listener. Both these cases can provide favorable opportunities for development.

Let me draw your attention to the fact that any work of art can be assessed according to the *scale of coarseness-subtlety*.

And every high-quality work of art should be used for refining attunement. Or, at least, it has to show the way from *tamas* (that is, from the initial coarseness, dullness, ignorance) — through *rajas* (the stage of active search of the way out to the light of Truth, when man transforms from a dully suffering person into a fighting one) — to *sattva* (purity, harmony, subtlety) — and higher.

In relation to the above said, let me emphasize that on the path to Perfection one cannot skip the stage of sattva. One cannot become perfect at once, starting from tamas or rajas! One cannot "leap" over the stage of sattva! The path of refinement, development of inner harmony and the ability to love — is necessary for everyone! No one should think that "it is not for me, let *others* be engaged in this, but I will achieve Perfection in another way". No! The law of the evolution of man expounded, in particular, by Krishna in the Bhagavad Gita *consists in gradual advancement through the stages-gunas mentioned above, so that one may come then to higher stages of work on oneself.*

With the help of art one can also train energy, vigor; this corresponds to maturing at the stage of rajas. Let us take rock, for example. Non-coarse, dynamic dances of youth — who opposed them? The people of tamas, who are far from real pure energy! Opposed those who are angry about everything new, or inert, irresolute people who lack energy themselves! Had they danced rock'n'roll or similar dances in their youth, they would live their lives more actively now.

Non-coarse energy (vigor) is very needed on the spiritual Path, because it develops the *personal power*, allows one to accumulate strength that can be used for various needs, for meditative work, for example.

So, with the help of an adequate dynamic music and dynamic dance one can develop in oneself these missing qualities.

With the help of other kinds of music and dance one can master higher states: calm, inner quietness (*hesychia*).

Painting, poetry, oriental kinds of art such as ikebana, "philosophical landscapes", etc. can also be helpful in mastering these states.

Yes, one has to master calm, not energy alone; this is essential on the spiritual Path! That is, one has to become universal: to be able to relax and to be maximally active when necessary.

With the help of works of art one can also exert a directed energy influence on the audience.

There are several possibilities of that kind. One of them is icons. Many people know from their own experience that through some icons one can receive flows of subtle energies. Different icons transmit different flows — different both by their intensity and by their level of *coarseness-subtlety*. By the way, I saw icons of some pseudo-saints which radiated very coarse, devilish energies...

There are also non-icon pictures that radiate energies. Such pictures are necessarily created by a strong artist. For example, such are the paintings of Nicholas Roerich. All such paintings can be assessed according to the *scale of hydrogens*, and they can be assigned corresponding numerical values. By the way, the paintings of Roerich are rajas. On a certain stage of development, they can have a strong positive influence, but later they have no such effect.

There can be more directed influence through art — the influence not on man in the whole but on man's bioenergy structures. Through music, vocal, or dance, one can induce resonant states in a particular chakra of the listeners or viewers, or in a certain meridian. In particular, these structures can be developed simply by letting into them the vibrations coming from the artist.

For example, if we listen to a vocalist who concentrates in anahata, then our anahatas passively attune with vocalist's anahata and this produces the corresponding emotional state.

This phenomenon is called *svara*; this is a Sanskrit word. There is a book by R.Menon *Indian Music: The Magic of the Raga*. It describes svara as a mystical phenomenon, whose mechanism has not been understood yet. In fact, the mechanism of *svara* consists in work of the performer with the bioenergy structures. The performer simply moves the concentration of the consciousness into a certain chakra or other energy structure and if this is done strongly enough, then the listeners enter the resonant states.

The same mechanism works in dance when we watch a dancer who possesses *svara* mastery.

It is quite interesting that through sounds produced by musical instruments one can create resonant states in the chakras and meridians of the listeners. An example of this is the tango of Oscar Stroke, the "tango king". He empirically found this effect and created his musical compositions in such a way that all the notes in his tangos affect the vishuddha chakra, activating it. Due to this, the vishuddhas of the listeners get "overflowed"; his music evokes pungent, strong emotional states of ecstasy, joy.

Now, too, there are musicians who use no single note that can cause resonance in the head chakras. To listeners such music is relaxing, freshening, especially to people who do intellectual work.

... Spiritual seekers who have established themselves in the state of *sattva*, who have got rid of the possibility of entering coarse emotional states — such seekers can try using the method of *laya*.

There is a branch of yoga called Laya Yoga. *Laya* means disappearance, dissolution of oneself in the Harmony of the Absolute. This implies turning off the mind, which resides in the head chakra ajna, — so that the organism may begin to act not under the mind's commands but under the control of God. An example of this is spontaneous dance performed in the state of the *latihan* meditation, which is the most typical example of training in Laya Yoga.

There are other methods. For example, one can "yield to laya" one hand holding a dowsing rod and with the help of this rod discover that which cannot be seen by the eyes or heard by the ears: to get answers about ore deposits or about underground communication lines, to perform medical diagnostics, and do many other things. Dowsing is also Laya Yoga, its particular case.

In the same way, you can learn to paint — when your hand as if by itself draws a pencil or a brush. In the same way, one can learn to write texts... In all such cases the hand is controlled by some spirit, and if we deserve it, then it can be the Holy Spirit.

I mentioned about dance. There are special methods that can help learn to yield the body to *laya*. For example, if the arms are raised, then it is easier for the body to begin moving, for the backbone to bend. Then it is very easy! On the contrary, if the arms hang down, then it is difficult to begin dancing in this state.

It is the same with any direction of art where we want to apply the principle of laya: one has to know the basic methods, to be an expert in this area to some degree. For example, in order to paint, one has to know how to mix dyes, how to apply them on the canvas or paper. Of course, in order to dance, one has to know the principles of plasticity of the body. And one has to be able to hold a pen to write with it.

In regard to laya, I have to warn the readers about the non-critical attitude towards what we do in this state. The loss of critical attitude can easily make us a laughing stock. This happens when one violates the ethical principles, because the ethics is the foundation of Harmony. On the contrary, if everything is all right with ethics, then Harmony with everything and everyone including God can become perfect.

... With the help of art one can stimulate the intellectual process as well. Let us think: how to do this?

Basic Principles of Teaching Psychic Self-Regulation to Children and Adolescents (lecture)[31]

Our experience accumulated in various forms of teaching psychic self-regulation to children and teenagers allows formulating the following recommendations:

1. Dedicated ethical work, which every instructor must do on the background of teaching psychic self-regulation, must lay the foundation of morality in students.

2. Groups of students can be formed either of children only or can include adults as well. In the latter case,

---

[31] From the book [17].

the program is created for children, but parents willingly participate in such classes. One of the advantages of the second option is that it creates common interests in such families and helps to overcome separation between the parents and children.

3. One should not teach children and adolescents the exercises of work with the chakras and meridians (some basic exercises with anahata can be an exception) if there are no special medical indications for this. The reason for this is that these exercises are not compatible with alcohol consumption during or after the course. One cannot be sure that children and teenagers will observe this rule in the future.

4. The emphasis in this work has to be put not on achievement of high results, but mainly on broadening the students' horizons, on informing the students — in order to help them to choose their way of life when they grow up. Enrich the classes with esthetics and sports. One can supplement them with choreography, music, photography, paintings, tourism, ecology, literature, philosophy — depending on the competence of the instructor.

One can also enrich the classes of different profiles with the elements of psychic self-regulation.

5. One should not teach shavasana to children younger than 12 years old, because some children have difficulties coming out of deep relaxation. (Exceptions from this rule are allowed only in case of medical indications. Such sessions must be conducted by a certified physician.)

6. There can be exercises of work with the chakras and meridians used by trained physicians to treat neurological and psychiatric disorders in children. It is especially effective for correcting social disorders.

7. Most easily children and teenagers master exercises with mental images. Mastering the concentration

is usually more difficult for them. However, training them in concentration is especially important for their progress in the school. Very helpful in this respect is to exclude "killed" food (that is prepared of bodies of killed animals) from children's diet, and at the same time to increase the amounts of proteins found in milk and eggs. The same recommendation is useful in every respect for all people without exception.

8. An interesting positive effect can be achieved if children are present (but do not participate on equal rights) on out-of-town classes of groups where their parents study. If there is no obtrusive attitude towards them, children turn on the important mechanism of training — imitation. They learn a careful attitude towards nature, as well as towards any manifestation of life; they master skills of life in a tent, building a fire and preparation of food on it, learn discipline (waking up early in the morning, morning exercises, morning bathing, etc.), learn to see the beauty of nature and attune to it, easily master exercises for tempering the body, for example, they insist on participation in *winter swimming* together with adults.

Regarding the practice of *winter swimming* for children, let me note the following: this method helps to increase the range of temperatures comfortable for the body for the whole life; it "tempers" the body. Yet it must be used under the following conditions:

1. Fully voluntary attitude of the child, with no persuasion from adults: the children themselves know best when they are ready for it;

2. Favorable emotional state of all present adults;

3. Making no attempts to treat with *winter swimming* (as well as with showers of cold water) children who are weakened by prolonged illnesses.

Winter swimming as a medical procedure is effective for treatment of some local disease processes in those children who are in general full of health. The healing mechanism in this case is bioenergetic stress in response to "cold impact". But in the body weakened by a prolonged illness there is no that potential of energy which can turn on the needed energy process.

In such cases, the opposite is effective — for example, hot bathes, saunas [64].

Art of Being Happy
(forest lecture for film)

The ability to attune emotionally to the BEAUTY and SUBTLETY of living nature allows us to gain inner harmony, which is essential for finding HAPPINESS IN LIFE. This is also one of the most important components of spiritual development.

This BEAUTY is an element of God's Creation.

It is important to understand this! Only if we have learned to love His Creation, can we fall in love with the Creator Himself! And without such a sincere love — is it possible to be happy?

Love necessarily has to be mutual! God's love alone is not enough for being happy! No, we have to strive to become not *loved* but *loving*! And our love must not be an egotistic parody of true love (I mean primitive sexual desires that non-spiritual people call by the word *love*). No, it must be an aspiration to GIVE ONESELF TO HIM!

Love for God begins with the desire to cognize Him — first only with the mind — and then in all fullness — so that the emotions of my love merge with the emotions of His love! And then, gradually, comes the fullness of Mergence — when one merges with Him as a consciousness developed in the process of searching Him and serving Him!

... Also it is very important to have like-minded friends on this Path. It is much easier to be happy of doing creative work if one works in a spiritual group, in a community, even a little one!

Morally healthy people feel satisfaction when they GIVE knowledge, skills, all of themselves — to others, seeking to make others happy!

It is thanks to this process of giving oneself and seeing its positive results that such a person feels happy!

What does one need to do to find good friends? — One needs just to offer oneself: to show to others one's usefulness! And then let everyone share with others what he or she knows and can do!

... For happiness, it is also important to have good health.

What does good health depend on?

There is an opinion that our suffering and calamities are caused by the sin committed by Adam and Eve... This ill fantasy is even called by a special term — *the original sin*... I suggest viewing this opinion as a sign of feeblemindedness of those who believe it, say nothing of those who preach this idea...

Some people blame doctors for diseases, blame the contamination of the environment — or blame others — those who made me feel stressed or be nervous...

No, it is only we who are to be blamed for our troubles!

It is hard to understand this for those who are ignorant in religious philosophy! Yet the truth is that these problems are caused by God Who loves us and through them points out our inadequacy to us: the inadequacy to what He wants us to be!

In simple terms, one can say that if we do unjustified harm to other beings — we program similar situations in our own life, in our own destiny — and this time we will be the victims. This is called the *law of karma*

— the law of destiny formation. In this way God teaches us not to do evil deeds, teaches us to be compassionate to the pain of others — He teaches us through our own pain.

The operation of the *law of karma* is not limited by the time of one incarnation; its effect manifests itself in the next lives as well... This is why, in particular, sick children are born...

One may ask: why does He need this? Why does He need us to be good — as He sees it?

We discussed this subject — the meaning of human life on the Earth — in every book published by us. Now I will only say briefly that we are particles of the evolving universal Consciousness, which is called the Absolute. It is in our bodies, in particular, that the Evolution of the Absolute takes place! This is why He values every soul so much! This is why He watches everyone and all the time tries to correct, to help everyone — except for those who proved to be completely hopeless; He sends such souls to hell — to the "cesspool" of the Evolution...

... So, in order to control one's own destiny, one has to learn the rules of life suggested to us by our Creator. He gave these rules to us through His Messiahs and prophets.

In order to fulfill these rules, one has to learn to control one's own emotions.

We have to accustom ourselves to living in subtle and pure emotional states — independent of the circumstances! Then we will be pleasant to friends; then we will ensure the health both of the body and soul; then we will achieve paradise or even higher abodes!

And coarse emotions like anger, irritation, envy, jealousy and other similar states are not only unpleasant and destructive for one's own health and for the health of others, but they also predetermine one's life in hell after the death of the body!

How can one learn to control one's own emotions? This is described in detail in our books and demonstrated in our films. Now I will mention only that the correct formation of the emotional sphere is based on the development of the spiritual heart.

The spiritual heart, which is located initially in the chakra anahata and begins its growth from this chakra, is a bio-energetical organ that generates subtle positive emotions of love.

Many Divine Teachers including Jesus Christ taught about the development of the spiritual heart.

It is thanks to its development that we can gain health, find good friends, and approach by the state of the soul that state in which God lives — the state of God in the aspect of the Holy Spirit and the state of God in the aspect of the Creator!

It is through this that God becomes a Reality that we cognize!

... I can give myself as an example. I am completely healthy despite being more than 60 years old. Moreover, my body has been growing younger since sometime now! How old, do you think, my body looks?... Forty years? Or maybe even thirty?

When my body was 59 years old, I heard how passers-by said: "He is so young — but wears a beard already!"...

I feel young, vigorous — and mature! I always live in a calm, pure, joyful state!

For a long time, I have not felt anger, irritation, envy, sorrow, anxiety, fear, and so on! I have been living and live now without anger and desire to revenge myself even on those who years ago tried to kill me; after this incident, I was dying painfully half a year and two times was in the state of clinical death. I do not feel anger, fear, and desire to revenge also on those who threatened me to "burn me alive" for my books — the books about God, about the joy of cognition of Him.

Moreover, I became so close to God that I can freely converse with Him. And I can fill my body with Him.

Do we all want to live like this?

If yes, then let us walk this well-explored Path which was paved for everyone who wants to walk it!

* * *

On places like this, it is very good to meditate, to merge with the subtlety of the morning beauty of nature, with the subtlety of the Holy Spirits — our Divine Teachers, Who control our destinies...

We necessarily have to master this if we decide to walk the spiritual Path, that is the Path of development of oneself, the Path of love for the Creation and the Creator, the Path of searching for Him — Whom we have to find and cognize!

For this purpose, one also has to read books about Him, about the Path to Him.

Many people go to temples and participate there in rituals. This can help in the beginning if one does not get infected there by the ideology of hatred from evil people. Unfortunately this happens quite often... But in general, taking part in public worship services helps beginners to take their attention away from the objects of the material world...

And what does one have to do then? — one has to understand that God is present in temples no more than outside of them. And it is not in a crowd of praying people but in the situation of being one-to-one with God, in solitude in nature — that we can feel the blissful TOUCHES of God, can begin to HEAR His thoughts directed to us and to learn to SEE the Divine Teachers — Holy Spirits, to EMBRACE Them, to enter into Their non-material bodies, to MERGE with Them...

... What do many people in Russia do when they stay in nature? They drink alcohol, inject heroin, kill and maim living beings, leave all kinds of garbage on the places where they stay, defile the QUIETNESS of nature with loud sounds of radio or CD players, they themselves yell...

It is obvious that this way of behaving brings one closer to hell rather than to the happiness of the cognition of God...

... For cognition of God and for one's own development, it is very important to master the state of INNER QUIETNESS. In this state one can know the BLISS OF CALM and QUIETNESS found in the Abode of the Creator...

Singing of birds, rustling of reed or leaves of trees do not interfere in this process but make the QUIETNESS OF DAWN more vivid, more bright emotionally!

Yet, the feeling of the beauty of nature in all its fullness can be achieved only by a well-prepared spiritual seeker. And only such a seeker can cognize the Creator and His Representatives — Holy Spirits. One has to prepare oneself for this, both in the intellectual-ethical aspect and through cleansing and development of the bioenergetical structures of the organism — the chakras and meridians.

... Also one can collect edible gifts of nature. They are mushrooms, berries, various herbs. They can be used for food right now or stored for future use.

For example, instead of tea one can brew various herbs. One can also dry herbs for brewing them in winter.

For making herb tea, one can use mint, fireweed, leaves of currant in autumn — when the plant does not need them. If you find a fallen birch — you can collect and dry leaves from it. Conifer needles and young cones that fall from coniferous trees are also suitable for brewing. (But one should avoid making too strong brewing of them, because our human stomachs are unused to high concentration of resin — unlike stomachs of wood grouses; conifer needles are one of the main kinds of food of wood grouses).

Or take, for example, nettle. Many people hate it because it stings. But it stings because these people do not eat nettle! Nettle is both delicious, when young, and possesses important medicinal properties: it stimulates the immune system of the organism, helping, in particular, to get rid of many diseases!

One can dry it for winter — and brew it then.

One can also use it in this way: wash nettle, chop it into pieces, put in boiling water, boil for a minute, allow to cool a little, and then eat with mayonnaise! It is very delicious!

In a similar way, one can store other plants: goutweed, fern dryopteris. One can dry for winter even common wood sorrel — and then use it for cooking soups.

One can add to meals other herbs uncooked: garden angelica, coltsfoot, and even young shoots of fireweed (grown-up, they become bitter).

We also store forest berries with sugar: cowberries, cranberries, raspberries, bilberries — in the form of slightly boiled jam.

We make honey of flowers of bird-cherry tree or meadowsweet. How? I will describe to you.

One has to collect flowers, fill with them large saucepots, fill these saucepots also with cold water (water must not be hot to allow insects that were accidentally collected with flowers to escape), then bring water to a boil, and set aside for the night.

Next day, squeeze the flowers and discard them. Strain the liquid and pour it into saucepots filling them to 2/3 of the volume. Bring to a boil and add sugar so that it fills the remaining 1/3 of the volume. Stir to allow sugar to dissolve, bring again to a boil, and pour into hot jars that were sterilized with boiling water. Put on hermetic caps.

In this way, we make very delicious and good-for-health honey!

As for mushrooms, we use them for food all year round. In home we store and eat salted mushrooms. During our camping in the forest, when no new mushrooms grow, we use dried mushrooms. Dried mushrooms are lightweight; therefore, it is convenient to carry them in backpacks and then to boil or even to fry them in a camping pot on a fire.

How to dry mushrooms?

For this purpose one needs a mushroom dryer. If one dries mushrooms on a fire, the dryer can be made collapsible so that it is convenient to put it into a backpack: for example, it can be made of two wide stripes of roofing iron. Such a dryer must have a bottom, otherwise mushrooms become sooty. For drying, we skewer mushrooms on spits made of steel wire.

Edible mushrooms grow virtually everywhere: in the tundra, in the forest, in the mountains, in the steppe. They are not only delicious but also provide us with important proteins. The testimony to this is our own health: we have been using mushrooms for food for many years! And this allows us not only to survive in the conditions of financial insufficiency, but also to BE HAPPY!

One can even fry mushrooms on a fire, putting them on a twig. First one has to warm the mushroom to the state when it produces juice. Then put some salt onto it: the salt sticks to the juice and does not fall off. And then one just needs to boil the mushroom in its own juice. Thus it becomes very delicious!

… In the season when no mushrooms grow in the forest, we fry cheese sandwiches on a fire. For this purpose, one can use special forks like this. Of course, we never make such forks by cutting living branches from trees. We use dry branches. Try it! It is also very delicious!

... This is the way we live — in unceasing TRUE joy!

Why do I stress the word TRUE? — because joy is not only about fried mushrooms and sandwiches! But one has to bring all the life into HARMONY WITH GOD. Namely one has to live:

— without causing harm to others, when possible,

— constantly developing oneself spiritually,

— living under the guidance of God,

— giving to others all the good that one can share!

I wish you success on this Path!

Sattva of Mists
(forest lecture for film)

Peace to you, friends!

Did you like this beauty? Have you managed to *experience* it, to *attune* to it, to *merge* with it?

... Once we met near a forest lake a professional photographer and for a long time admired together with him a similar mist, which was dancing gently in the rays of the rising sun...

He said to us, "Having seen *this*, I am ready now to die!"

His emotion (the emotion of an atheist, unfortunately) was understandable for us! But would it be right to end the incarnation, having known this *super beauty* of the Creation, but have not known the Creator?

... Let us think together: what is the meaning of human life?

This is not at all a pseudo-question, that is, the question to which there is no answer, as it was claimed by some materialistic philosophers!

No, there is a complete answer to this question — an answer from the standpoint of the modern biological science, the science about LIFE. I am going to talk with you about this as a scientist-biologist, who, together with colleagues, dedicated our lives to studying this question.

To start with, one can formulate the answer as the following: the meaning of life consists in development of oneself as a soul, as a consciousness.

And now let us talk about this in more detail. In particular, one has to answer the following questions: for what reason it is needed? For what reason one has to develop oneself? For what reason one has to become better?

First of all, one has to destroy in oneself the false religious ideas asserting that we are separated from God by an impassable abyss and that God is just a terrible Judge, Who punishes us, sinners. And that the highest and almost unrealizable dream of man is the dream of going to paradise... And that, in order to make this happen, one has to dedicate one's life only to begging zealously forgiveness from God (they call this "praying") and to participation in certain rituals; there is also a point of view that for this purpose one also has to torture and kill "infidels" and "heretics"...

But in reality all this is not true.

We are not separate from God. To make it more clear, we have to clarify the meaning of the word *God*: because among people there is no common understanding even in this; people understand this word differently.

This word can mean *Absolute* — that is, *Absolutely Everything*: the Creator coessential with His multidimensional Creation. And every one of us is His integral part, as for example, a blood cell has a certain freedom inside the body, where it lives and which it serves; but, at the same time, it is a part of this body.

The other meaning of the word *God* is the Creator, the Primordial Consciousness, Which is called also God-the-Father and by other names. He abides in the very *depth* of the multidimensional Absolute. He is infinite. He fills with Himself the immense universal space. He is present inside our bodies. Yet, He exists in the *other dimension of space* — in relation to those dimensions where most of us live.

He is not cognizable for people who seek Him in a wrong place: in the sky, in other planets, etc.

But He is cognizable for those who follow His directions about how we should live on the Earth, those who really love their Creator, who fall in love with Him, who seek to become similar to Him by growing themselves as love...

"God is Love," — taught Jesus Christ!

This means, in particular, that in order to become closer to Him in the state of the soul, we have to grow ourselves as love.

And those who grow themselves as coarseness, hatred, disdain, and haughtiness towards other manifestations of the Life of the Absolute — those go to hell. Hell is the most coarse spatial dimension, the place inhabited by souls who developed in themselves the qualities opposite of the qualities of the Primordial Consciousness.

On the contrary, paradise is a subtle spatial dimension, the place where live souls who developed themselves on the path of subtlety, tenderness, care, caress: that is, on the path of love.

But *how* does one develop oneself on the path of subtlety?

The point is that our *emotional states* are the states of ours as consciousnesses, as souls. And we can accustom ourselves to living in certain emotional states: more coarse or more subtle. By this we predetermine our place in the multidimensional Absolute: hell, paradise, the Abode of the Creator...

This is what Jesus Christ taught to His disciples. And this part of His Teaching was described by a personal disciple of Jesus — Philip the Apostle in His Gospel.

Philip writes that people who developed themselves in the right direction are accepted by the Creator in His Abode; they merge by the developed consciousnesses into Him, become His integral Parts.[32]

And then Those, Who have attained this, can come out from the Abode with a Part of Themselves in order to help the embodied people. Coming out thus, They manifest Themselves as Holy Spirits. (These *Manifestations* of the Creator are called, in the aggregate sense, the Holy Spirit).

Sometimes They, with the same purpose, even incarnate again in human bodies...

Such an incarnation of God in a human body is called, in different languages, — Messiah, Christ, Avatar.

* * *

What does one have to do in order to progress in this direction? This is also described in the Teaching of Jesus Christ and in the Teachings of other Divine Teachers.[33]

First, one has to accept the principle of not causing harm as much as possible: not causing harm to other embodied beings.

We cause such harm not only by killing or by causing physical pain. We cause harm by slandering, by deceiving in other ways, by stealing, by treating others with-

---

[32] [6,11].
[33] [6,11].

out due respect, by backbiting, by being jealous, by refusing to help without reason, and even by being in coarse emotional states! With our emotions we create energy fields — favorable or unfavorable for other beings! Therefore, our "internal" state is not our "internal affair"!

The second step is mastering volitional regulation of own emotions. This is called the art of *psychic self-regulation*. And this is not difficult if one knows *how* to do this.

Efficient control of the emotional sphere can be achieved only through mastering the functions of the chakras, for it is the chakras — bioenergy organs — which determine our psychic states, our emotions, our physical and mental abilities, etc.

And the level of the development of the chakras and the level of their energetic purity determine, to a great extent, one's health...

All chakras and main meridians of the organism have to be pure and functioning properly. The main chakra is anahata. It is in this chakra that the *spiritual heart* can grow (this part of the multidimensional organism is the most important on the spiritual Path). Because it is only the *development of the spiritual heart* that allows us to transform ourselves into Love, to grow to the state where we receive the right to become closer to the Creator and to enter His Abode.

All this was described by us in detail in the books and films created by our research group.

And in no case should one try to use drugs with "mystical" purposes, for example, for getting into *other worlds!* You will get into the embrace of hellish beings; you will destroy the body and soul! Moreover, one should not aspire to get into the *other worlds*, but into the Abode of the Creator! And for this purpose, there are other methods! We have studied these methods, described them, and even demonstrated in our films.

* * *

There is an important and true principle of Islam: "There is no God besides (one) God!" This short formula reflects the principle of *monotheism*. In relation to this, it is appropriate to consider whether there is a contradiction between this principle and that which I said before.

Let us consider this subject in relation to the two meanings of the word *God* mentioned before.

What concerns the first meaning (God as the Absolute) — everything is clear about it: the Absolute is One Universal Living Organism, and there can be no other one — this follows even from the definition of this concept.

What concerns the second meaning (God as the Creator, God-the-Father, the Primordial Consciousness) — again we have to abandon the false and primitive notions of God-the-Father as of an old man sitting on a cloud! This lie about God is presented to many people as, allegedly,... Christianity! However, this is a feature of the most primitive paganism, i.e. foolish and false "folk" beliefs, which oppose the true scientific knowledge!

In reality, the Creator is as infinite as the Absolute. He is truly *akbar*, that is, great, immense, infinite!

And this formula of Islam: "*Allah akbar!*" directly stimulates *reasonable* followers to study the INFINITE GREATNESS OF THE CREATOR, and — through this — to *direct quantitative growth of souls*, to worshipping Him, to "sinking" with the consciousness in the Boundless Ocean of the *Divine* Consciousness!

The Creator is the *deepest* (in the sense of the multidimensionality of space) and *fundamental* Part of the Absolute. He calls Himself — the *Heart of the Absolute* (the word *Heart* here means not a pulsating anatomical organ but the Spiritual Heart, the most Essential Part).

The criterion of one's belongingness to this *Heart of the Absolute* is one's abiding in It constantly. At that, All Who abide *there* live in a *mutually dissolved, merged* state. That is, the *Heart of the Absolute* is indeed one Structure common for the entire Absolute.

Their Individualities are restored when They come out with a Part of Themselves from this One *Heart of the Absolute*.

(This is not just my or someone else's fantasies: all this can be observed directly if one deserves it.

And we observe this!)

In other words, the Creator is *One* but consists of *Many*. And these *Many* are constantly supplemented by Those newly coming into the Creator and enriching Him with Themselves.

This constitutes the *Life* of the Universal Organism called the *Absolute*; this constitutes Its Evolution.

And if we love God, we have to strive to participate in this process by developing ourselves and by helping others in this.

Love for God is similar to love between two people: it implies striving for cognition of the beloved, striving for mergence with Him, striving to give oneself to Him.

The opposite of this is pseudo-love, which some perverted people call "love". It consists of *wanting* something from the object of one's lust (that is, primitive egoistic passion) and the desire to *possess* individually this object...

* * *

So, this constitutes the highest *meaning of our lives*. And now we have to clarify some methodological details.

The love for God necessarily implies studying Him. Without knowing the object of our love, we cannot love Him in all fullness!

Initial knowledge about God can be gained from books, from lectures, or from conversations with other people. And it is good that beginners in religion seek like-minded people, seek conversations with them, in particular, during divine services, religious meetings, which are often accompanied by rituals.

During rituals, the mind, which usually wanders from one petty thought to another, gets distracted from such wandering and becomes calm — and this allows one to receive the first experience of mystical *touches* by which *non-incarnate beings* try to draw our attention. And in response to questions arising in us in such moments, we may receive answers coming as if from "nowhere".

(By the way, they are not necessarily answers and touches from Divine Teachers — the Holy Spirits; they can be signs from lesser developed souls or representatives of hell: it depends on the ethical status of the *object* of such influence).

But then — after some time passes — it will be good if a positively developed seeker enters on the next, third stage of studying God — outside of material temples, on the expanse of the Creation: in fields, woods, steppe, water expanse — where one can expand and flood with the spiritual heart to all sides — in the environment favorable for this! With the help of such possibilities, one can grow oneself quite quickly as a spiritual heart to the size of kilometers and then — to the size of hundreds and thousands of kilometers...

It is in such conditions that we learn to love not only the living nature with all its best manifestations, but also — through this — its Creator. It is not possible to fall in love with the Creator without loving first His Creation!

It is in these conditions and through relationships with our companions that we learn in the best way the true ethics and love-care!

Here we learn also to overcome difficulties, gain the necessary strength of consciousnesses and bodies.

Here we have the best opportunity for developing correctly the emotional sphere through attunement with the *beauty* of living nature.

Moreover, by studying the energies of the surrounding space, by finding positive and negative *places of power*, by training oneself through this in practical studying of the principal differences inside multidimensional space — we gradually gain insight about the structure of the Absolute.

And on many positive *places of power* we find for ourselves the possibility of direct and easy communication — verbal and visual — with the Representatives of the Holy Spirit, Who become our Divine Teachers and guide us further into Their Abode: into the Abode of the Creator.

This direction of research is one of the branches of ecology — the science about relationships of an organism with its environment. It is called *ecological psychology* (or *ecopsychology*).

* * *

Let me repeat once again:

By reading books, attaining lectures and religious meetings, we receive the opportunity to get some preliminary information (true or false) about God.

By the way, what do I mean by false information about God? For example, that He is not the boundless Ocean of Consciousness, but a flying person, very bloodthirsty in some sects, and that He is our servant, who has to satisfy all our earthly whims… And therefore, all we need to do is to keep pestering Him with our requests: "Lord, give! Lord, give!…"

Yet, this is a disgusting lie! True love for anyone including God is not *wanting from* them! Love is, first of all, sincere aspiration to give oneself to serve for the good of the Beloved!

And God is ready to bring closer to Him not those who achieved "perfection" in development of parasitic qualities in themselves, but those who renounce personal interests and serve Him selflessly!

* * *

Let us consider the further possibilities of spiritual development of man.

Mastering the art of psychic self-regulation in classes, which can be conducted in home or in other conditions, allows one to make oneself better and to prepare oneself for really serious spiritual work — that is, for the state when one possesses not *faith* but *knowledge* about God!

Yet, direct cognition of God and living communication with Him-Teacher becomes really and fully possible only in ecopsychological work.

It is only on the various *places of power* in nature that one receives the opportunity for full development of the chakras and meridians, and for curing all physical diseases, for spreading the spiritual heart outside the body, and for further learning from concrete Representatives of the Creator, Whom one hears and sees well; and then living communication with Them becomes similar in its easiness to communication with embodied people!

And it is absolutely impossible to achieve this inside buildings!

It is also impossible — other than on corresponding *places of power* — to cognize paradise (as a place of living) during life in the material body and master living in it! And it is even more impossible to master many variations of entering the Abode of the Creator, to learn not only to live in it but also to come out from it!

* * *

And the last advice to help you to avoid being mistaken: let us not forget the words from the New Testament: "God is *Light*, and in Him there is no darkness at all" (1 John 1:5). Yes, the Representatives of the Creator, when coming to us, assume Forms consisting of the subtlest white *Light*, because the Consciousness of the Creator and of Holy Spirits is the *most subtle* state of all existing in the universe.

And only those souls can contemplate Him, communicate with Him directly, who have become closer to Him on the path of subtlety. It can be done, in particular, through attunement with similar mists permeated with the light of the tender morning sun!

(Let me remind you that about all this you can read, hear, and see in our books and films).

I wish you success on this Path!

Our Creator is very close to us — inside and outside our bodies, and we just have to make the right efforts in order to become convinced of this, to cognize Him... and merge with Him!

Jesus, in particular, said (this is written in *The Book of Jesus* by Ben Cullen) that the distance from every one of us to the Creator is not larger than the thickness of the finest paper. And this is true indeed: this also becomes obvious on corresponding *places of power* within the work on the program of ecopsychology!

Jesus also said about this the following: "Blessed are the pure in heart, for they shall see God" (Matt 5:8).

And Krishna in the Bhagavad Gita (11:54) said the same: "Only love can contemplate Me in My innermost Essence and merge with Me".

"The most important thing is a *loving heart*. The first meditation is the meditation of *love*; in it you should settle your heart aspiring to the good of all beings," — these words are from the preaching of Gautama Buddha.

The same was said by Divine Teachers through the *Living Ethics* of Agni Yoga: "First, one has to accustom oneself to subtlety of emotions, in order to fill the spirit with the aspiration for the world of beauty. In this way, the conventional concept of the standard (of beautiness) is replaced with true understanding of the *beauty*...

"Subtlety of emotions has to be introduced into life.

"In forest seek My instructions.

"In mountains listen to My call.

"In murmuring of a brook listen to My whispering.

"Love Me — and your power will grow with *love*!

"The entire world is God's Body. And My *Heart* is *Home* for you."

The same is taught by our Contemporary, Avatar Sathya Sai Baba: "There is nothing in the world that is not a Manifestation of God. Do not doubt that the entire cosmos is pervaded with God and that everything (existing) is contained in Him. There is not a single atom in the universe which is not permeated with the Divine!

"I tell you about Love; I guide you on the Path of Love.

"The *heart* is the most important of everything!

"... The destiny of man is to go from the human to the Divine.

"The purpose of life is to grow in love, to multiply this love, and to merge with God, Who is Love itself; and the best way to achieve this is by serving. There is no better means for getting rid of egoism than service.

"We have to... *love* until we become Love ourselves and merge with God Who is Love. Everything is that easy.

"God is Love, and the quickest and straightest path to Him goes through love in action, through selfless service to people.

"Seek Him with your *heart* and not with the eyes directed at the outer." [34]

Sattva of Spring (introduction to film)

Peace to you, friends!

Now we are going to saturate you with subtle beauty!

What for? The point is that this is one of the most important methods of spiritual work.

From the evolutionary standpoint everyone starts their personal history in paradise. It will be more clear if you study the scheme for studying the structure of the Absolute[35]. Souls get formed and start developing in paradise. They are not human souls yet; they are germs of human souls that go through the initial stages of their evolution in vegetal and then in animal bodies.

But having reached after many such incarnations the possibility to become humans, we, for some reason, begin to develop attachments to material objects and grow egocentrism in ourselves. It gets manifested as arrogance, contemptuous attitude towards other living beings, and so on.

Since it is impossible to satisfy completely the vicious desires of possessing the objects of our longing, it provokes in us persistent negative emotions and results in formation of such qualities as irritation, angriness, jealousy, touchiness, and so on.

In this way most of people lose paradise...

---

[34] [6,11].
[35] See in the end of this book.

... And souls living in paradise are those who accustomed themselves to pure, subtle, loving, tender states of consciousness.

And hell is the destiny of coarse people, who got used to living during their life in the physical body in coarse emotional states.

The paradisiacal states are called sometimes sattvic, the hellish states — tamasic, and the intermediate — rajasic.

So, to come back to paradise — once we come to know about these laws — we have to master psychical self-regulation with the purpose of rooting out all coarse states in ourselves and cultivating subtle states by all means.

More details about the most efficient methods of psychical self-regulation can be found in our books. And now — one of the most important methods of psychical self-regulation — *attunement to the Beautiful*!

We find the beautiful, first of all, in living nature.

... Moreover, it is possible to cognize God in the aspect of the Creator only from sattva — from the paradisiacal state of the soul.

The Creator is the most subtle part of the Universal Consciousness!

And sattva is the closest to the Divinity state of the soul!

God is really cognizable for people who follow this knowledge!

And He is indeed incognizable for those existing in the gunas tamas and rajas!

... And another very important point — God is Love! And one can approach Him only through cultivating in oneself the emotions of love — first for the sattvic beings and phenomena, and then for Him, for God.

So, let us begin immersing into sattva by attuning to it, merging with it, becoming it!...

Keys to the Secrets of Life.
Achievement of Immortality
(forest lecture for film)

Why do we live on the Earth? What is the meaning of our lives?

From the history of philosophy, we know some unsuccessful attempts to find answers to these questions.

For example, the founders of existentialism asserted that the life of every one of us on the Earth is nothing more than a chance event. Moreover, no one of us gave permission to live here. They lamented the life on the Earth and regarded suicide as the only correct way out of this situation.

They were atheists.

But many contemporary believers, people who believe in the existence of God, never ask this question at all. They... just dream about earthly well-being and about avoiding going to hell after the death of the body... And what does one have to do for this? They believe one has to participate in various religious rituals, to repent one's real and imaginary sins, also to pray — which means, first of all, to beg salvation from hell from God or from various deities and saints invented by particular religious movements.

This kind of absurdity was always preached in such religious movements. Priests instilled in the minds of their "flock" the ideas about wrathful God who punishes people; therefore, one has to fear Him! And we, priests, are your intercessors: we "pray" God to forgive you and teach you how to "pray" in the right way...

Why do I call such a form of pseudo-religiosity — absurdity? Because in reality, we, according to the Will of God, have to DEVELOP OURSELVES as souls in accordance with His Teachings — rather than moaning to Him about our sinfulness! And we should not beg earthly favors from Him but we have to strive to become "perfect as our Heavenly Father is perfect" — as Jesus Christ commanded!

And another point: is it fear that helps to establish good relationships? No! It is love! It is not by chance that Jesus and all other Divine Teachers teach us not to be afraid, not to hate, but to LOVE!

There is another attempt to explain the meaning of our lives. It is also a wrong one, though of a higher level. I consider it to be of a higher level because it has some positive meaning, though quite little. According to it, we appeared on the Earth because God was bored of being alone in His Abode... and thus decided to divide a part of Himself into small particles — souls. For what? Just for fun, just to be able to look from the outside at Himself, to entertain Himself in this way... And what do we need to do then? We just need to become aware of our coessentiality with Him.

How should we regard these naive ideas?

They slightly resemble the truth... though in a very poor way!

Why poor? Because this tale misses the DESCRIPTION OF GOD. Therefore, it does not provide even a hint as to where one has to seek God in order to realize this coessentiality with Him...

The reason for this kind of misunderstanding is that the majority of the embodied people are psychogenetically young souls, who are not capable of comprehending with the mind such phenomena as the multidimensionality of space, for example. And without correct understanding of this concept, one cannot understand the essence of God and the way of cognition of Him.

We discussed this subject in our books; please read them! Now I am going just to say briefly that the spatial dimensions are strata of the Absolute, which differ among themselves by the levels of the *coarseness-subtlety* scale.

The Creator (or God-the-Father, the Primordial Consciousness, Ishvara, Tao, Allah and so on — He may be called differently in different human languages) is the most subtle Part of the Absolute — Its MAIN Part, which is INFINITE in size and exists ETERNALLY.

On the other end of the *coarseness-subtlety* scale, there is hell — the abode of the most despising souls: aggressive, malicious, consisting of dark energies.

* * *

In reality, individual souls originated not as particles of the Primordial Consciousness, but as particles of another component of the Absolute — so-called protopurusha.

The task of these souls (including everyone of us) is to advance in their development to the Primordial Consciousness, the Creator.

It will be more clear to you if you look at the scheme for studying the structure of the Absolute, which shows in particular the dynamics of processes within the Absolute.

In the end, souls who have achieved Perfection infuse into the Creator and thus enrich Him with themselves. Having settled forever in the Abode of the Creator and living now in Mergence with Him as His integral Parts, these Divine Souls continue to work by providing help to other evolving beings. In the world of embodied people, They appear as Representatives of the Creator, Who are called Holy Spirits (in the aggregate sense, They are called the Holy Spirit).

This constitutes the meaning of the existence of the entire Creation, including the meaning of our lives and the lives of all beings!

As for those who do not follow this path, who on the contrary develop in themselves coarseness, aggressiveness, cruelty — their destiny is hell.

The information I am telling you now was not invented by me. No, this knowledge was imparted to people by God; the Holy Spirits taught this knowledge to embodied people in the past and teach it now.

Among such Teachers we know, in particular, Thoth-the-Atlantean (He was Hermes Trismegistus in His next Divine Incarnation), Pythagoras, Krishna, Gautama Buddha, Jesus Christ, the Divine Teachers of later epochs and our Contemporaries. (This information is presented most fully in our book *Classics of Spiritual Philosophy and the Present*).

* * *

So, what do we need to do in order to advance successfully to our true and ultimate Goal?

We must:

— study the will of God and aspire to ethical purity,

— develop ourselves intellectually,

— take care about the energetic purity and health of the organism, strive to make it as pure as possible,

— master the methods of psychical self-regulation which allow one, in particular, to transform oneself into a growing spiritual heart and to refine oneself as a consciousness. Invulnerability of the consciousness, by the way, is its inability to leave subtle and pure states, independent of the circumstances,

then we must:

— gain the ability to live in the state of inner quietness (hesychia), because successful meditative work can be performed only against such a background,

— then one has to develop oneself quantitatively (as a consciousness); an individual consciousness can be grown to giant sizes — thousands or million times larger than the size of the human body,

— then one needs to explore the structure of the Absolute with the developed consciousness, to settle in more and more subtle strata of the Absolute up to the Abode of the Creator,

— and to help others on this Path.

Let me note right away that attempts to use drugs with the purpose of going to "other worlds" are wrong: they result in destruction of the health both of the body and of the consciousness.

Probably, some points mentioned above need to be commented.

For example, one may say: "Now everything is clear to me! Now I will go to God! I will learn to meditate! Now I understand that there is no need to finish school, there is no need to go to university!" Yet, this would be a wrong conclusion. All forms of education not only enrich us with various information, but they also develop the THINKING FUNCTION OF THE CONSCIOUSNESS. And without a well-developed intellect, one cannot traverse the entire Path: one will UNAVOIDABLY go astray from it and will be lost.

* * *

As for avoiding contamination of the organism and cleansing it, the following advice is helpful. One needs:

— to wash the body daily with soap, if possible,

— to eat food containing a complete set of necessary amino-acids and vitamins; food cooked of bodies of killed animals has to be excluded completely: such a nutrition is wrong from the ethical standpoint and from the energetic standpoint as well, because it prevents the refinement of the consciousness and causes manifestations of gout and other diseases,

also one needs:

— to avoid close emotional relationships with energetically coarse people; such contacts are especially unfavorable in sexual relations,

— one needs to be in nature often, especially in the morning and evening; attunement of the consciousness with the subtle beauty of nature is a powerful purifier of the soul; we demonstrated this in our previous films,

— there are also special techniques of Raja Yoga which allow one to achieve quickly the purity of the energy structures of the organism, that is the chakras and meridians,

— and then, on the stage of Buddhi Yoga, one continues the work on removing bad energies from the organism and on MAKING THE CELLS OF THE BODY DIVINE.

* * *

By the way, what is the difference between Raja Yoga and Buddhi Yoga?

Raja Yoga is the stage of cleansing the organism and further self-development within the physical body and the energy cocoon around the body.

When everything necessary is done on this stage — one can continue the work on the stage of Buddhi Yoga, that is the work on the development of oneself as a consciousness outside the body and the *cocoon*. It is the methods of Buddhi Yoga that help one to become a Mahatma — a Great Atman. They also allow one to enter the Abode of the Creator — provided one knows how to do it and the Creator allows entering. After that, one continues to live in the Abode in the state of ETERNAL MERGENCE WITH THE CREATOR.

It is important to understand that one can exit from the physical body into the Divine strata of the Absolute only if the body is cleansed to the necessary level of purity. If the body is contaminated with coarse energies, then one can exit from it only into coarse non-material dimensions. Therefore, it is inadvisable to make attempts to go outside the body if it hasn't been cleansed well enough.

The methods of refinement and growing of the consciousness, increasing its ability of acting in the non-material worlds, also the methods of direct exploration of the multidimensional Absolute are called meditations. There are many of them. Of the higher meditations described in the ancient literary sources, one can mention the meditation *Cross* which Jesus Christ taught to His closest Disciples (this meditation is mentioned by Philip the Apostle in His Gospel), the meditation *Pyramid* described by Thoth-the-Atlantean, the meditation of Krishna from the Bhagavad Gita *Supporting all living beings with the hands of love*, meditation of Lao Tse *Ocean*. (You may read about them in the book *Classics of Spiritual Philosophy and the Present*). Of course, in order to perform these meditations one needs serious preparatory training.

By the way, the ability of the consciousness which is free from the material body (though the body, at that, remains living, healthy, and able) — depends first of all on the size of the consciousness. The size of an individual consciousness defines also the so-called *personal power*.

It is very important to understand that on the Path to higher spiritual achievements, only the consciousness which is subtle can grow and develop successfully; the state of subtlety has to become natural, basic. If one has not achieved this status, it is quite easy to fall back to coarseness — and then such a person goes to hell rather than to the Abode of the Creator. In such cases, quite often one cannot notice one's own degradation and coarsening...

Yet there are special techniques that help make the consciousness subtle. One of the techniques consists in working with so-called Mahadoubles of Divine Teachers. A Mahadouble is a Divine Consciousness that assumed a giant anthropomorphic form standing over the ground. In this form, our Divine Teachers appear to us.

A consciousness refined to Their Divine level of subtlety is capable of SEEING these Mahadoubles and TALKING with Them. For such an advanced spiritual seeker, They become personal Divine Spiritual Teachers. Filling the form of Their Mahadoubles with oneself provides one with invaluable initial experience of Mergence with God.

Yet this is only the beginning of the path to the achievement of Divinity.

Then one has to learn — with the help of the Divine Teachers — to live in Their common Abode: in the Abode of the Creator, in the state of firm Mergence with Him.

This Goal can be and must be realized during life in the physical body. This cannot be done after the death of the body, because it is the material body that allows the transformation the energy derived from the ordinary food into the energy of the growing consciousness.

* * *

In the works left by some incarnate Divine Teachers — that is Messiahs, Avatars — there is information about the possibility for man to achieve Immortality. What does it mean?

There are two forms of such Immortality.

In the first form, one abandons the cycle of births and deaths, that is, one does not need to be born in a body on the Earth and to die any more. This form of Immortality is achieved through the firm and full Mergence with the Primordial Consciousness in Its Abode. Further incarnations of such Divine Souls may take place — but only voluntarily and not for the sake of personal self-development but with the purpose of providing the most efficient help to incarnate people.

Yet, there is another form of Immortality — when on the basis of the achievements mentioned above, one achieves also the immortality of the physical body. This requires that the cells of the material body be brought to the Divine level of subtlety.

It was described in our book *Classics of Spiritual Philosophy and the Present*. Among Those possessing such immortal bodies we know Jesus Christ, Adler, and Thoth-the-Atlantean. They explained to us how one can achieve this goal — and it seems quite feasible.

* * *

Hopefully, I managed to inspire you to make efforts on the spiritual Path. Walk it! By doing so we realize the Will of the Creator, Who sent us to live on the Earth!

Now, once we have understood the meaning of our lives — doesn't it make sense to dedicate all our time and efforts to the realization of this meaning?

Walk this Path! Even if one manages to traverse not the entire Path but only some part of it — anyway this makes one's life happier in the current incarnation, and it will be much easier to continue walking the Path the next time!

General Conclusion

1. About the History of Religion

1:1. Throughout the history of mankind on the planet Earth, people capable of philosophical thinking have been undoubtedly raising questions about the meaning of their lives, about the possibility of living in the unembodied state, and about the existence of God.

Such thinkers have been inventing more or less adequate philosophical concepts, organizing philosophical and esoteric groups, schools, and even religious movements.

1:2. God — on His side — has been repeatedly giving them His Teachings through His Messengers (Messiahs, Avatars) and prophets. Each time the information was presented in the form that was adequate for a concrete group of people — according to the level of their philosophic and religious awareness and the conditions of life in that particular historical period (whether it was a period of war or peace, first stages of religion's formation or existence of established religious tradition in the particular region).

1:3. But at each of those epicenters of religious knowledge established by God, people inevitably distorted His Teachings. For example:

— religious duties of people got reduced to mere participation in "saving" rituals; bodily movements and standard prayers gradually became the main religious occupation of believers, substituting for real efforts on the path of personal spiritual evolution;

— so-called religious fundamentalism appeared, where the religious life was considered not as accumulating knowledge about God and the meaning of our life, not as mastering of the methods of spiritual self-development and helping others in doing it, but was reduced to crude, violent forcing of people to keep certain "rules of behavior" that have no religious value;

— false concepts of "national religions" and of "national Gods" formed, whereas in reality God is One — not only for all people of the Earth but for the whole Universe;

— such degeneration very often resulted in hatred towards "heretics" and "infidels" becoming the main essence of the religious ideology, which led to terror and aggressive wars.[36]

1:4. For all rational people of our planet it should be clear that there is a necessity for studying, accepting, and instilling in the mentality of people of all countries a religious concept based on the modern scientific knowledge and on recapitulation of the religious experience accumulated throughout the history of mankind, as well as on what God is teaching us now.

2. How the Word *God* Is to Be Understood

2:1. First of all, it is necessary to accept the fact that the Universe is multidimensional — in reality (and not only mathematically). Its dimensions (eons, lokas) can be cognized by an advanced human consciousness. Such a level of consciousness can be attained through proper spiritual training. One of the components of this training should be a multi-stage practice of meditation.

2:2. There are dimensions of hell and paradise and those serving as "depositories of construction material" for forming solid matter and souls. There is also a dimension that represents the Abode of the Creator.

2:3. Historically it happened that the word *God* has several meanings and people often get confused by them.

2:4. The principal meaning of this word is the Creator, the Primordial Universal Consciousness, dwelling in the primary spatial dimension. This Consciousness

---

[36] How religious movements degrade is described in the book [9].

Also it is important to mention that the succession of traditions (*paramparaness*) of particular religious teachings does not imply that these teachings are true ones. In fact, one observes the contrary situation — the original Teachings get distorted and perverted even during the life of their Founders and even more after They pass away.

represents the subtlest state of all energy states in the universe — on the *coarseness-subtlety* scale. The inhabitants of hell are on the opposite end of this scale: they live in the coarsest states of consciousness.

2:5. The second meaning of the word *God* includes the Creator with His entire multidimensional Creation, which is brought into existence by Him, is based on Him as on a foundation, and is incapable of existing without or being separated from Him. In this sense, God is *Absolutely Everything* (the Absolute) — Everything, except for hell and its inhabitants. (By definition of Jesus Christ, hell is the *outer darkness* — outer in relation to God-Absolute).

2:6. The concept of *God* includes also Manifestations of the Creator in the Creation which people call the Holy Spirit (Brahman).

The Holy Spirit most often manifests Himself for incarnate people in the form of Divine Teachers that come out from the Abode of the Creator.

They can, in particular, condense the energy of the Consciousness to the perceivable for us level or even visible to regular eyesight.

2:7. Manifestation of a Divine Teacher on the material plane through incarnation into a human body is called Messiah, Christ, Avatar.

Such a Teacher, as well as the Holy Spirit, is an Integral Part of the Creator (Primordial Consciousness).

2:8. The statement "God is One" is true. All Those dwelling in the Abode of the Creator are merged integral Parts of the One Primordial Consciousness.

The criterion here is that Their Abode is the primary spatial dimension. Every One of Them comes out from it into the world of the Creation only with a part of Oneself, at that remaining coessential to the Creator.

2:9. Numerous individual manifestations in the world of the Creation (objects; bodies, including ours; embodied and non-embodied souls, except for hell inhabitants) should be considered as cells of the infinite multidimensional Universal Organism of God in the aspect of the Absolute.

2:10. The essence of all processes that take place in the universe is the Evolution of the Universal Divine Consciousness, the Evolution of the Absolute.

2:11. The concept of *God* must not include mythological (fairy-tale) and fictitious characters of national religious folklore (those sharing such naive and essentially false conceptions are called *pagans*, that is those holding primitive folk beliefs)

Attempts to present God as an invisible flying being with a human-like appearance are also naive and false.

God should be thought of as neither "information" nor "information field", nor "collective human intellect", nor should He be given other similar superficial and incompetent definitions.

Cognition of God has nothing to do with "conversations with aliens", "astral traveling", spiritism, magic rituals or astrological fantasies.

Describing God as a malicious monster punishing people for their sins is a striking perversion that turns people away from loving Him and hinders their advancement on the spiritual Path.

Likewise, bringing devil and other intimidating factors into the center of attention is a gross religious distortion. Cultivation of mystical fear — as opposed to cherishing creative Love — is the main cause of spiritual degradation and development of mass psychopathology among the followers of such forms of pseudo-religion.

2:12. Thus, the concept of God includes:

— the Creator, Who is called in other languages and other religious schools God-the-Father, Primordial Consciousness, Allah, Ishvara, Tao, etc.,

— the Absolute,

— non-incarnate (They are countless) as well as incarnate Divine Teachers coming out from the Abode of the Creator.

This is the essence of the true, monotheistic conception of what God is.

2:13. From His Abode the Creator creates "islets" of matter throughout the infinite space of the universe and after some time — when they are no longer necessary — He dematerializes them.

The purpose of this process is to create conditions for embodying new souls on material substrates in order to present them with an opportunity for development.

Having grown to the Divine level, these Souls merge into the Creator and enrich Him with Themselves.

2:14. Incarnations in the material world are necessary for the development of souls, since it is in the physical body that the energy needed for growth of the "lump" of the consciousness is produced. This energy is derived primarily from ordinary food — the one that we eat.

But not any kind of material food provides the organism with the energy eminently suitable for growth of the soul in the proper direction: the most adequate quality of energy is supplied by the *killing-free* diet, i.e. the one that does not contain meat, fish, and other products made of bodies of killed animals.

Nutrition that involves killing of animals is incompatible with high ethical principles and often results in situations when the souls of killed animals enter the bodies of people who killed them or of those who ate their flesh. Such enterings (called *possessions*) cause various psychic and somatic disorders, and diseases, including cancer.[37]

---

[37] The mechanism of oncological diseases is a local distortion of the genotype of a group of cells. It results in formation of a tumor and other kinds of pathologies.

The factors causing such disorders can be exposure to radiation,

The natural food for people is various edible plants, milk and milk products, and bird eggs.

2:15. The evolution of each individual soul begins when its germen is formed in a mineral. Then follows numerous incarnations in bodies of plants — small in the beginning, then of larger size; then — into animal bodies of increasing size and species complexity; and finally — into human bodies.

Each of us, humans, has previously lived in bodies of various plants and animals.

And now, in the bodies of plants and animals, we should see other growing souls. We have to learn to respect their lives and in every possible way avoid doing any unnecessary harm to them.

The *killing-free* lifestyle in regard to people and animals, as well as restraining from harming plants unnecessarily must be a norm for every individual.[38]

2:16. God in the aspect of the Creator — and this is really perceivable by a developed human consciousness — can be depicted as an Ocean of Blissful, Most Tender, Subtlest Light of Consciousness.

Man has to learn to love Him, to fall in love with Him — and this will be a prerequisite for cognizing Him and for merging with Him. As a result of personal evolu-

---

hereditary genetic disorders, chemical carcinogens, possibly a viral influence, but also possessions. In the latter case, the spirit-animal begins to adjust the part of the human organism, where it has settled, to make a "nest" for itself. It does it by changing and adapting for itself the tissues of the body.

This statement is not a fantasy or a "scientific hypothesis" but a fact observed with clairvoyance in many cases of diseased people. Repentance for committed killings and for gluttony results in getting freed from the possession and in quick recovery — especially if it is combined with healing and sanative measures (including winter-swimming).

[38] With the exception of cases of self-defense, for example, against aggressive animals or insects.

tion, each individual soul has to merge into the Universal Soul of the Creator, which is the Main Part of the Absolute.

3. What Is Man

3:1. Man is not a body. Man is a lump of energy of consciousness (a soul), capable of self-comprehension, remembering, thinking, moving, growing qualitatively and quantitatively, and of degradation.

An incarnation consists in binding a soul with a body (soon to be born) performed by God.

The death constitutes a complete separation of them.

3:2. People are embodied into material bodies by God in order to undergo consecutive stages of personal evolution. They possess a considerable amount of free will, i.e. the right to choose the strategic direction of the personal evolution (to the Abode of the Creator — or to hell), as well as ways of solving daily problems and tasks.

God — in the aspect of the Holy Spirit — constantly suggests ways to improve, to become better to everyone. In this way He expresses His Love-Care for everyone.

But He extremely rarely interferes "by force" with people realizing their desires.

In this way, God — as the Supreme Shepherd — "shepherds" us on the surface of the planet Earth — as if on His "pasture". He is interested that we develop in the direction preferable by Him: namely, we have to become Perfect Souls and merge with Him in His Abode, and thus to enrich Him with ourselves.

And if someone does not live the Earth's life in the way preferable by God, He inflicts pain to that person through illnesses or various calamities. As a result, some of us start to reflect on it and then reform. But others only grow more embittered and, unfortunately, degrade at even a higher rate.

In this way — through realization of the *free will* — natural selection goes on among the souls embodied by God.

He takes the best ones into His Abode. Good souls get in paradise for some time, and after that they get embodied again in the conditions favorable for further development. The abode of the worst souls is hell. Some of those souls are given an opportunity to be embodied again, to try one more time, while the worst of them, hopeless in God's opinion, get destroyed, annihilated forever (this is where the ideas of "blazing inferno" and "infernal fire consuming sinners" originate from).

3:3. We have to become aware of ourselves not as of the body or mind but as of an embodied soul (consciousness): only from this standpoint it is possible to understand correctly how to live on the Earth.

The expressions "my soul", "his (her) soul", "their (our) souls" or the likes are incorrect. Let us realize — we *are* souls.

3:4. People of all nationalities and races, and of both sexes — are equal in the face of God. What really makes them different from one another is the age of the soul and the degree to which they have developed certain positive and negative qualities.

The basic principles of spiritual advancement are the same for all people regardless of sex, nationality, and other similar characteristics, though the methods of spiritual work must be different depending on: a) the age of a person in the current incarnation, b) the psychogenetic age (age of the soul), c) present level of ethical and intellectual development, and d) the portion of the spiritual Path that an individual soul has already successfully traveled.

3:5. The supreme prospective task of each human being is to cognize God in all of His aspects and Manifestations, then, upon achieving spiritual Perfection, to merge with the Creator in His Abode, and then to continue taking part in the Universal Evolutionary Process from there, by assisting the embodied beings in particular.

But what one should begin with is the intellectual development and ethical self-transformation.

4. Methodological Principles of Spiritual Self-Development

4:1. The Perfection of the Creator has three main aspects. They are — Love, Wisdom, and Power. Therefore, each of us in the course of the personal evolution has to develop these three qualities.

4:2. Everyone should begin with accepting the following main ethical principles:

"Don't do to others whatever you would not want them to do to you!"

and

"Help everyone in everything good!"

Then it would be appropriate to begin mastering the functions of the spiritual heart — an organ producing the emotions of love.

4:3. The spiritual heart is a bioenergetic structure originally located in the chest. The first step of its development is mastered when it has filled the whole chest, what makes one capable of living in the state of stable concentration of the consciousness in the spiritual heart, of perceiving the outer world with it, and of acting *from it*, including speaking.

When this is accomplished, and as long as one abides in the spiritual heart with the concentration of the consciousness, one is no longer able to enter emotional states other than variations of heart love.

This radically changes one's relationships with the environment, including other people. Also one's health gets improved dramatically.

Those, who have settled in this state, who got used to and will continue living in it until the end of their incarnation, after leaving the body are going to appear among other blissful souls in paradise.[39]

The methods of realization of everything said above have been developed by us; they are described in detail in our books and demonstrated in our films.

4:4. In order to succeed in spiritual development, one has to transform oneself into a large soul consisting primarily of the spiritual heart.

One has to learn to live so that one almost never abandons the emotions of love: tender freshness, tactful care, willingness to help other people in everything good sincerely and selflessly, respect to all worthy ones, gratitude to anyone who helps, forgiveness of offenders, willingness to abandon oneself and sacrifice oneself for the sake of others. And even when fighting for the sake of others' good, one must not leave the state of love.

Let everyone strive for ridding themselves of all kinds of arrogance, selfishness, greed, violence, and of all kinds of emotions of anger, including the emotions of condemnation, revengefulness, irritation, envy, and jealousy. These emotional states must be considered as an adversary to Love.

Gaining full control over one's own emotions is possible through intellectual work on struggling with one's own vices (including repentance) and on cultivating missing positive qualities. For this purpose, it is very helpful

---

[39] It should be clear to the reader that the incorrect understanding of the term heart as an aggregate of all emotions including sexual passion (lust), hatred, and so on has nothing to do with spirituality. Figures of speech "to live according to the heart", "to live by heart" have to be understood as "to live in love, with love" and not as "to follow emotions uncontrolled by the mind".

Unfortunately, the latter meaning became a part of the "classic" literature, and this does not contribute to the spiritual culture of the readers of such books.

to master the methods of psychic self-regulation, which are based on working with the structures of the human organism responsible for generation of emotions.

4:5. "God is Love", taught Jesus Christ. He Himself was Love. And He commanded that we, too, become It.

In order to be able to approach our Creator — Who is Love — we have to transform ourselves into Love. There is no other way.

And this is not just a slogan made up of nice words yet unfeasible, but a comprehensive system of knowledge and methods thoroughly tested and verified by numerous spiritual seekers.

4:6. The development of the intellect is a crucial element of one's spiritual advancement. Children must be given education of as high quality as possible. Adults should always seek ways to acquire new knowledge — preferably that, which will be useful on the spiritual Path.

4:7. It makes sense to devote the professional activity not to striving for money and accumulating material wealth, but to learning as much as possible in the beginning of our lives in order to use the acquired knowledge and skills in the future to serve God through serving people.

4:8. Doing good deeds by helping other souls in their evolution — let this be the major incentive of everyone's social activity!

Let such activity be sincere giving! Then other people — the best of them — will begin to respond by giving back. It is in this way that groups of true and reliable friends with common spiritual goals form.

4:9. Giving birth and proper upbringing of children is also a service to God.

4:10. In educating children, special techniques can be successfully used, which are quite helpful in preparing them for serious spiritual work in the future.

4:11. Children should be involved in creative work at the level adequate for their age.

Let them help parents in their work, let them take a paid job outside of school time. Let teaching them various labor skills become a part of school educational programs.

Through this, children must learn to create and to value everything good created by others.

Otherwise, many children become destructive when they grow up.

4:12. Marriage and education of children provide numerous excellent opportunities for self-perfecting, for development of such aspects of love as caring, tenderness, and altruism.

This experience also significantly contributes to the intellectual progress of an individual soul by providing numerous psychological lessons in particular.

God — as a Teacher — is the "Supreme Psychologist". Thus, we have to master psychology as well.

4:13. The prevailing opinion that the main task of man in relation to God consists in sole praying and that nothing else is necessary is deeply erroneous and harmful. One must realize that God does not need our prayers, which are begging, in essence.

What God wants from us in the first place is righteousness expressed in ethically correct attitude towards all living beings, including other people, as well as towards Him. In particular, He wants us to seek Him, serve Him, learn to love Him, and strive for developing ourselves to such a degree that we can offer ourselves to Him as a gift, as perfect as possible.

It is this gift that God will be pleased to receive as an offering from man.

4:14. He does not need any killing of animals and plants as an "offering to God". Those killings are but criminal acts and are not in any way "pleasing to God".

4:15. Introduction of the ideas of irreparably sinful human nature, nothingness of man who is destined to remain an eternal antipode to God is an error and a transgression in the face of God. It contradicts the very Intention that the Creator has for us. It creates a huge obstacle for the spiritual growth.

4:16. It is better to begin the development of the power aspect of the soul through engaging in manual labor. If this is currently impossible, then various kinds of athletic training can be helpful.

It is necessary to have a strong and healthy body in order to advance successfully on the spiritual Path.

The power aspect of the consciousness can be developed further through special methods of development of the energy structures of the organism and special meditations. But they can be taught only to intellectually mature people, who have gained the required subtlety of the consciousness and the ability to remain in the emotional state of love for a long time.

4:17. The opinion that people attain paradise or end up in hell as a result of some particular action (or actions) is erroneous. Actions significant from the ethical standpoint determine one's destiny only for the periods of embodiment — in the current or future incarnations.

But what determines the place, where we abide after the death of the body — be it hell, paradise, or other spatial dimensions (including the Abode of the Creator) — is the state of the consciousness to which we accustomed ourselves during life in the body.

People who get used to living in coarse emotional states, upon leaving the body continue to exist in these states among other beings similar to them.

Those who live (including the recent period before departing from the body) in subtle and pure heart love, after the death of the body find themselves in paradise.

But in order to reach the Abode of the Creator from the "starting" point of the paradisiacal state, one needs to go through a long and difficult meditative practice guided by one or several Divine Teachers.

One has to dedicate the whole life to this in order to succeed.

Let us emphasize that nobody can pass this part of the Path on their own. The errors made here can have grievous consequences. For example, it is possible "to get lost" in spatial dimensions... Or to break down as a result of some stressing factor and to lapse into coarse emotional states... This can wipe out all one's positive meditative achievements and cause serious diseases.

4:18. Spiritual work cannot be successful for people who use substances called drugs, including alcohol and tobacco products.

4:19. The human organism is multidimensional, and in this respect it is similar to the multidimensional Absolute. Therefore, the process of self-cognition coincides with the process of cognition of the Absolute.

4:20. One of the main tasks of spiritual work is to transform the human egocentrism to God-centrism — both mentally and in meditative realization.

4:21. The final steps of spiritual ascent can be mastered only in monasticism.

4:22. Monasticism is unidirectionality of spiritual seeker's attention focused on only one Goal — full cognition of God and merging with the Creator in His Abode, also helping all worthy ones walking this Path.

4:23. The tasks of a true monk cannot be accomplished by mere wearing special clothes, accepting new names, kow-towing and saying standard prayers. All this has nothing to do with the true monasticism.

4:24. Leading a parasitic way of life which is sometimes extolled as a virtue by adepts of some degenerated religious schools is in fact a vicious practice that has a detrimental effect on the destinies of the followers of this distortion.

God considers panhandling as an indecent occupation [6,11].

4:25. Celibacy (complete refraining from sexual contacts) is by no means a necessary attribute of the true monastic life. It rather does harm than helps on the spiritual Path, creating a sexual "dominant" (a dominating idea of sexual dissatisfaction) — instead of one's having the Creator and the care for people as a sole dominant. Celibacy hinders the development of such important variations of love as sexually tinged tenderness, attention and care in relationships with the spouse and children.

Celibacy also can be harmful to health causing sometimes adenoma of prostate in men and neuroses based on sexual dissatisfaction in both men and women.

4:26. Having sex is not a "sin" by itself, as long as

a) no violence or doing harm is involved,

b) partners are adequate,

c) sex does not overshadow the more important aspects of life.

A harmonious sexual life is absolutely normal for all healthy adults, even for those who have devoted their lives completely to the attainment of the highest spiritual goals.

But people entering into a marriage should be at similar stages of their spiritual advancement [11].

4:27. Recent popularization of the idea that "the more sex — the more spirituality" is another extreme, no less harmful for spiritual development. In this case sex is brought into the center of attention, instead of the Creator, multi-aspect self-development, and participation in the Evolutionary Process through service to God. This service consists in helping other people in their existence on the Earth and facilitating their spiritual progress.

"Where your treasure is there your heart will be also", taught Jesus Christ (Luke 12:34).

5. Structure of the Human Organism and Structure of the Absolute

5:1. Man is not a body. Man is a consciousness (a soul) embodied into a material body for a limited period of time.

5:2. The organism (but not the body!) of incarnate man is multidimensional. (It should be noted that the "seven bodies" scheme, which is described in some books, is methodologically wrong. It would be more correct to talk about a potential representation of every human in all principal layers of the multidimensional Absolute; it is this potential that man has to realize. By the way, this is the concept described in the Bible as likeness of man to God — God in the aspect of the multidimensional Absolute.

5:3. The above said may be easier to understand if one considers the scheme for studying the structure of the Absolute presented at the end of this book.[40]

This scheme is not so easy to understand since it is impossible to illustrate adequately in picture the multidimensionality of space. Thus, in order to understand it, one needs to keep in mind that each layer of multidimensionality shown on the scheme as lower, in reality is located *deeper* on the multidimensional scale. And the deeper the layer the *subtle* it is.

The Abode of the Creator is located in the *deepest*, that is the *subtlest* energy layer of the multidimensional Absolute. This is where we should seek Him.

And the refinement of the consciousness (starting with mastering the regulation of the emotional sphere) is the methodologically correct direction of work here.

5:4. Further esoteric work may consist in learning to move with the concentration of the consciousness be-

---

[40] This scheme was first published in the book [10].

tween all layers of this scheme (not in imagination but in the real multidimensional space), like one moves with the concentration of the consciousness inside the body.

5.5. This entire educational process of ours (including both theoretical and practical studies, also exams) is conducted under the guidance of the Holy Spirit; He leaves no one without His attention and His help, and nothing can happen that would be beyond His awareness or out of His control.

6. What Religious Associations Should Do

6:1. Ritual forms of religious practice can be well used by beginners. But one should understand that rituals are useful only for helping people remember about God's existence.

Participating in rituals — whatever they are called or whatever value people assign to them — cannot by itself solve the task of realization of our purpose of life.

6:2. Activities of religious associations should not be limited just to performing rites. It is necessary to explain to people what God is, tell them about the meaning of their lives and the way of its realization. Great focus should be on ethical work involving discussions on ethical principles, practice of conscious and sincere repentance, and collective analysis of ethical problems — using specific examples from life, books, newspapers, films, and other sources.

Esthetics, including attunement to the subtlest manifestations of living nature and to certain works of art, can be extremely helpful. Sublime and inspiring beauty of human body may also play an important part in this work.

Spiritual work becomes much more effective when complemented by lessons on ecology, sport training, and discussions about healthy lifestyle, as well as mastering healing and self-healing methods.

The methods of psychic self-regulation should be taught with the emphasis on mastering the functions of the spiritual heart.

6:3. Serious meditative techniques must not be taught to children and ethically and intellectually immature adults, especially the methods related to the power aspect of the development of the consciousness. Breaking this rule can lead to serious mental disorders that stop positive evolution of the soul.

Initiations into spiritual knowledge must be done strictly on a step-by-step basis — new stages must be given only after disciples have mastered the previous ones.

6:4. The main qualities of God are Love, Wisdom, and Power.

Thus, the one who seeks Perfection has to develop these qualities in oneself.

For this purpose, there are three closely related directions of spiritual work: ethical, intellectual, and psychoenergetic ones.

The ethical aspect of the development is the main one on the spiritual Path.

Therefore, it is the basic ethical principles of a religious organization that serve as the criterion for judging whether its religious orientation is correct or incorrect.

The motto "God and Love!" is true.

Hatred towards anyone, preaching of violence, making killing of people and animals a "norm", alcoholism and using other kinds of drugs, as well as self-interest, aggressiveness, self-admiring, falsity, and arrogance of leaders — this is wrong, this is evil, is not of God and does not bring one to God.

6:5. Thus, the main principle of the evolutionary development of man is multi-aspect LOVE which

— begins with compassionate attitude to all manifestations of life,

— is guided by the true understanding of the religious and philosophic aspect of our existence,

— is based on the development of oneself as a spiritual heart,

— guides us — through love for the Creation — to love for the Creator.

6:6. Love for the Creator allows us to cognize God in all of His aspects and Manifestations and merge with the Creator.

6:7. This Victory concludes the individual evolution of the soul on its human stage of development.

All Those Who Achieved this continue to live as Integral Parts of the Creator.

6:8. One of the Manifestations of the activity of Those Who Achieved is help which They as Holy Spirits provide to incarnate beings.

In some cases Representatives of the Creator incarnate in human bodies again — to help embodied people more successfully.

Bibliography

1. Agni Yoga. Community. "Detskaya Literatura", Novosibirsk, 1991 *(in Russian)*.
2. Agni Yoga. Fiery World. III. "Detskaya Literatura", Novosibirsk, 1991 *(in Russian)*.
3. Agni Yoga. Hierarchy. Naberezhnye Chelny, 1991 *(in Russian)*.
4. Agni Yoga. Supermundane. "Sfera", Moscow, 1995 *(in Russian)*.
5. Akinfiev I.Y. — Vegetarianism from Biological Standpoint. Ekaterinoslav, 1914 *(in Russian)*.
6. Antonov V.V. — God Speaks (Textbook of Religion). "Polus", Saint Petersburg, 2002 *(in Russian)*.
7. Antonov V.V. — How God Can Be Cognized. Autobiography of a Scientist, Who Studied God. *"New Atlanteans"*, Bancroft, 2009.
8. Antonov V.V. — Sexology. *"New Atlanteans"*, Bancroft, 2008.
9. Antonov V.V. — Spiritual Heart. The Religion of Unity. *"New Atlanteans"*, Bancroft, 2010.
10. Antonov V.V. — The New Upanishad: Structure and Cognition of the Absolute. *"New Atlanteans"*, Bancroft, 2011.
11. Antonov V.V. (ed.) — Classics of Spiritual Philosophy and the Present. *"New Atlanteans"*, Bancroft, 2008.
12. Antonov V.V. (ed.) — Dobrynya. Byliny. "Drouk", Odessa, 2006 *(in Russian)*.
13. Antonov V.V. (ed.) — God Speaks. Book 2. Divine Teachers — about Themselves. "Vilna Ukraina", Lvov, 2005 *(in Russian)*.
14. Antonov V.V. (ed.) — How God Can Be Cognized. Book 2. Autobiographies of God's Disciples. "Vilna Ukraina", Lvov, 2005 *(in Russian)*.

15. Antonov V.V. (ed.) — Practice of the Modern Hesychasm. "KP OGT", Odessa, 2004 *(in Russian)*.
16. Antonov V.V. (ed.) — Spiritual Heart: the Path to the Creator (Poems-Meditations and Revelations). *"New Atlanteans"*, Bancroft, 2010.
17. Antonov V.V. (ed.) — Spiritual Work with Children. *"New Atlanteans"*, Bancroft, 2008.
18. Antonov V.V. (ed.) — Tao Te Ching. *"New Atlanteans"*, Bancroft, 2008.
19. Babaji the Unfathomable. "Libris", Moscow, 1997 *(in Russian)*.
20. Bennett T.G. — Concerning Subud. "Hedder & Stoughton", 1958.
21. Bezobrazov P.V. — On the Animals' Rights. Moscow, 1904 *(in Russian)*.
22. Blofeld J.E. — The Tantric Mysticism of Tibet. "Dutton", N.Y., 1970.
23. Castaneda, Margaret — A Magical Journey with Carlos Castaneda. "Myth", Kr., 1998 *(in Russian)*.
24. Chertkov V.G. — Malicious Entertainment. Reflections on Hunting. "Posrednik", 1890 *(in Russian)*.
25. Cullen B. (compil.) — The Book of Jesus. "Polus", Saint Petersburg, 1997 *(in Russian)*.
26. Danilov B.A. (compil.) — Sides of Agni Yoga. Vol. 7. "Algim", Novosibirsk, 1995 *(in Russian)*.
27. David-Neel A. — Magic and Mystery in Tibet. "Univ. Books", N.Y., 1958.
28. Demin V.N. — Secret Ways of Slavic Tribes. «Fair-Press», Moscow, 2002.
29. Dowling L.H. — The Aquarian Gospel of Jesus the Christ. "Society for Vedic Culture", Saint Petersburg, 2001 *(in Russian)*.
30. Dymshits E.O. — On Vegetarianism. "Izdatelstvo Rozenberga", Yekaterinoslav, 1911 *(in Russian)*.
31. Gorky M. (Peshkov A.M.) — Confession. Collected works in 30 volumes. Vol.8. "Khudozhestvennaya